DATE DUE

NOY 5-31-11

Polish Chicago

Our History, Our Recipes

by

Joseph W. Zurawski

Recipe Coordinator - Julita Siegel • Recipe Photography - Katherine Bish

G. Bradley Publishing, Inc., St. Louis, Missouri • www.gbradleypublishing.com

Publication Staff

Author . . . . Joseph W. Zurawski
Introduction . . . . Dominic A. Pacyga
Foreword . . . . Edmund Gronkiewicz
Epilogue . . . . Jan Lorys
Recipes Coordinator . . . . Julita Siegel
Recipes Photography . . . . Katherine Bish
Photo Editor . . . . Michael Bruner
Book Design . . . . Diane Kramer
Dust Jacket Design . . . . Michael Bruner
Project Editor . . . . Diane Gannon
Copy Editor: . . . . Gloria Baraks
Publisher . . . . G. Bradley Publishing, Inc.

Use of Abbreviations

Several organizations are frequently mentioned in the text. We have used the following abbreviations often adapted by these organizations in their own publications.

PMA   The Polish Museum of America
PNA   Polish National Alliance of the
               United States of North America
PRCUA   Polish Roman Catholic Union
               of America
PWA   Polish Women's Alliance

Generally, we identified members of religious orders of women as Felician Sisters, Franciscan Sisters of Chicago, and Sisters of the Resurrection without an initialized suffix. We found this use prevalent in contemporary literature with few references to the full titles of orders such as Congregation of the Sisters of St. Felix of Cantalice Third Order Regular of St. Francis of Assisi, sometimes abbreviated as CSSF. CR is used to identify priests of the Congregation of the Resurrection.

Dedication

It is with overwhelming pride for our Polish ancestors that I dedicate this book to my parents, Walter and Zofia Zurawski, and other Polish immigrants whose indomitable spirit led them to embark on a new life. Leaving their home, friends, and family they overcame all the odds against them. They not only bettered their own lives, they have ultimately enriched ours and, indeed, the City of Chicago.

Publisher's note: We chose not to include diacritical marks on Polish words used in this book. We wanted to retain the integrity of the English language for both Polish Americans and non-Poles. Also the possible release of a Polish language version of Polish Chicago *is being considered.*

A graduate of Eastern Illinois University School of Journalism, Katherine Bish has been telling stories through pictures since 1998. Her award-winning food photography is regularly featured in *St. Louis Magazine* and *the St. Louis Post-Dispatch*. Her work has also been featured in *National Geographic Traveler, Food and Wine, Gourmet,* and *Bon Appetit*. Katherine was the food photographer for the *Greektown Chicago* and *German Milwaukee* books by G. Bradley Publishing.

Julita Siegel was born in Kielce, Poland and came to the U.S. after graduating from the University of Adam Mickiewicz in Poznan with a master's degree in Art History. She works at the PMA cataloging and digitizing documentary photographs in the museum's collection. This suits Julita perfectly as it combines her love for photography and art with an interest and respect for the past, as well as for Polish culture and heritage.

Julita continues her education in photography and graphic design. She freelances as a professional photographer and was responsible for many photos in the New Polonia section of this book. She and her husband, Bart, share a passion for ethnic home cooking and small, family-owned restaurants. They currently live in the suburbs of Chicago but dream of moving to the old Polish Triangle neighborhood. Photo by Bart Siegel

ISBN 978-0-9774512-2-7
Printed in the U.S.A.

Table of Contents

DISCARD

Introduction to Polish Chicago

Polish immigrants and their offspring have long played a role in the history of Chicago. From the city's beginning, Poles have made their way to the shores of Lake Michigan to make their fortunes. Various waves of immigration have drawn these men and women to Chicago's many neighborhoods. The first before the Civil War included refugees from Poland's insurrections against occupation by her neighbors in 1831, 1846, and, later, in 1861. These politically driven migrations paved the path for vast economic immigration, known in Poland as *Za Chlebem* or "For Bread." The latter migrations transformed Chicago and created the largest Polonia or Polish immigrant community in the United States. This largely peasant migration lasted for 60 years from the beginning of the American Civil War until the cutting off of European immigration in the 1920s. These several waves emanated from first German-occupied Poland and then the Russian and Austrian partitions.

To meet community needs, the pioneers established a socially viable network and a strong church foundation. The first Polish Roman Catholic parish in Chicago, St. Stanislaus Kostka, appeared just after the Civil War. It became the mother church of all those large Polish churches that quickly spread across the prairie. By the time the Poles were finished building churches, more than 60 Catholic and Polish National Catholic Churches dotted the Chicago landscape.

During World War I, Chicago's Polonia began to flex its political muscles. The community contributed to Poland's army in exile fighting alongside the French and Americans on the Western Front. In turn, Polish workers joined the Armed Forces of the United States, and on the Home Front, contributed to the vast Liberty Bond campaigns that helped pay for the war effort. In the end, the community's goal of a free and independent Poland was accomplished with the Treaty of Versailles.

Unfortunately, war shaped much of Poland's and the Chicago Polonia's history in the 20th century. On September 1, 1939, the German army once again crossed Poland's borders and began World War II. Again, Chicago's Polonia came to the homeland's rescue by sending aid to its beleaguered populace. Again, after Pearl Harbor large numbers of Polish Americans joined the Armed Forces of the United States. The war ended with a Soviet-supported regime in power in Poland and with another wave of Polish migration to the United States and Chicago. These "displaced" persons rejuvenated the city's Polish communities breathing new life into ethnic institutions while, at the same time, Polish Americans were becoming more assimilated and moving to the suburbs.

Eventually, yet another most recent wave of immigrants would come to the city and suburbs, the so-called Solidarity immigration. These would again revitalize many neighborhoods. Today, well over 70 percent of Polish Americans in Northern Illinois live in the suburbs. This hardly meant an end to Chicago's Polonia. It can still be seen and experienced along Milwaukee Avenue on the Northwest Side and Archer Avenue on the Southwest Side. Polish is still the language of choice in many Chicago neighborhoods and Polish masses attract throngs at churches such as St. Hyacinth's and St. Bruno's. Polkas still rattle wedding halls, and a new generation of Chicagoans continues to have appreciation for Polonia's great heritage.

This book traces the history of this intricate community so involved in the lifeblood of Chicago. Joseph Zurawski has written a wonderful synopsis of the Chicago Polonia in all its phases. In addition, the historical photos, "windows to the past," as well as the tantalizing recipes offer the reader the sights, aromas, and tastes of Polish Chicago. I hope that this book will lead the readers to discover more of these sensations in a wonderfully diverse Chicago.

Dominic A. Pacyga, Ph.D.
Columbia College/Chicago

FOREWORD

Polonia, as the Polish community in Chicago is known, is not and never has been a monolithic or static community. Polonia today is a far cry from the Polonia that existed in the 19th century, the time of its origins, or for that matter, even the Polonia of 20 years ago.

No longer is the initial immigration solely confined to certain "first stage" neighborhoods. In fact, quite often, recent immigrants have moved quickly to the suburbs where the Polish population now exceeds that of Chicago proper. The multiple Polish parishes of old, the core of yesteryear's Polonia, have given way to parishes with a strong sense of Polish preservation where religious services are often provided in Polish. Furthermore, marriage with non-Polish Americans diversified not only the nature of the neighborhood but also the families themselves.

The very ebb and flow of immigration, often dictated by various motivations, plus the integration of generation after generation within the framework of Chicago and its environs created, and continues to create, different needs, different values, and different perspectives. Immigration has always been a major catalyst in the formation of the climate of Polonia in Chicago. Recent arrivals are more educated, more technically qualified. However, the booming economies in Ireland and Great Britain are also attracting Polish immigrants, who find opportunities there closer to Poland. This allows them to travel back and forth to Poland, even for extended weekends, in a manner not practical in Chicago. This diversion of Polish immigrants will impact on the tide and type of immigration from Poland to Polonia in Chicago.

Polonia has become many different things to many people. *Polish Chicago: Our History, Our Recipes* should be of important interest to each of us who share this heritage. As Polish Americans we will be reminded of our past and of our community's origins. We will be made aware that our current Polonia is still, and likely will continue to be, in a continual stage of growth and development.

While others may note our Polish history shows a constant streak of individualism, often impeding constructive steps in unity, we have been and remain Polonia, no matter which generation, no matter which neighborhood, no matter what economic class. A publication such as this reminds us not only of our roots, it also calls attention to our very being.

I look with awe at Joseph W. Zurawski's undertaking. His dedication, research, and hard work have resulted in a single volume presenting the most comprehensive analysis ever attempted of Chicago's Polonia. Nevertheless, this work is a "product of human hands." I suspect some may question editorial approach. Others will criticize selection of subject matter, the lack of, or the overabundance of, coverage of certain topics. I applaud such views. Do not two Poles with strong opinions in a heated discussion about politics, form three political parties by the end of the evening? Will not Chicago's Polish American community reportedly to be 750,000, have at least 750,001 opinions of this work. Certainly! Let such energy and probing spur further research resulting in future volumes that will unravel the many dynamic facts of our Polonia.

For this, and for future generations, this work will remain an important source. It will serve well the serious researcher, general readers seeking information of Polonia, and all who enjoy richly illustrated, well-written works which provide a comfortable, enjoyable evening.

Edmund Gronkiewicz
Attorney at Law

Maps of Poland

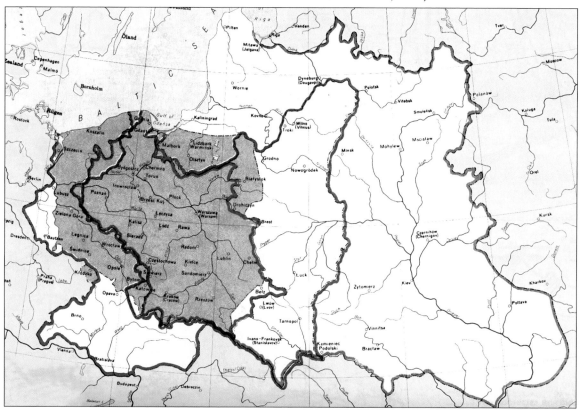

The shape of Polish territories has changed considerably over the centuries.

Orange line = Polish boundaries in 1018.

Gray line = Polish boundaries (Crown and Lithuania) in 1634.

Blue line = Polish boundaries in 1939.

Pink shaded = Territory of today's Poland.

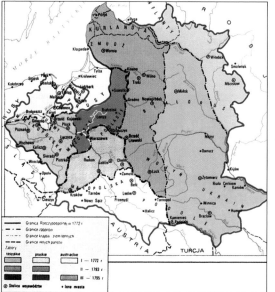

In 1772, Poland's three powerful neighbors, Russia, Prussia and Austria, each wanted to own Poland. This was all but impossible without risking war with each other. They finally settled their dispute by dividing a weakened Poland among themselves in a series of agreements called the Three Partitions of Poland effectively wiping Poland off the map by 1795.

Contemporary map of Poland.

Slavonic tribes roamed, and eventually occupied, vast areas of land east and west of the Vistula River in central Europe as early as the first and second century. A group of tribes were known as the "Polanie," which can be loosely translated as "dwellers of the field." Their territory included Gniezno, which was to become the first capital of Poland, and Poznan, the seat of Poland's first bishop.

Piast, a peasant, was the first king of Poland. In 962, his grandson, Mieszko I, married Dabrowka, a Christian Bohemian princess who influenced her husband to embrace Christianity. Mieszko was baptized in 966. Although the official founding of the Polish state is generally listed as 963, the millennium of Poland's history was observed with elaborate ceremonies throughout the world in 1966 proclaiming to all that Poland's history and development were closely aligned with the jurisdiction of the Holy See in Rome and that its cultural and social vision embraced the philosophies of Christian western Europe.

During the fourteenth century, Casimir III, the only king in Poland's history known as "The Great," created a central administration which safeguarded commercial interests and imposed military duty on every landowner to insure protection for all Polish towns. Casimir built numerous churches. He constructed 40 new fortress towns to protect the frontiers. His crowning achievement, however, was establishing a university at Krakow in 1364. By 1394, some 4,300 were enrolled. Mikolaj Kopernik, better known as Nicholas Copernicus, would become its most famous student. By the 15th century, the time at which Copernicus attended, more than 18,000 students had already received instruction and the university

deserved acclaim as one of Europe's leading academic centers, a distinction it enjoys to the present day.

During this time two important trade routes crossed Poland. A north-south route from the Baltic Sea to the Mediterranean and an east-west axis from western Europe to the Black Sea, Turkey, and eastward to India. These routes were highly profitable and since Krakow was an important trade center it became a welcome, if unlikely, member of the Hanseatic League.

The Jagiellonian dynasty, which followed the Piast dynasty, is highlighted by the union of Poland and Lithuania. The Polish queen, Jadwiga, married the great duke of Lithuania, Jagiello, in 1385.

Copernicus

Lithuania officially accepted Christianity and the Polish-Lithuanian Commonwealth became the strongest and largest state in central Europe. In a major conflict of the Middle Ages, the Polish-Lithuanian army defeated the Teutonic Knights and the threat of the Teutonic Order was forever crushed. As the stability of the Commonwealth became less of a concern, Poland embraced the Renaissance ideals of humanism and significant artistic and cultural expression became a hallmark throughout Poland.

In the 16th century, Poland successfully checked the duchy of Moscow, prosperity flourished, and Poland and Lithuania agreed to be ruled by one king and one parliament. This was Poland's "Golden Age."

Other notable kings of Poland were Stephen Batory who created courts of appeal and established a university at Wilno (1579) and John Sobieski who decisively defeated the Turks at Vienna (1683). That battle often has been heralded as saving Christendom in Europe from all future Turkish attacks.

However, over time, the central authority of Polish kings slowly, but very definitely, eroded due to the political concept of "liberum veto." This practice granted any Polish noble the right to defeat any proposed legislation. As Polish kings sought to maintain control of the state, Prussia, Russia, and Austria exploited the weakness of Polish internal rule and began to

Poland's King Mieszko I, shown with a crucifix in this famous painting by Jan Matejko, accepted Christianity in 966. This event initiated Poland's deep commitment to Christianity for more than 1,000 years.

King Casimir III was the only king in Polish history to be called "The Great." When he came to the throne, neighbors did not recognize his title and instead called him "King of Krakow". He rebuilt the economy bringing prosperity to Poland. By the time of his death he doubled the size of Poland.

annex Polish territories. This first partition of Poland in 1772 sparked a determination in Poland to strengthen the state. The last Polish king, Stanislaus August Poniatowski, enacted a national board of education, granted privileges to towns, and adopted the Polish democratic constitution of May 3, 1791. These actions provoked Russia and Prussia which again absorbed Polish territories in 1793. Thaddeus Kosciuszko, who returned to Poland after making significant contributions to the colonial cause in the American war for independence, led an unsuccessful national uprising for Poland's independence. The insurrection was crushed and Poland was erased from the map of Europe with the third and final partition in 1795.

Throughout the nineteenth century Poles attempted to re-establish their independence. Casting their lot with Napoleon, and contributing some 80,000 troops to march with the French army on its assault on Moscow in 1812, Poland saw its hopes for independence dashed as Napoleon's Grand Army was decimated in its disastrous retreat from Russia. After the Napoleonic episode, Russia increased the brutality of its rule with Prussia also moving to tighten control in Poland.

With its political and military leadership severely depleted, Poles were unsuccessful in launching insurrections throughout the nineteenth century. However, the spirit of Polish nationalism was constantly being kept alive, in fact, inflamed, by Poles throughout Europe.

Although in Paris, Adam Mickiewicz, a poet, became the true national leader of the Polish

Adam Mickiewicz was the national poet of Poland. During the 19th century, when Poland existed only in the hearts and minds of Poles since it did not have a country, Mickiewicz kept alive the spirit of an independent Poland with his poetry.

nation. He was a source of Polish patriotism in the 19th century and would serve as an inspiration a century later when the Poles were again struggling for their independence. In his poem, the underlying theme for Polish independence was religious, if not Messianic. Only by death and suffering, as Christ died and suffered, could Poland resurrect gloriously as Christ had risen. In *Forefather's Eve*, Mickiewicz's great national epic, the poem ends with a promise of the nation's deliverance.

During this same period, Poland lived in the music of Frederic Chopin. As one observer was to write a century later, "[Chopin's music] became familiar, like that of a friend who understood unutterable thoughts, a friend whose touch stirred secret confessions of joy, of pain, of longing, and of purpose. Oddly enough, though the very identify of Poland was forbidden, everybody knew this voice, this touch was Polish."

Poland lost its land, its government, its country in the 18th century. However, Poles very definitely discovered what it meant to be a nation and the spirit of nationalism dominated Polish thought throughout Europe. Toward the end of the century and the early years of the 20th century, Poles in the United States did what they could to aid the cause of regaining Polish independence.

The Great War, later to be called World War I, did not last the few months which most early combatants believed. After four years of unprecedented destruction (Russia's casualties numbered more than 15 million) Germany would be subjected to accept guilt for the conflict,

Frederic Chopin wrote the music that has come to typify the Polish spirit. Intense, yet graceful, Chopin's music is still popular throughout the world today.

while Austria was reduced to a shadow of its former might. These former powers were not at the treaty discussions which ended the war but Polish representatives were.

Thanks to the efforts of United States President, Woodrow Wilson who included independence for Poland as the thirteenth of his Fourteen Points for peace after the war, Poland achieved its independence. Not fully prepared for statehood, Poland, almost immediately, found itself engaged in a war against the Bolsheviks, who assumed power in Russia during the Great War. Poles were successful in that conflict. In 1926, Jozef Pilsudski, took command of the Polish government and made significant strides in economic and social areas until his death in 1935. Afterwards, a time known as the "Reigns of the Colonels," the government was not able to meet the growing threat of German militarism. Germany invaded Poland, September 1, 1939, to launch World War II.

Soviet troops invaded Poland from the east two weeks later. By the end of September, Poland was no longer able to defend itself and surrendered. German and Russian troops would control the country until the war's end. The Polish nation experienced six years of unimaginable horror and devastation as a result of the war. Six million, in a population of some 30 million, died as a result of Nazi extermination or Soviet forced labor. About 400,000 left Poland between 1939 and 1946. In the early phases of the war, 420,000 prisoners of war were kept in German camps; later 17,000 Home Army insurgents would join them in 1944; 1,700,000 were deported to Siberia; 200,000 were forcibly conscripted into the German army; up to 3,000,000 were employed as slave laborers in the German war economy; 68,000 were captured and placed in captivity as a result of the Warsaw Uprising; 350,000 were in Soviet camps and prisons; and 190,000 were captured by the Soviets in 1939. It was estimated that six million Polish citizens were outside of Poland at the end of World War II.

Allied victory, and Poland was a very active ally throughout the war, resulted in Soviet domination of Poland. Agreements made by the United States, Great Britain, and Russia at Teheran and at Yalta sealed Poland's fate. Although the future of Poland was determined at these meetings, no representative of Poland was present. With the Soviet army entrenched in Poland after the war, fraudulent elections in 1947 firmly established Soviet rule in Poland as a satellite, more accurately, a "captive" satellite, of the Soviet Union. The following year, Arthur Bliss Lane would explain the political status of postwar Poland in his book, *I Saw Poland Betrayed: An American Ambassador Reports to his People.*

Soviet occupation, although brutal, never achieved its objectives. Poles again found solace in their faith. Soviet officials quickly learned that the more they attacked religion and the Catholic church, the stronger and more forcefully did Poles proclaim and practice their faith.

Poles also strongly resisted the economic dictates of forced collectivization. Peasant farmers on small private plots frequently out-produced larger, state-owned farms.

Culturally, the Soviet Union's "socialist realism" invited scorn to the point of ridicule. The massive Palace of Culture, built by the Soviets as a gift to the people of Poland, was "accepted" as the most beautiful area in Poland. As Poles explained, "It's so beautiful to look out over Poland from the Palace of Culture because that's the only place in Poland you can be and not see the Palace of Culture."

True leadership for the Polish nation began to emerge in the person of Stefan Cardinal Wyszynski. In 1953, the cardinal protested the oath of loyalty bishops were to take to the Polish People's Republic. Said Wyszynski, "We cannot retreat further. To retreat further would mean complete surrender." Wyszynski's arrest increased his power and influence.

Attempts at liberalization and the so-called "Polish Road to Socialism" were an unwelcome backward

Walter Krawiec, cartoonist for the Dziennik Chicagoski, *one of Chicago's popular Polish-language dailies, portrays Germany's attack on Poland, September 1, 1939, signaling the outbreak of World War II.*

Jozef Pilsudski effectively led the Polish nation between the two World Wars. Although many criticized his methods as forceful and too militaristic—it is believed he wanted to enjoin the Allies in a war against Hitler in the 1930s—his passing in 1935 weakened this resolve and Poland was invaded by Germany, September 1, 1939.

step Soviets had to take in 1956 fearing proliferation of violent outbreaks earlier in the year.

Riots in Gdansk and other areas and the worker's strikes in 1970 helped establish the Committee for Defense of the Workers in 1977 and the Free Trade Union Committee in 1978. After the Gdansk shipyard strike in 1980, Solidarity was officially registered as a trade union with Lech Walesa elected chairman the following year.

Walesa, an unemployed electrician at the shipyards, and his Solidarity movement would prevail over the threat of Soviet invasion. As the Solidarity movement increased in power and influence—even Communist party members were joining—the Soviet-imposed government in Poland was toppled

Stefan Cardinal Wyszynski was not only Poland's spiritual leader during the Communist occupation following World War II, he also clashed with the Soviet-imposed government in Poland over government policies. Not allowed to invite Pope Paul VI for the observance of Poland's Millennium of Christianity in 1966, Wyszynski was able to convince Communist leaders to permit John Paul II to visit Poland in 1979. At right, the Cardinal meets with Marcia Zurawski in October 1976. Both were in Rome for the investiture of John Paul II.

and Walesa was recognized as a national, and international, hero.

Walesa was awarded the Nobel Peace Prize in 1983. Egil Aarvik, Chairman of the Norwegian Nobel Committee, commented in presenting the award: "Lech Walesa made Solidarity more than an expression of the unity of a group campaigning for special interests. Solidarity has come to represent the determination to resolve conflicts and obliterate disagreement through peaceful negotiations where all involved meet with a mutual respect for one another's dignity."

As dominant a figure as Walesa was, another Pole, Karol Wojtyla, (to many an obscure figure "from a far country,") was thrust into headlines around the world October 16, 1978, with the announcement, *Habemus Papam.* Almost immediately, as George Weigel, the Pope's biographer, wrote, "John Paul's Polishness was of intense interest to the media."

The world would quickly learn that a century earlier Juliusz Slowacki, a Polish poet, wrote, "Behold the Slavic Pope is coming." It was Wojtyla who broke ground October 14, 1967 at Nowa Huta to build Poland's largest church in what was planned as the model atheistic Communist city. Moreover, Wojtyla had represented the church in official capacities throughout the world in the decade preceding his election.

After his election to the papacy, John Paul II no longer resided in Poland. However, Poland and its struggle for independence remained within his focus and he used the influence of his office to involve others, notably the United States, to assist Poles or to deter Soviets in their control of Poland. As his biographer has written, John Paul II's visit to Poland, June 2-10, 1979, resulted in "Nine days that changed the world." The Pope was in Poland encouraging Poles to reclaim their Polish history and identity, to go towards the future. Indeed, he seemed to echo a popular motto that had developed throughout Poland, "Let Poland be Poland." As the Pope prepared to leave "my Poland," his final words implored Poles: "You must be strong with the strength of faith… Today more than in any other age you need this strength… You must be strong with the strength of hope…. You must be strong with love… I beg you: never lose your trust… Never lose your spiritual freedom."

As the Vatican, Soviet, and other archives release documents, the role of John Paul II in the collapse of Communist regimes which controlled Russia and central and east European nations will be more fully revealed.

John Paul II died in 2005. Although severely wounded by an assassination attempt and hampered by illness in his final years, Karol Wojtyla had one of the longest Papal reigns in history. In his first 20 years in office he made 84 foreign pilgrimages, traveling 700,000 miles. No individual in history has spoken directly to as many people as has John Paul II.

Throughout history Poles have yearned for a leader who would reflect the romantic heroism they cherish so dearly. Karol Wojtyla provided that heroism not only for Poles, but to millions around the globe earning respect, if not admiration, for his faith, his homeland, and his vision for the dignity of every human life.

Lech Walesa led the Gdansk shipyard strike in Poland which forced the Communists to capitulate and negotiate the Gdansk agreement of August 31, 1980. The Solidarity union became a legal reality in Poland and marked the beginning of the end of Communist rule. Shown here is Andrew Gedlek with Walesa during the latter's visit to Chicago in 1996.

John Paul II began his first pilgrimage to the United States with stops in Chicago, Boston, New York, Philadelphia, Des Moines, and Washington, D.C. During his visit to Chicago from October 4-6, 1979, he attracted large crowds wherever he went. John Paul II celebrated Mass in Grant Park before an estimated 1.2 million people.

In 1476, King Christian I of Denmark commissioned a small flotilla of vessels that left Copenhagen. It did reach and explore today's Greenland, with some sources claiming it discovered Labrador. The ships sailed south to the area of the Delaware River before returning to Denmark. The pilot of the expedition, John Scolvus, was believed to be a Pole, John of Kolno (a town in Poland), who died on the return trip to Denmark.

Since Poland was prosperous, culturally advanced, and socially stable during the period of early explorations of the American continent, there was little motivation or desire to establish colonies. However, skilled workers from Poland were brought to North Carolina in 1585 to assist Sir Walter Raleigh in the production of pitch. In 1608 more skilled workers from Poland came to Jamestown. Others followed. Eventually a total of 50 helped to establish the first permanent English settlement in America.

Thaddeus Kosciuszko

Captain John Smith wrote in his *True Travels*, "they and the Dutchmen were the only ones who knew what work was." In 1609, the Poles saved Smith's life when Indians set an ambush to kill him.

Although Polish workers produced the first commercial goods in the colonies and quickly became free citizens, they were not granted full voting rights by the first session of the Virginia House of Burgesses in 1619. The Poles protested and suspended work in their glass factory, tar distillery, and soap plants. Since almost all the profits of the London Company came from the resale of the products produced by Poles in Virginia, the Virginia governor declared that the Poles "shall be enfranchised and made as free as any inhabitants."

Many Poles came to the colonies and achieved distinction. Karol Kurczewski (Alexander Curtiss) was appointed schoolmaster in New Amsterdam in 1659 and founded the first Latin school in today's New York City. He was also one of the city's first physicians. Olbracht Zaborowski acquired large tracts of land in New Jersey and was appointed as the first Justice of the Peace for upper Bergen County, New Jersey. Anthony Sadowski (Sandusky) and his sons, Jacob and James, explored and established trading posts in territories that would become Ohio, Kentucky, and Tennessee.

During the Revolutionary War, Poland's highly-skilled and trained soldiers were recruited to assist in the colonial attempt to win independence. Thaddeus Kosciuszko came to Philadelphia in 1776 and was appointed colonel of engineers. Eventually he had the title of chief of engineers, and is credited with directing the construction of defenses which resulted in important victories for the colonists. He built the fortifications at West Point which would be studied by future generations of United States military officers. After West Point Military Academy was officially opened, the first texts used were those written by Kosciuszko. For his services, the U.S. Congress granted Kosciuszko U.S. citizenship and awarded him large tracts of land in today's state of Ohio.

Kosciuszko also received distinction as a pioneer of negro emancipation. Before leaving America he granted freedom to Agrippa Hull, a negro, who was presented to Kosciuszko at West Point as his personal servant. Kosciuszko drew up a will in which he authorized Thomas Jefferson to dispose of the properties granted to Kosciuszko by the United States and "to employ the whole thereof in purchasing Negroes …and giving them their liberty… in having them instructed for their new condition in the duties of morality which may make them good neighbors, good fathers and mothers, husbands and wives, in their duty as citizens; teaching them to be defenders of their liberty and country…."

Count Casimir Pulaski, often called the "Father of the American Cavalry," commanded four regiments of cavalry during the American Revolution. He is credited with saving Washington's troops at Brandywine and at Warren's Tavern. His Pulaski Legion became the model for development of other legions during the war. Pulaski was killed during the siege of Savannah on September 25, 1779.

The contributions of Kosciuszko and Pulaski towards American independence have been, and are today, shown numerous expression by a grateful nation. Towns, counties, schools, and other public areas across America bear their names. In Chicago, a prominent statue of Kosciuszko was placed in Humboldt Park. At its dedication on September 11, 1904, more than 100,000 were in attendance. In 1978, the statue was relocated to a more prominent area on Solidarity Drive in the shadows of Soldier Field on Chicago's lake front. Illinois commemorates Pulaski with an official state holiday. An annual program at The Polish Museum of America in Chicago attracts the state's and city's principal elected officials who pay homage to his deeds and lay a wreath beneath a massive painting showing Pulaski being wounded in Savannah.

Free of foreign domination, the United States was successful in establishing a permanent government and constitution. In Europe, Poland's central government was crumbling and foreign domination of Poland was achieved by Prussia, Russia, and Austria by 1795. An unsuccessful insurrection in 1830-1831 resulted in many exiles seeking refuge in the United States. The United States Congress approved settlement of 22,040 acres near Rock River, Illinois for arrivals from Poland. That Polish colony never materialized but proved to be the impetus for Poles to make their way to Chicago which, within a century, would garner the largest concentration of Poles in the United States.

Captain John Napierski, who took part in the 1831 insurrection, is believed to be the first Pole to reside in Chicago. Major Louis Chlopicki, nephew of Louis Chlopicki, who led the 1831 insurrection, also came to Chicago in 1834. Voting records reveal that A. Panakaske and J. Zaleski voted for William B. Ogden in Chicago's 1837 mayoralty race. Two Polish physicians also made their way to Chicago in the 1850s, Dr. Jacob Cert and Dr. Edward Hartwich.

Most accounts, however, agree that it was Anthony Smarzewski-Schermann who should be credited as the founder of Chicago's Polonia. Over the years, this term, Polonia, was frequently used to signify a specific local Polish settlement or the entire Polish American community in the United States. Smarzewski came to Chicago with his wife and three children in 1850. Listed as a carpenter, he quit that trade to open a grocery store on Noble and Bradley streets to serve a growing Polish population. He added the name "Schermann" to his Polish surname to attract the well-established German community.

By 1860, there were, depending on which sources one accepts, at least 109 but probably closer to 500 Poles residing in Chicago. Edward Wilkoszewski, an industrious entrepreneur, arrived in 1861 and provided employment for hundreds of Poles during the 1860s and 1870s.

Poles were arriving in larger numbers as a result of unsuccessful insurrections, revolutions, and ever-increasing restrictions imposed by the occupying powers in Poland.

Poles distinguished themselves in the Union Army during the Civil War. Captain Bernard F. Stampoffski organized Company F of the Ninth Illinois Cavalry. Edmund T. Hulanicki attained the rank of captain of the Twelfth U.S. Heavy Artillery and his brother, Thomas, commanded Battery L of the Second Illinois Light Artillery.

Peter Kiolbassa served in the Confederate Army having resided, since 1855, in the emerging Polish colony at Panna Maria in Texas at the outbreak of hostilities. He was captured by Union forces and taken to Illinois. He enlisted as a private and rose in rank to be Captain of Company E, Sixth U.S. Colored Cavalry.

Having studied at a business college in Texas, Kiolbassa was also a schoolteacher and organist at the village church. While in Chicago, Kiolbassa contacted Rev. Leopold Moczygemba, CR (Congregation of the Resurrection, a religious order that was most prominent in establishing Polish parishes throughout Chicago), asking him to leave his Texas mission, come to Chicago, and help establish a "permanent organization" for Chicago Poles. Moczygemba arrived in 1864 and, at the home of Smarzewski-Schermann, the Society of St. Stanislaus Kostka was formed. Plans were drawn which resulted in the first Polish Catholic parish in Chicago, St. Stanislaus Kostka. Smarzewski-Schermann was elected president of the society and Kiolbassa, vice-president. Joseph Niemczewski served as secretary with John Arkuszewski and Andrew Kurr, committee members.

St. Stanislaus Kostka Church was formally opened in 1867. It organized under the leadership of Rev. Vincent Barzynski, CR. He arrived in 1874 and the parish community rapidly expanded to become the largest Catholic parish in the world. By 1899, St. Stanislaus Kostka had about 40,000 members and some 50 church societies, a few with as many as 4,000 members. Mother Caroline of the School Sisters of Notre Dame in North America was invited to organize a school. She came with three sisters and a candidate in 1874. By the turn of the century more than 4,000 students were enrolled in the school.

Peter Kiolbassa

Holy Trinity Church, a short walk from St. Stanislaus Kostka, opened in 1872. It closed for a few years, but then rapidly increased in membership. St. Hedwig's, about a mile to the north, opened in 1888. These three churches, along with other major Polish organizations, formed the heartland of the Polish community or, as it was often called at that time, "Polish Downtown." This area had the largest concentration of Poles in Chicago with some neighborhoods or specific blocks with 90 per cent or more of the residents Polish.

A second Polish community developed in Pilsen west and south of "Polish Downtown" with the opening of St. Adalbert's Parish in 1873. As the Polish population began to move west, other churches opened: St. Casimir, St. Ann, St. Mary of Czestochowa, Good Shepherd, and St. Roman.

Bridgeport provided the home for a third distinct Polish community. St. Mary of Perpetual Help, organized in 1883, was opened within the geographic boundaries of Bridgeport with two branches of the Chicago River and two railroad tracks defining the boundaries. Just outside this geographic entity were the stockyards which attracted Poles to the area. St. Joseph Parish was established in 1887 to serve this growing Polish population. St. John of God Parish (1906) and Sacred Heart Parish (1910) were also provided for workers at the stockyards while St. Barbara Parish was opened in Bridgeport in 1910.

On Chicago's far south side, along the lake, the steel mills were becoming an important industry. Seventy Polish families got permission to build a church and Immaculate Conception organized in 1882. St. Michael Parish (1892), St. Mary Magdalene (1910), and St. Bronislaus (1920) also served the Polish population as it increased alongside the booming steel industry.

Although Poles could be found in all areas of the city, two patterns emerged. Poles settled near two of the city's major diagonal streets, Milwaukee

Avenue to the northwest and Archer Avenue to the southwest. Over the years, churches were built near these commercial venues.

Polish American fraternal societies, which grew quickly and numbered well over 100,000 members within a generation, were established in Chicago with the founding of the Polish Roman Catholic Union of America (PRCUA) in 1873 and the Polish National Alliance of the United States of North America (PNA) in 1880. Since the Congregation of the Resurrection was instrumental in launching the PRCUA, allegiance to the Catholic faith was emphasized. When the PNA was formed, it announced it would strive for the material and moral development of the Polish element in the United States and stressed the necessity of helping Poland. A prominent historian of the time wrote, "For some time neither Catholics nor Poles existed in America; but only Unionists (PRCUA) or Alianists (PNA); who was not a member of the Alliance, him the Polish National Alliance did not regard as a Pole; while whoever was not a member of the Polish Roman Catholic Union, the PRCUA did not regard as a Catholic." For the most part, most Poles remained Catholic and continued support, whenever possible, to assist Polish causes in partitioned Poland.

A definite schism developed in the Polish community over the control of church properties. Some individual Poles were reluctant to give up ownership of "their" church to either the archdiocese or an individual pastor, and the Polish National Catholic Church, which retained ownership of the church properties with the people of the parish, did number about 6,000 adherents in Chicago by 1918.

A prolific Polish press emerged in Chicago. Upon arrival in the city, most Poles continued to use the Polish language at home, church, in stores, were entertained in Polish, and usually were employed where everyone seemed to speak, or understand, Polish. The following is a partial listing of Polish newspapers published between 1873 and 1908. The list is meant to be representative rather than exhaustive. Dates of publication are indicated: *The Catholic Gazette* (1874), *Chicago Polish Gazette* (1873-1913), *The Friend of the People* (1876-1884), *The Country Squire* (1874), *Harmony* (1881—still published), *The Chicago Gazette* (1885), *Chicago Polish News* (1873-1913), *Grain* (1886-1903), *Daily Journal* (1887), *The Chicago Courier* (1887), *Chicago Times* (1887), *The Aspergillum* (1887-1888), *Faith and Fatherland*, which became *The Polish Nation* (1888—still published), *The Free Voice* (1889-1890), *Poles in Chicago* (1890), *The Polish Daily News* (1890—still published today but not with the same line of ownership), *The Reform* (1891-1892), *The Polish Gazette* (1892-1895), *The Chicago Telegraph* (1892), *The Standard* (1893-1902), *The Labor Gazette* (1894), *The Polish Women's Voice*, (1900—still published), *Daily Alliance* (1908—still published).

Caution must be used before accepting circulation figures of these publications. Many newspapers ceased after a few editions. Others combined. Early statistics are difficult to locate. In 1920, the Polish Statistical Bureau reported that the circulation of all Polish newspapers in the Chicago area was 1,340,000. These figures were probably inflated by editors who were trying to attract advertisers since, for the same year, the same editors reported circulation of 1,000,000 to the U.S. Post Office to determine mailing costs. Further discrepancies can be noted when checking N.W. Ayers publications which are often cited as authoritative. In 1916, for example, Ayers calculated circulation of several Polish publications as 160,000 while editors for the same publications stated 400,000 as their circulation.

Book publishing in Chicago's Polish community was also impressive. Helena Chrzanowska, an employee of the former Smulski Publishing Company on Noble Street which became the Polish American Publishing Company, recalled "a typical monthly requisition (February 1913) which came from shipping to my desk: 25,000 copies of *Smulski Primer*, 25,000 copies of *Dyniewicz Primer*, 20,000 copies of *Szopinski Primer*, 20,000 copies of *Smulski First Reader*, 20,000 copies of *Smulski Second Reader*, 20,000 copies of *Dyniewicz Second Reader*, 10,000 copies of *Smulski Third Reader*, and 10,000 copies of *Dyniewicz Third Reader*. Five different catechisms totaled a printing of 75,000 copies from 1903 to 1930. Copies of Polish Bible histories, Polish New Testament histories, the history of the Catholic Church and Liturgies all topped 55,000 annually. Histories and other works about Poland averaged about 36,000 a year. Polish grammars, spellers, and other schoolbooks totaled 30,000 per year." Chrzanowska estimates a grand total of 375,000 to 400,000 Polish volumes were printed annually between 1903 and 1933 at the Polish American Publishing Company. Combined with the Polish Publishing Company specializing in Polish prayer books, "the output was staggering." Add to this the thousands of Polish American dictionaries, novels, poetry, popular almanacs published during this same period along with Polish plays, sheet music, Polish "dream books," and fortune-telling cards one can conclude that Poles appreciated and cherished the printed word.

Polish theatrical presentations began in Chicago in 1873. Each parish had its own hall and many of the productions were performed by amateur players. However, there were up to as many as eight theatrical companies who staged regular performances in several different venues. Admission was usu-

Dziennik Chicagoski announces its 50th anniversary in December 1940.

ally 25 to 50 cents with a ball following the performance. Audiences frequently included English, Irish, and Germans residents from the local area and others were known to travel hundreds of miles to attend performances. A random sampling of the Polish theatre's repertoire in Chicago until 1890 included: *Emancipation of Women, The Nightingale, The New Don Quixote, The Lobzowians, Wanda or The Perfection of Woman, On the Bug River, The Wedding on the Electric Current, The Peasant Aristocrats, The Master Cobbler of Noble Street, Money or The Individual, Kosciuszko, The Carpathian Mountaineers, Sobieski at Vienna, The Polish Uprising of 1863,* and *The Torch Parade.*

A popular, even though usually referred to as a "forgotten playwright" in the Polish community, was Anthony Jax. He arrived in Chicago in 1889, perhaps earlier. Author of at least 35, with other sources claiming as many as 50, plays, Jax was an extremely private individual. He did not direct his own

The first issue of Free Poland *was published by the Polish National Council at the PRCUA building in Chicago on September 1, 1914. The publication was printed in English and directed at a general audience to promote independence for Poland at the end of World War I.*

plays and neither sought attention nor reviews. However, managers were quick to discover that staging a play by Jax was always profitable. Jax wrote tragedies, dramas, comedies, operettas, farces, and at times featured a single actor in a variety of performances. A few of his titles may indicate the wide range of Jax's appeal: *Freedom and Slavery, A Professor's Wig, The Cousin from Russia, Virginal Vows, Genevieve, The German Scythe-bearer, Fools Are Not Sewn, His Lordship in America, The Mouse Tower, The Degenerate Daughter* (acclaimed as Jax's best work), and *Polish Uncle Sam.* Jax's works have

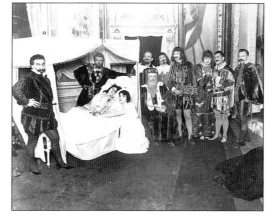

Othello *and other plays of non-Polish playwrights were often performed in Polish by Polish American theatrical groups throughout Chicago during the early decades of the 20th century.*

Anna Pedicini popularized a role in Mr. Ogorek *(Mr. Pickle), a play written and performed in Chicago in the early 20th century. Plays of this type were based on the life of a Polish peasant in America. They included* Siekierki *and* Bartek Bieda *which were widely popular on the stage and later on radio broadcasts.*

been aptly summarized as, "a precious but unpolished gem."

Each parish had its own elementary school. St. Stanislaus Kostka High School was affiliated with the parish. The Congregation of the Resurrection established St. Stanislaus College in 1891 which grew to an enrollment of 210. After a new building was purchased in 1929, the former building was renamed Weber Hall and by 1931 the school

was referred to as Weber High School. Holy Trinity High School was founded in 1910 and a new facility was built in 1927. Weber and Holy Trinity were open to boys, while girls attended, directly across Division Street on which all three schools were located, Holy Family Academy, which opened in 1885.

Other social agencies were formed. The Franciscan Sisters from Poland established St. Joseph's Home for the Aged in 1898. Most Rev. Paul P. Rhode, the first Roman Catholic Bishop of Polish origin consecrated in the United States, founded St. Hedwig's Orphanage in Niles in 1910. Both institutions were instrumental in adding a cohesive element to Chicago's Polish American community.

Peter Kiolbassa, elected to the state legislature in 1877, would, over the years, hold several elected offices. Elected Chicago's city treasurer, he was the first to return interest on city funds, contrary to keeping it for private use as did former treasurers. John Smulski, elected Chicago's city attorney in 1903 and Illinois state treasurer in 1906, also turned over all money earned as interest to the state.

The increasing flow of immigrants from Poland to the United States was directly related to the oppressive policies of the Prussian, Austrian, and Russian overlords in the former Polish territory. For example, Otto von Bismarck, Chancellor of

Prussia, wrote, "Nothing is left for us but to exterminate the [Poles.]" Although Bismarck was impressed with the loyalty and fighting capabilities of the Polish peasants, his compulsory military service provided further inducement for Poles to leave Poland.

Henryk Sienkiewicz, prolific 19th century novelist whose work recalled Poland's past, explained the massive migration with two words, "For bread." Another factor was the active recruitment, such as by the Illinois Central Railroad, for workers who were needed for the rapid U.S. industrialization which commenced in earnest toward the end of the 19th century.

Numerous scholars have challenged statistics maintained at Ellis Island and by the U.S. Census for arrivals from Poland, the country that did not exist on the political maps of Europe after the Civil War and before World War I. Many Poles coming to America during this period were counted as Prussians, Russians, and Austrians. Most could not speak English. Many had minimal formal education.

However, once settled in Chicago, the Polish American population could be more accurately recorded. By 1918, it numbered 383,000 organized in 38 parishes with 35,909 children attending parochial schools. Church property was valued at $10,363,000; there were 4,096 Polish businesses, industrial and commercial enterprises, and 26,630 Poles owned their own homes valued at $335,000,000. By 1928, the number of Poles in Chicago rose to 424,725, representing the largest ethnic group in the city. On the eve of the Great Depression, Poles had accumulated savings held by building and loan associations of some $366,720,000.

After the United States entered World War

Most Rev. Paul P. Rhode

John Smulski

I in April of 1917, Poles rejoiced at Woodrow Wilson's "Peace Without Victory" speech to the U.S. Senate, January 22, 1917. Said Wilson: "No peace can last or ought to last, which does not recognize and accept the principle that governments derive all their just powers from the consent of the governed, and that no right anywhere exists to hand peoples about from sovereignty to sovereignty as if they were property. I take it for granted, for instance, if I may venture on a single example, that statesmen everywhere are agreed that there should be a united, independent and autonomous Poland, and that henceforth inviolable security of life, of worship and of industrial and social development should be guaranteed to all people who have lived heretofore under the powers of government devoted to a faith and purpose hostile to their own." Poland would be free and independent after an Allied victory.

From the beginning of the war, Poles raised funds to assist their Polish brethren in Europe. World-famous pianist, Ignace Jan Paderewski, who would become Poland's first premier after the war, committed himself to numerous concerts throughout the United States with all proceeds contributed to assisting Poles in Europe. On September 20, 1917, the Polish Central Relief Committee met in Chicago to determine military support from the United States for the Polish Army in France. After the Germans surrendered in 1918, recruitment ceased with 38,108 men applying for service and 22,395 accepted. An authority on the subject summed up the efforts of the "Military Commission [which enabled] Polonia to contribute significantly to resurrecting Poland."

Although Chicago had the nation's largest Polish American community, radio broadcasts in Polish were first heard in Cleveland in 1926. A year later the "White Eagle Hour" made its debut on

Chicago radio. A Golden Age Committee, composed of Polish American activists in Chicago, organized programs for Polish-speaking audiences in 1928. Joseph Migala, who has written extensively on the subject, credits the committee with making "great contributions to the development of Polish radio in the early, most difficult years."

Polish language broadcasts could be heard on several stations, and were sponsored by merchants (Association of Polish Merchants and Manufacturers, Grand Leader Department Store, Ritter's Furniture Store, Star West Wash Laundry,) major industries (Evans Fur Company, Wonder Cut Bread, Vervena Co.) and Polish American organizations (Grunwald Society of the Polish National Alliance, White Eagle Drama Circle). Almost all followed a format which announced their program as "Radio Hour of...." By the 1930s many Polish radio programs were broadcast every day. In 1936, the *Alliance Daily* indicated that a poll revealed that the Grunwald Hour, Early Birds, and Ritter's Hour were listener favorites, while audiences selected The Siekierka Family, Bartek Bieda, and Ogor-kowa as the most interesting dramatic or comedy sketches.

A group of Polish radio personalities formed a Polish Radio Syndicate and registered with the State of Illinois on February 20, 1938. Its aim was

Ignace Jan Paderewski

"to organize the advertising market to eliminate unhealthy competition among radio broadcasters and to improve the quality of programs." The outbreak of World War II limited its scope of effective activity.

Adolf Hitler's Third Reich launched World War II when German forces invaded Poland in 1939. Stunned, as was the rest of the world, the Polish American community anguished as Poland was again occupied by its powerful neighbors, Germany and the Soviet Union. After the war, another, and quite different group of

Poles, would begin to make its way to the United States. They would discover, as others had been discovering for almost a century, what it meant to be a Polish American in this land of opportunity.

Sociologist, Theresita Polzin, summarizes the impact of the late 19th and early 20th century Polish immigration movement on American society: "The Poles as a group made two specific unique contributions to the culture of the United States…. What was urban, industrial, democratic (that is, economic and political—though far from "equality"), the Poles accepted and adopted from the new environment; what was cultural—institutions, traditions, values—they kept from a heritage enriched by centuries of talent, toil, trial, and religious values…. The second major unique contribution of Poles to American culture… was the stability of the Polish American population that prompted John Kennedy to acknowledge: "…longer than most immigrant groups they kept their language, their customs, their dances."…The outstanding testimony to Polish American stability was home ownership. It might be called "a passion for owning a home" or "the hallmark of the Polish American." It was concrete evidence of the Poles' preference for stability…. It may be this very stability that resents deeply any social disruption, such as movement of populations which make for changing neighborhoods…. The Poles of any generation appreciate America. They hide often among other Americans because in many aspects of life, including physical appearance and language, they are like other Americans. However, a goodly segment of them have retained many customs, traditions, beliefs, values, and some patterns of behavior traceable to the land of their forefathers. Their lingering influence is most pronounced in the areas of family and religion. Here they stand visible."

Fire was always a threat to two- and three-story wooden building flats in the area around St. Michael the Archangel Church on Chicago's southeast side. Residents observe the destruction being caused by a July 23, 1919 fire in the neighborhood.

A major celebration at St. John of God Church brought together numerous parish societies and guests from the entire Back of the Yards neighborhood.

Talman Savings and Loan Association, at one time the largest savings and loan association in Illinois, sponsored a very popular Polish Festival on its grounds. Many groups appeared in traditional Polish folk costumes such as the ladies below at the 1973 festival.

The Polish Constitution Day Parade, at first, was observed on the Sunday closest to May 3rd (Polish Constitution Day). It stepped off at Holy Trinity Church, marched past the headquarters of the PNA, headquarters of the PRCUA at Augusta Boulevard and Milwaukee Avenue, then proceeded west about two miles on Augusta Boulevard (shown right) to the memorial statue of Thaddeus Kosciuszko in Humboldt Park.

Coming Over

"New York, 19 November [1906]

Since early morning on Saturday one could sense the bustle of activity among the passengers of the America. People were packing quickly. Later, at breakfast, the normally tranquil dining room was buzzing like a beehive … in general the mood was one of joy. But here and there I could see sad-faced people engrossed in their thoughts and looking wistfully back. Those were the people who in a few hours were to set foot in the New World for the first time in order to build themselves a new future. They devote these final moments to nostalgia, their families and thoughts of their native land. What does the future hold in store for them—they ask, before they are sucked into the bewildering, topsy-turvy whirl of a hard struggle for existence …"

Emigrants from Poland leave for New York at the turn of the century.

Polish immigrants await a ship at a German port to begin their journey to a new life in America. Note the signs communicating in several languages.

"And so a physician examines our eyes, an immigration official asks why we have come to America, a customs official attempts to establish what we are bringing in. When I tell them my nationality, everywhere I see a cordial smile and hear the comment: "Aha, Polish, Polish," indicating that the Poles enjoy a good reputation here. Occupation: journalist; destination: through America, and they don't even bother to ask how much money I have with me.... The formalities are over, I walk out on deck."

Mrs. Wanda Rozmarek, far left, wife of Charles (PNA president) was present to greet this group of displaced persons from Poland arriving in Chicago in 1949.

Polish immigrants in New York after arrival at Ellis Island.

"The customs inspection is much ado about nothing. In the enormous hall everybody stands beneath the first letter of his surname. When all his luggage had been removed from the ship, he takes the proper tag to the inspector seated before the letter A for example (in my case that entailed a hike of half a verst there and back) and finds an official who sticks on a card, for my trunks were not even opened."

Quotes from Ludwik Wlodek,
In The Land of George
Washington: Travel Impressions,
The Poles in America, 1907

List of Polish Churches founded prior to 1956

St. Stanislaus Kostka	1867
Holy Trinity	1872
St. Adalbert	1873
Immaculate Conception B.V.M	1882
SS. Cyril & Methodius	1883
St. Mary of Perpetual Help	1883
St. Josaphat	1884
St. Joseph	1886
St. Hedwig	1888
St. Casimir	1890
St. Andrew the Apostle	1891
St. Michael	1892
Ascension	1892
St. John Cantius	1893
St. Stanislaus B&M (Cragin)	1893
St. Hyacinth	1894
St. Stanislaus B&M (Posen)	1894
Sacred Heart	1895
Sts. Peter and Paul	1895
Our Lady of Czestochowa	1895
St. Mary of the Angels	1897
St. Salomea	1897
St. Isidore	1900
Assumption	1902
St. Ann	1903
Holy Innocents	1905
St. Florian	1906
St. John of God	1906
Five Holy Martyrs	1908
St. Francis of Assisi	1909
St. Barbara	1910
St. Mary	1910
Sacred Heart	1910
Transfiguration	1911
Immaculate Heart of Mary	1912
St. Wenceslaus	1912
St. Helen	1914
St. James (Hansen Park)	1914
St. Ladislaus	1914
St. Constance	1916
St. Bronislaus	1920
St. Fidelis	1920
St. Camillus	1921
St. Blasé	1921
St. Pancratius	1924
St. Bruno	1925
St. Susanna	1927
St. Bronislawa	1928
St. Roman	1928
Mother of God	1956

Today, as in generations past, value in the Polish American community is measured by what is holy, sacred, and enduring. The Catholic faith has crystallized this thinking for Poles and Polish Americans as they continue to openly embrace the Church's teachings and Sacraments.

Wladek, an enduring diminutive of Walter (Wladyslaw), provides insight into the motivations of Polish migration to America as well as Poles adapting to their new homes in America in William I. Thomas' and Florian Znaniecki's *The Polish Peasant in Europe and America*. This four-volume work, published in 1924, provides a detailed and comprehensive account of Wladek's childhood and early adult life.

Wladek's deep-seated religious beliefs were a daily reality. As with generations of Poles before, Wladek's chronological calendar was not kept with days or months. Dates and events were remembered by their relationship to Christmas, Easter, Pentecost, saints' feast days, and other days considered holy such as homage to Our Lady of Czestochowa and All Souls Day.

Unable to find steady employment, Wladek is attracted by the lure and promise of America. He leaves for Chicago in 1913 to join his sister and others from Poland who had settled in Chicago.

Wladek's words are very personal. He makes frequent references reflecting his religious beliefs. Those beliefs are as vital today as they were to Wladek more than a century ago.

"When the priest came in every one of us children greeted him by kissing his hand; he talked a little with everybody and wished us a merry 'Alleluiah.'"

– Wladek

"On Sunday we had to pray from our prayer-books after breakfast, every one from his own; for as soon as any of us knew how to read a little he received a small prayer-book as a gift."

– Wladek

"St. Constance Parish on the northwest side of Chicago, where I served as Pastor from January 1, 2001, until June 30, 2003, after being appointed auxiliary archbishop of Chicago, provides a fitting illustration of the demographic trends that occurred in Polonia during the twentieth century. Founded in 1916 as a non-territorial Polish parish, St. Constance in those early years was essentially a Polish-speaking parish. By the 1970s, the children and grandchildren of those first immigrant parishioners no longer spoke Polish, and St. Constance became a predominantly English-speaking parish with only one Polish Mass on Sunday. With the influx of new immigrants from Poland in the 1990s, by the time I became Pastor of St. Constance Parish at the start of the third millennium of Christianity, there were two Polish Masses with overflow crowds in a church that seats 1,000 people, So I added two Polish Masses, and now over 4,000 people attend four Polish and four English Masses every weekend at St. Constance Parish."

Most Rev. Thomas J. Paprocki, A Pastoral Plan for Polonia in the New Millennium

> *"I always considered disobedience a great sin and I could not understand how it was possible not to listen to one's parents. I listened not only to them but also to my older brothers and sisters, and if they ordered me to do anything I did it, not only from fear but also from conviction that I was doing right."*
>
> – Wladek

Rev. Vincent Barzynski, CR., was an effective organizer of Chicago's Polish American community. Pastor at St. Stanislaus Kostka from 1874 to 1899, he helped organize many parishes in the Chicago area for new arrivals from Poland. His funeral, one of the largest in Chicago history, attracted 10,000 marchers, 500 funeral carriages, and 150 clergy.

Rev. Casimir Sztuczko, CSC, was appointed pastor for Holy Trinity Parish in 1893 when he was 26 years old. He served in that position for 55 years.

Rev. Leopold Moczygemba, CR., the first Polish priest to preach and offer sacraments to Polish Americans in Chicago, later became PRCUA's president from 1875 to 1878. He also devoted considerable efforts to raise funds in Chicago for a seminary to train priests to serve Polish Americans. Moczygemba established Punna Maria in Texas, the first Polish settlement in the United States.

> *"My father was a very God-fearing man. As far as I remember he never omitted any divine service. So he educated us also very religiously. Every morning we had to kneel down all together and say the prayer. And father sat near us and saw to it that we did not hurry too much."*
>
> – Wladek

Current List of Churches with Mass in Polish

–Chicago–

St. Adalbert
St. Ann (S. Leavitt)
St. Bruno
St. Camillus
St. Constance
St. Daniel the Prophet
St. Ferdinand
St. Fidelis
Five Holy Martyrs
St. Florian
St. Frances Assissi
St. Francis Borgia
Sacred Heart Mission
St. Hedwig
St. Helen
Holy Innocents
Holy Trinity Polish Mission
St. Hyacinth Basilica
St. James (W. Fullerton)
St. Jane De Chantal
St. Joseph
St. Ladislaus
St. Mary of the Angels
St. Monica
St. Pancratius
St. Pascal
SS. Peter & Paul
St. Priscilla
St. Richard
St. Roman
St. Stanislaus Bishop and Martyr
St. Stanislaus Kostka
St. Thecla
Transfiguration
St. Turibius
St. Wenceslaus

–Suburbs–

St. Albert the Great (Burbank)
St. Andrew the Apostle (Calumet City)
St. Blase (Summit)
SS. Cyril & Methodius (Lemont)
St. Fabian (Bridgeview)
St. Gertrude (Franklin Park)
Holy Spirit Chapel (Northbrook)
Immaculate Conception (Waukegan)
St. John the Baptist (Harvey)
St. John Brebeuf (Niles)
St. John the Evangelist (Streamwood)
St. Joseph (Summit)
St. Joseph the Worker (Wheeling)
Santa Maria Del Popolo (Mundelein)
St. Mary Margaret (Algonquin)
St. Mary of Czestochowa (Cicero)
Our Lady Mother of the Church (Willow Springs)
Polish Missions Churches (Lombard/Wood Dale)
St. Rosalie (Harwood Heights)
St. Stephen Deacon and Martyr (Tinley Park)
St. Thomas Becket (Mt. Prospect)
St. Thomas Villanova (Palatine)
Transfiguration (Wauconda)
St. Zachary (Des Plaines)

St. Stanislaus Kostka Church, school, rectory, and convent was established in 1867 to serve Polish immigrants to Chicago. By 1899, the church had 40,000 parishioners and a school enrollment of 4,000.

The interior of St. Stanislaus Kostka Church.

The area in front of St. Stanislaus Kostka Church was cleared of homes and businesses in 1913 to make way for Blackhawk Park.

"I was the oldest [son] at home after my brother left. I now served at mass alone and I was very proud of this."
– Wladek

The fire at St. Stanislaus Kostka Church in 1906. Records of the PRCUA were completely destroyed in the blaze. Since the PRCUA was growing rapidly, a decision was made to build a separate facility for the PRCUA at Augusta Boulevard and Milwaukee Avenue after the fire. That facility remains in use until the present time.

Photo left: Holy Trinity Church as it appeared in the late 19th century. It was getting too small for the growing congregation, so a new church was built, photo right, and dedicated October 6, 1906.

Photo right: Holy Trinity Church dominates the area cleared by urban renewal of all businesses on Noble Street south of Division Street. Many older homes were demolished and Noble Street was closed to traffic.

The 900-seat Holy Trinity auditorium was the scene for many dramatic, choral, and other presentations for the Polish American community in the early decades of the 20th century.

Poles Return to Holy Trinity

Holy Trinity parish was organized in 1873 in the heart of Chicago's rapidly emerging Polish American community. It was closed for several years and functioned sporadically until 1893 when Rev. Casimir Sztuczko, CSC, was appointed pastor. After the present church was built in 1905, and consecrated in 1906, the parish grew rapidly. During the decade from 1910 to 1920, baptisms averaged well over 1,000 per year along with 300 to 400 weddings. A noticeable decline began in the mid-1930s when baptisms averaged about 180 annually and weddings at about 130. There was a slight resurgence in the late 1940s but a dramatic decline after 1975 when Rev.

Casimir Czaplicki, the last pastor from the Congregation of the Holy Cross, left in 1975. In the decade from 1975 to 1985, baptisms and marriages averaged less than eight per year.

In 1986, when Sunday Mass attendance dropped to an average of 860, Joseph Cardinal Bernadine moved to establish a Polish Pastoral Mission at Holy Trinity Church. Within two years, baptisms and weddings began to increase dramatically, a trend which continues until the present day. Attendance for the five Sunday Masses has increased to 5,000 and an estimated 10,000 took part in Holy Week Services in 2007.

Walenty and Agnieszka Kowalski, pioneer settlers in Cragin, were founders of St. Stanislaus Bishop and Martyr Parish. In 1893, when Cragin was still a farm community, the Kowalskis organized a committee to petition the archbishop for a Polish priest. After setting aside ten lots, the new church was dedicated June 18, 1893 by Rev. Vincent Barzynski, CR. The Kowalskis allowed their home to be used for the first school classrooms and provided meals for the teachers and administrators from the school and parish office.

"Solemn days were Christmas, Easter, mother's and father's name-days."
– Wladek

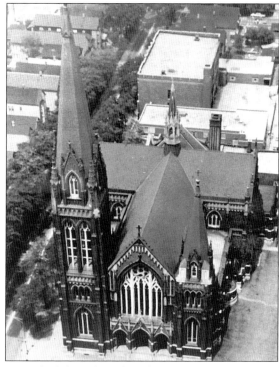

St. Michael the Archangel was built near Illinois Steel South Works. Construction began in 1907 under the leadership of Rev. Paul Rhode who, in 1908, became the first Polish Roman Catholic Bishop in the United States.

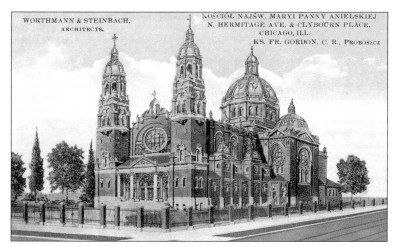

Work on St. Mary of the Angels, shown above, began in 1911, but due to labor strikes and building material shortages, it was not completed until 1920.

St. Hedwig's first church, shown here, was blessed December 3, 1888, with the first Mass said five days later for the Feast of the Immaculate Conception. By 1918, the parish population was 20,000.

St. Adalbert Church was built in 1873 as Polish Americans formed a community south of their main settlements near St. Stanislaus Kostka Church. By 1918, it grew to a total of 20,000 parishioners. The second church, with its 185-foot towers and copper domes, was designed by Henry J. Schlacks and completed in 1914.

"On Easter morning at 6 father awakened everybody for the "Resurrection." I have never seen the holidays celebrated with greater solemnity than in my parents' home."

– Wladek

The Polish National Church organized in Chicago in 1895. The issue separating "Polish" Catholics from "Roman" Catholics was ownership of parish property, the former claiming parishioners, the latter insisting it should be the diocese in which the property was located. Rev. Anthony Kozlowski, assistant pastor at St. Hedwig was excommunicated from the Roman Catholic Church in 1895 and established an All Saints Parish and Church, with most of the congregation being former members of St. Hedwig. Shown at right is All Saints Cathedral which served Chicago's Polish National Catholic community from June 1931 until October 1993 when the present All Saints Cathedral at 9201 West Higgins was dedicated.

Holy Innocents Parish was organized in 1905 and the church pictured was built in 1910. It was one of the first parishes and churches administered by the Archdiocese of Chicago. Today, the facilities also house the Alfred A. Abramowicz Seminary which prepares priests, many of whom arrive from Poland, for service in the Polish American community.

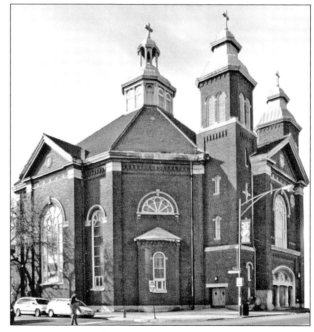

When St. Casimir's Church was founded in 1890, it housed a church and school in a frame building. This larger church, near 22nd Street and South Whipple, was dedicated December 21, 1919. Rev. Stanislaus Bona, pastor from 1921 to 1932, was consecrated a bishop in 1932.

Carnivals were a popular fund-raising activity for many Polish American parishes. Sometimes, lasting as long as two weeks, live bands, large mechanical rides, bingo, and other games of chance, as well as food and refreshments attracted thousands such as this 1967 centennial carnival of St. Stanislaus Kostka.

CHICAGOLAND OBSERVANCE
SOLDIER FIELD
AUGUST 28, 1966

St. John Cantius Church served the parish organized by Rev. Vincent Barzynski, CR, in 1893. The church building was dedicated December 11, 1898.

In 1966, Poland's Millennium of Christianity was observed in Polish American churches throughout the Chicago area, at a large banquet at McCormick Place, and culminated with a capacity crowd at Soldier Field for a concelebrated Mass.

St. Hedwig's Polish National Catholic Church was founded in 1940 on Chicago's southeast side.

After the prayer we kissed our parents' hands after every meal.

– Wladek

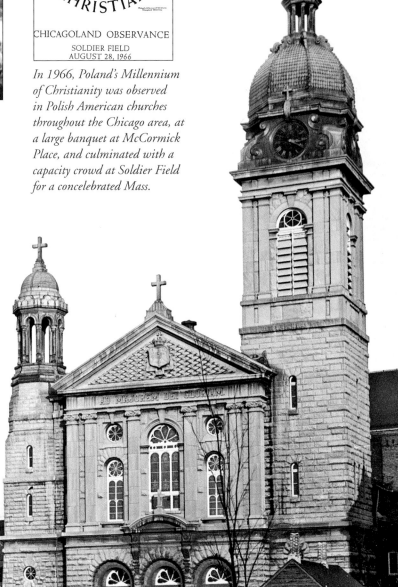

Mother Celine Bozecka, foundress of the Sisters of the Resurrection, made her last visit to the United States and visited with the First Communion Class at St. Casimir Parish, June 27, 1909.

Boze Cialo *(The Feast of Corpus Christi) commemorates the institution of the Holy Eucharist. Many Polish American churches observed the feast with a procession and then placement of the Eucharist at an altar inside or outside the church as shown here at St. Mary of the Angels Church in 1941.*

"Father ordered me to tell the priest everything, even things I did not consider sinful. But I told only things which I considered sinful myself. For example, when I stole anything from my parents I did not consider it a sin and did not tell it."

– Wladek

Polish Americans receive the sign of the cross on Ash Wednesday which marks the beginning of Lent. This illustration was by Walter Krawiec, a very popular cartoonist for Chicago's Polish Daily News. *His cartoons, which covered a broad range of topics, were printed daily in the center of the newspaper's front page. Although born in Poland in 1889, Krawiec has gained recognition as the foremost artist of the American circus. Between 1927 and 1949 his paintings of circus scenes were often displayed at the Art Institute of Chicago. Although Krawiec passed away in 1982, his* Circus Rider *and* The Cage Wagon *were recently sold at auction in 2001 and 2003 and the Threadway/Toomey Galleries were listing his work in 2005.*

Outdoor processions were very common at Polish American churches such as this Palm Sunday procession at St. Hedwig's Church.

"Christmas had more importance for us, because every child was presented with a gift, measured according to our parents' love."

– Wladek

The church choir of St. John of God around 1920.

Altar boys often wore elaborate garb for religious services. Notice the two boys on the left indicating, perhaps, junior or senior standing.

Zuawi (a reference to a unit involved in the Polish insurrection of 1863), was a group dressed in Swiss guard uniforms similar to those worn in the Vatican, and organized on May 1, 1915 at St. Stanislaus Kostka Parish. The group participated in church observances for the New Year, 40-hour devotions, Christmas, Zielone Swiatki (Green Holidays), First Communions, Corpus Christi, Holy Week, and Easter.

As this cartoon of Walter Krawiec illustrates Mother of God (Matka Boska), and Mother Earth (Matka Ziemia), were as highly revered as our dear personal human mother (Matka Rodzaju Ludzkiego).

"As to swearing, I was not foul-mouthed. Nobody of my acquaintance or family had ever heard from me the word 'psiakrew' [dog's blood]. My only oath was 'psiakosc sloniowa' [dog's bone of an elephant (parody of the first)]. In the worst wrath I sometimes expressed myself, "A co do pioruna" [Let the thunder strike it], and this was the extent of it."

– Wladek

"During Easter, on Good Saturday, we had [food to be consecrated]; placeks, babas, mazureks, veal, ham, sausage, eggs, cheese, butter, horse-radish, vinegar, pepper and salt. In the middle of the table was a swine's head adorned with frosting, and holding in its mouth a painted egg."

– Wladek

St. John Brebeuf Parish was established in Niles in 1953. Recent estimates indicate the parish is about 40 per cent Polish American, up from ten per cent just ten years ago. Two of the priests at the parish are from Poland, one of whom was assigned there after completing theological studies at the Archbishop Abramowicz Seminary in Chicago. Previously there was one sparsely attended Polish mass, now there are four with attendance more than 1,500. A newly formed Polish Children's Choir sings at some of these masses and takes part in an outside Corpus Christi procession visiting four altars. A Queen Jadwiga Society arranges an annual *Oplatek* (sharing the wafer) and also helps in arranging a New Year's Eve party or Sylwester.

Sylwester

Sylwester is the name given to New Year's eve in many Polish American communities. St. Sylvester, a pope who died in 335, according to legend, saved the world from Leviathan, a dragon who, had he escaped, would have destroyed humanity and set heaven ablaze. This all would have happened on January 1, 1000, had Sylvester failed. Thanks to Sylvester it did not and his feast day is December 31st.

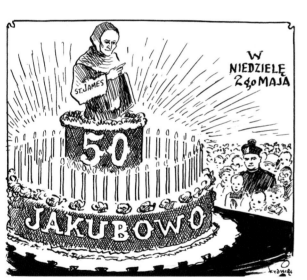

St. James Church on West Fullerton and North Menard avenues celebrated its 50th anniversary in 1954. The anniversary cake highlights *Jakubowo, with the suffix "owo," frequently used by Polish Americans to suggest an entire parish community including other institutions, commercial businesses, as well as all residents. Rev. Edward Przybylski, pastor, on right, can be discerned in this cartoon by Walter Krawiec.*

The interior of St. Hyacinth Basilica is decorated for the Christmas season.

Frances Siedliska was born in partitioned Poland. Although her parents were rather well established, Frances decided on a religious vocation. In 1875, with the permission of Pope Pius IX, she founded a new order which came to be known as the Congregation of the Sisters of the Holy Family of Nazareth.

Mother Frances came to Chicago in 1885 in response to pleas from pastors of Polish parishes for help in establishing schools. Thanks to Mother Frances' organizational skills, some 28 schools were eventually opened and staffed by the sisters. On her second trip to Chicago in 1889, Mother Frances became aware of the critical need of a hospital to serve the Polish speaking community. The sisters were given a deed to property at 1714-22 West Division Street in 1892. Two years later they opened a 24-bed hospital. Mother Frances insisted the hospital accept patients of all religions, races, and nationalities. The sign on the door read, *Szpital Polski* (Polish Hospital).

By 1899, 20 beds were added. Nevertheless, admissions kept rising rapidly. A new hospital was planned for a square-block bounded by Oakley Boulevard and Haddon, Leavitt, and Thomas streets. On October 27, 1900, the day the foundation was laid, a Polish language newspaper wrote, "This hospital will be a first-class hospital…and will become the pride of *Polonia Chicagoska* (Chicago's Polish American community).

To insure the highest medical standards at the new 297-bed St. Mary of Nazareth Hospital that would open in 1902, the sisters worked closely with Dr. Albert Ochsner who became chief of staff at the new hospital for 31 years. Dr. Ochsner, known as a "master in the operating area," invented and was the first to use forceps, had attending surgery staff change their garb from black to white, and invited direct observation of clinical procedures by other surgeons and staff. Dr. Ochsner also encouraged the sisters to establish a school of nursing which opened in 1900 as St.

30

Mary of Nazareth School of Nursing. The school grew rapidly and, by 1986 when it closed, had some 3,000 graduates. Over the years, the hospital also conducted schools of nurse anesthetists, radio technology, and medical technology.

Continued demands for the hospital's services resulted in 13 major renovations and additions by 1975. However, a tiny crack at the foundation which expanded to a few inches five floors above, proved difficult to repair effectively. After considerable prayer, planning, and reflection, the sisters made a decision to build a hospital in the immediate area.

The proposed hospital received a $34-mil-

The first class at St. Mary of Nazareth School of Nursing graduated in 1903. At that time, nursing candidates had to agree to remain for the three-year course of studies and be on duty from 7:30 a.m. to 7:30 p.m. daily. Two hours on week days and three hours on Sunday were "allowed for recreation." Students were paid an allowance of $5.00 per month, received room and board, a "reasonable" amount of laundry work, and "during illness [were] cared for gratuitously."

lion-FHA grant, the largest in Illinois history, plus two other grants totaling almost $10 million. On January 5, 1975, John Cardinal Cody dedicated the new 490-bed St. Mary of Nazareth Hospital's $43 million facility. A feature that attracted national attention was the private room each patient would have.

In 1959, Sister Stella Louise Slomka was appointed chief executive officer. During her 40-year tenure, she guided the transition to the new hospital and is credited with numerous management, clinical, and dietary innovations in hospital operations.

Throughout the years, St. Mary of Nazareth Hospital has fostered close ties with the community. Numerous health fairs are conducted free of charge at the hospital and in the community. A Women's Auxiliary has invited the community to its many cultural and social activities for more than 100 years. Outreach programs for youth, seniors, and others resulted in positive community relations.

The hospital's mission has not changed. A century ago, the hospital's annual ledger revealed: 838 Polish patients, 460 German, 298 Irish, 298 "various," 232 Jewish, 82 Norwegian, plus one each Swedish, Lithuanian, Italian, Canadian, Syrian, Greek, Negro, Turkish, Bohemian, English, Hungarian, Scottish, French, Belgian, Persian, and Swiss. More recently, a hospital administrator commented, "We're not just a Spanish Hospital, a Polish hospital…. Our focus remains multi-cultural." In years past, as today, translators assist patients not familiar with the English language.

Within the past decade, St. Mary's explored joining with other hospitals or healthcare networks. The result was a cooperative agreement with the Sisters of the Resurrection, a religious Congregation tracing its origins to Poland, to form Resurrection Health Care, a system that is co-sponsored by the Sisters of the Holy Family of Nazareth and the Sisters of the Resurrection. Other hospitals have joined, making it the largest Catholic healthcare organization in the Chicago area. St. Mary of Nazareth Hospital today operates as one campus with neighboring St. Elizabeth Hospital. A major building program has been launched with construction of an emergency center underway at the site of the former St. Mary of Nazareth Hospital.

When St. Mary of Nazareth Hospital opened in 1902 (above), large porches were added on each floor on both the north and south wings. Measuring 12 feet by 50 feet, they could be enclosed in winter. Over the years, the porches became fragile and were all removed by the 1960s (photo left). The new 16-story hospital (below) dwarfs the five-story hospital which was leveled several days after this photo was taken. Today, on the site of the old hospital, stands a residence for the sisters, and, under construction, will be a new emergency center for the hospital.

Surgeries performed at St. Mary of Nazareth Hospital in the early years of the 20th century were often used as educational opportunities for other doctors and staff to learn the latest surgical techniques.

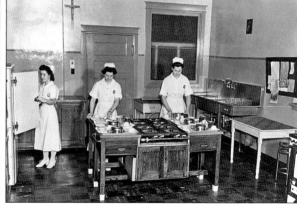

A sister records data as she aids a nurse attending to a patient at the hospital in the early 1900s.

St. Mary of Nazareth Hospital introduced several dietary services that attracted national attention. "Convenience food"—completely pre-packaged, heat-and-serve food—resulted in substantial cost savings and was utilized for 20 years after it was introduced in 1967.

Sisters worked in the laundry during the early years of the hospital.

The sisters provided a variety of entertainment for children spending the Christmas holiday in the hospital. They were usually joined by members of the Women's Auxiliary who distributed presents to each child.

The May Crowning of Mary, Mother of Jesus, has been observed by student nurses, and later, by nurses on each shift at the hospital. In earlier years, the ceremony was preceded by a procession to the chapel in the school of nursing, or to the chapel in the hospital, or to the statue of Mary on the grounds in the garden grotto.

Sister Stella Louise Slomka, CEO at St. Mary of Nazareth Hospital, chats with Sig Sakowicz, well-known radio personality at WGN radio, and Mrs. Dominic Chechile, president of the Women's Auxiliary, during a fashion show sponsored by the Auxiliary. Since its founding in 1904, the Auxiliary has invited the community to concerts, operas, fashion shows, theatrical presentations, bingo parties, bake sales, and numerous other events.

St. Mary of Nazareth Hospital was selected by the City of Chicago as the official welcoming site for a delegation of the Episcopate of Poland headed by Karol Cardinal Wojtyla. On August 20, 1976, Wojtyla was greeted at the hospital by Mayor Richard J. Daley and John Cardinal Cody. In the background, Sister Stella Louise, the hospital's CEO, waits with the traditional Polish welcome of bread, symbolizing material sustenance, and salt, signifying spiritual sustenance. In October 1978, Wojtyla was elected Pope and took the name, John Paul II.

The Franciscan Sisters of Chicago prepare to move into their first home (inset above and at left). The house, the original Dudzik family residence, was built in 1885 at 11 Chapin Street (later changed to 1341 Haddon). The sisters moved in December 8, 1894, the date of their founding. Holy Trinity Church looms in the background. On January 22, 1965, the home was demolished as part of the Chicago Department of Urban Renewal's Project Noble-Division.

The Franciscan Sisters of Chicago began moving to the Avondale area in the 1890s where they were developing a Motherhouse complex on Hamlin and Schubert Avenues. From the left is St. Vincent's Orphan Asylum Center, St. Joseph Home for the Aged and Crippled, and on the right is the Novitiate House.

Pioneer Sisters of the Franciscan Sisters of Chicago on the day of their First Profession of Vows, June 3, 1900. From left, Sister M. Anne Wysinski, Sister M. Angeline Topolinski, Sister M. Agnes Dzik, and Sister M. Theresa Dudzik.

The four-story building in the center was the second house of the Franciscan Sisters of Chicago. The Sisters and aged residents occupied the first and second floors shortly after the structure was completed in 1896. St. Stanislaus Kostka Church is in the right foreground and the residence of former Congressman Daniel Rostenkowski is visible on the left.

The Franciscan Sisters of Chicago cared for homeless children at the St. Vincent's Orphan Asylum, shown at left, erected in 1899. Originally built to accommodate 60, by 1911, as many as 117 orphans lived at the facility when it closed and all residents moved to St. Hedwig's Orphanage in Niles. The photo below shows the children at the orphanage in 1906.

St. Stanislaus Bishop and Martyr School was established in the former church of the parish in 1920 after a new church was built. The first parish school opened in 1897 with three grades. The Franciscan Sisters of Chicago were invited to teach at the school in 1902 when enrollment reached 65. By 1930, there were 1,365 students.

The Franciscan Sisters of Chicago administered the St. Elizabeth Day Nursery complex at Ashland Avenue and Blackhawk Street from 1904 to 1915 and from 1920 to 1959. When it opened it charged 10 cents per day for each child. The tuition included two hot meals for the 60 to 65 children who attended.

The Franciscan Sisters of Chicago opened Guardian Angel Day Care Center (formerly Guardian Angel Day Care Center and Home for Ladies) in 1917 at today's 46th Street and McDowell Avenue on Chicago's southwest side. During the Depression years, 1931-1932, the Sisters cared for more than 800 children at the center. Only half could afford the daily charge of 15 cents.

The campus of the Franciscan Sisters of Chicago in Lemont. The building at the top in the photo is the administration building. The second major building is the Our Lady of Victory Motherhouse. At the bottom in the photo is the Franciscan Village. The Franciscan Sisters of Chicago sponsor 16 senior living "communities" located in five states. They were ranked the sixth-fastest-growing provider of health and residential services for older adults based on 2005 U.S. statistics.

The Walker Mansion, circa 1936, became the first home of the Franciscan Sisters of Chicago in Lemont, Illinois. The 1868 abandoned mansion and 155 acres were purchased in 1925. A chapel was designed in the former living room. The building was also used as a convent and novitiate before it was converted into the Mother Theresa Museum.

Sr. Ann Strezelecka was one of four sisters who came to Chicago in 1900 to teach the 425 pupils at St. Mary of the Angels School. Sister Ann would become the first provincial director for the Sisters of the Resurrection after more sisters began arriving from Poland.

Pictured is the White House, the first building occupied by the Sisters of the Resurrection around 1913 as they continued to arrive in Chicago. The residence remained on the property until the 1970s when the current convent, built in three phases, was completed.

A circa-1930 aerial depicts the provincial house of the Sisters of the Resurrection. Among many other uses, the facility was occupied by about 75 sisters who taught at Resurrection High School and Boarding School and other institutions in Chicago.

Since February 1917 day-care services have been provided by the Sisters of the Resurrection in this building directly across the street from the entrance to St. Mary of the Angels Church.

A group of wide-eyed youngsters are helped by a caring sister.

The Mother Celine League, a women's auxiliary assisting the Sisters of the Resurrection, raised funds by sponsoring tag days at churches as well as bake sales, card and bunco parties, and other activities.

An annual tradition since 1922 is the elaborate May procession from Resurrection High School to Our Lady of Lourdes Grotto on the grounds of the Sisters of the Resurrection.

Talcott Avenue was a dirt road when the Sisters of the Resurrection purchased their first parcel of property in 1913. The sisters tended the cows, chickens, and horses and took care of the gardens and orchards until 1960 when farming was discontinued.

In the chapel, on the grounds of the Sisters of the Resurrection, juniors at Resurrection High School receive their class rings during Mass.

Sisters of the Resurrection taught numerous Polish American students at St. Casimir High School and Grade School in the early and mid-decades of the 20th century. Today, the school's name has changed to Our Lady of Tepeyac where 170, mostly Hispanic, students attend.

The first chapel of the Sisters of the Resurrection, built in 1913, was shared with Resurrection High School. It remained in use until 2003 when a new chapel, utilizing the original windows of the first chapel, was built.

Sr. Mary Edward Dira, Chicago Mayor Richard J. Daley, and Rev. John Iwicki, meet on the grounds of the Sisters of the Resurrection on Talcott Avenue.

The campus of the Sisters of the Congregation of the Resurrection on Talcott Avenue, around 1970, pictures the Queen of the Resurrection House of Prayer and the provincial house of the Congregation of the Resurrection, on the left; Resurrection Medical Center, center background; and Resurrection High School on the right. In later years a 500-room retirement home was added as were medical office buildings.

The Felician Sisters (Congregation of the Sisters of St. Felix) purchased 30.55 acres of property in 1921 on Peterson Avenue near today's Pulaski Road to build a new provincial house, chapel, facilities for the novitiate, Good Counsel High School and a chaplaincy. Construction began in 1925 and was completed in 1927 when the above photo was probably taken.

The rock garden situated in the Felician Sisters Provincialate was erected in the 1930s to make use of the property's natural pond which was stocked with gold fish. The retreat also features a gazebo, statues, and walkways.

The provincial superior of the Felician Sisters in Chicago and her councilors pose at the foot of the crucifix on the grounds of the Provincialate, circa 1940. The group includes Mother Mary Jolanta Pawlak, Sr. Mary Regina Przybylska, Sr. Mary Felicitas Kruczkowska, Sr. Mary Hermana Romanowski, Sr. Mary Seraphia Winnicki, Sr. Mary Xavier Wroblewska, and Sr. Mary Assumpta Rzepecka.

The Fourteen Stations of the Cross with an entrance arch and an exit crucifix on the grounds of the Felician Sisters Provincialate on Peterson Avenue were erected and blessed in the early 1940s. The project was sponsored by various chapters of the Mother of Good Counsel Auxiliary. Pictured is the Third Station of the Cross.

The Lourdes Grotto on the grounds of the Felician Sisters Provincialate on Peterson Avenue was built in 1931. It is used for May devotions, Corpus Christi processions, private reflection, and other religious observances.

An aerial view of the Felician Sisters Provincialate, circa 1970, includes the sisters' living quarters, chapel, Good Counsel High School and chaplaincy. This aerial captures the considerable growth in the surrounding area since the original building was completed in 1927.

GRAMATYKA
JĘZYKA POLSKIEGO

DLA SZKÓŁ PARAFJALNYCH
w AMERYCE

NAPISAŁA
S. M. CYRYLA

ZESZYT II.
Przeznaczony dla
stopnia piątego.

NAKŁADEM SS. FELICJANEK
3800 PETERSON AVENUE
W CHICAGO, ILL.

Gramatyka Jezyka Polskiego *(A Polish Grammar)
was one of 13 books written by Felician Sister
Mary Cyryla Tabaka and published by the Felician
Sisters. Besides the grammar, she wrote books on
Polish history, Polish culture, and the history of the
Church. The textbooks enjoy a wide circulation in
Polish American schools around the country.*

*Felician Sister Mary Rachael Czarnik published a
series of Christmas carols in Polish in 1944. The
title page of the work indicates that the carols were
specifically prepared for the "piano accordion," a
very popular instrument played by many youngsters
during this era in the Polish American community.*

BOHATER DWU ŚWIATÓW

Marcinek mieszkał na farmie. Razu
pewnego brat jego Adolf zabrał go ze sobą
do wielkiego miasta Chicago. Marcinek ni-
gdy takiego miasta nie widział. Nie mógł
się napatrzeć pięknym ogrodom, parkom
i ogromnym budynkom, co sięgały prawie
nieba.

— Co to za wysokie domy! Jak ludzie
mogą się dostać tak wysoko? — zapytał
brata.

A page from Moja Trzecia Ksiazecka *(My Third
Book) by Felician Sister Cyryla Tabaka, was published in 1936. In the short story entitled "Hero in
Two Worlds" (*Bohater Dwu Swiatow*) a brother
recounts the achievements of General Casimir
Pulaski to his sibling during his first sightseeing
tour of Chicago.*

*Ground was broken for new facilities for Good
Counsel High School, at left in photo, on June 23,
1963. Dedication of the $3,000,000 structure
took place on June 12, 1966. The school, adminis-
tered by the Felician Sisters, opened with an enroll-
ment of 600 and grew to 1,100 by the mid 1970s.
Due to declining enrollment, it closed in 2003.
Today the building has become the Northtown
Academy Campus of the International Charter
School Foundation.*

Felician Sister Mary Lucinia Szpak was one of the first religious sisters to teach hearing-impaired children in the Archdiocese of Chicago at the St. Mel-Holy Ghost Day School for the Deaf in 1954. The program emphasized the oral method of instruction.

A typing class at Good Counsel High School in 1946 is under the watchful eye of Felician Sister Mary Mericia Brongiel, head of the Commercial Department.

Felician College opened in 1953, with an enrollment of 50, as an independent school for the education of Felician Sisters. Lay students were enrolled in 1967. Eventually the college reached an enrollment of 560 in 1971. Felician College became Montay College in 1986 specializing in liberal arts, geriatrics, and drug education. Unable to maintain a steady enrollment, it closed in 1995.

The Good Counsel High School band took an active part in community events in the late 1970s. It performed in the Polish Constitution Day Parade, the Chicago Christmas Parade, and with glee clubs at numerous other schools.

Waves of Polish immigrants began arriving in the United States in response to the labor needs of America's rapid industrialization in the five decades following the Civil War. Although the rural life-style could be left behind by the masses of Polish peasants coming to this new land, they found that their sense of community, which helped them to survive in Poland, had to be adapted to an urban setting. Almost immediately, Poles began establishing churches with extensive religious, cultural, social, and educational activities which gave Polish Americans a new sense of community.

As the Polish American population rapidly increased in America's industrial centers, movements materialized to bring together all Polish Americans. A sense of "Polonia"—a nationally unified Polish American community–began to emerge as fraternal organizations such as the Polish Roman Catholic Union of America (PRCUA), the Polish National Alliance (PNA), and the Polish Women's Alliance (PWA) were launched with national headquarters in Chicago. Each of these fraternals published a national newspaper and sponsored national cultural, educational, and sports programs. Each supported the reestablishment of the Polish state following World War I and aided their Polish brethren during and after World War II.

Today, "Polonia" signifies the cultural and social unity of former Polish citizens and their descendants throughout the world. The emergence of America's "Polonia" is the result of thousands of activities sponsored by numerous Polish American groups which helped millions of Polish Americans.

Convened by fraternals during World War II, today's Polish American Congress, headquartered in Chicago, continues to elect leaders of Polish American fraternals to speak with one voice in articulating the aims and goals of Americans of Polish heritage.

Although the PNA and PRCUA were major fraternals which established their national headquarters in Chicago and developed large followings, the PWA was the first fraternal organized in Chicago. Shown above are delegates to PWA's first convention which met June 6, 1900. The emblem, superimposed in the photo with the statement, "First Convention of the Polish Women's Alliance in America," appears to be a near-replica of one used by the PNA. Polish American women attempted, without success, to actively participate as members in the PRCUA, PNA, and Polish Falcons of America, also a Chicago-based fraternal at the time. After they were flatly rejected for membership by these organizations, Polish American women formed their own fraternal. Within a year both PRCUA and PNA invited women to join their ranks.

Organizers of the Polish American Congress met in Chicago in March 1944. The aim of the Congress was, and continues to be, to unite all Polish Americans on matters of common concern. During World War II, Polish Americans became increasingly anxious about the fate of the Polish state after the war and the position of the United States about every nation's territorial integrity as expressed in the Atlantic Charter. Would the United States defend Poland's pre-World War II boundaries or would the United States recognize Russia's claim to Polish territories seized in the first month of the war? In the center, seated, is Honorata Wolowska, PWA president; to her right is PNA president, Charles Rozmarek; and to her left is PRCUA president, John Olejniczak.

The Early Years

When the founders of the three largest Polish American fraternals in the United States launched their organizations well over 100 years ago, each selected Chicago for its national headquarters. Although all shared similar goals and would continue to provide its members with almost identical mutual aid assistance such as burial insurance, each fiercely guarded its independence.

There were real differences in how each group was organized. Membership in PRCUA, as the name suggests, required being an active member in a Roman Catholic Church. PRCUA, founded in 1873, was an outgrowth of the St. Stanislaus Society, established in 1864, which led to the opening of St. Stanislaus Kostka, the first parish in Chicago that began serving the Polish American community exclusively in 1867. Rev. Vincent Barzynski, CR, pastor of St. Stanislaus, was also one of the founders of PRCUA and was instrumental in organizing other Polish American communities in Chicago where churches were being built to serve rapidly increasing Polish American poplulations.

The Polish Council, also a fraternal-aid society as was St. Stanislaus Society, was formed in 1866.

It reflected the aspirations of many exiles who fled Poland after failed Polish insurrections during the 19th century. Its primary goal was to promote the restoration of an independent Poland. The patriotic fevor of the Polish Council began to wither until Agaton Giller, a veteran of the 1863 insurrection, wrote an influential essay in Europe on "The Organization of Poles in the United States." It was widely reprinted throughout America. That document can be rightly called the spiritual foundation of PNA which was launched in 1880.

Below: The PRCUA headquarters was built after the 1906 fire at St. Stanislaus Kostka in 1906 where all the organization's records were kept. In its early years retail establishments occupied the ground floor, which now houses the library, at left, and offices on the right.

The PNA's first permanent headquarters was dedicated in 1896 at 1404 West Division. The above photo was taken in April 1901.

The national headquarters of the PWA, the largest Polish women's fraternal in the world, was remodeled in 1933 for the Polish Women's Congress. When the organization was founded members met in homes until 1905 when a private dwelling was purchased. A more permanent structure was built (photo above) on Ashland Avenue in 1911.

Since women could not apply for membership in the PRCUA or the PNA, Stafania Chmielinska called a meeting at her south-side residence in Chicago. She persuaded seven friends to form the Society of the Polish Women's Alliance in America. The date was May 22, 1898. The group's primary goal was to work for Poland's independence. On November 12, 1899, an officer of the PNA addressed the Society of the Polish Women's Alliance in America, St. Helen's Society, and Queen Wanda Society. He urged them to form a national organization similar to the PRCUA and PNA. Eight days later, on November 20, 1899,

these three societies and the White Eagle Society, adopted a constitution creating the PWA.

In the early years of the fraternal movement there were numerous factions, splinter groups, and new organizations forming, all within a tug-of-war scenario with the Catholics and patriots each trying to convince every member of the Polish American community of the primary significance of its position. PNA insisted the PRCUA was not patriotic enough and some priests would not bury PNA members.

Even though the PRCUA was structured to assist with the formation of churches to serve Pol-

ish Americans, the PNA, in 1886, responded with a proposed change in its constitution to promote, with loans, the building of new parishes for the Polish American community. The following year, a move to include "Catholic" in the name of the PNA, created such a stir at the PNA convention (highest authority venue within a fraternal society), that it was declared out of order. Many priests associated with the PNA left the organization when atheists were declared eligible for PNA membership. These priests joined with priests in the PRCUA to form the Polish Union of America, However, both the PRCUA and PNA insisted the

The Lily Garland of PWA group 67 in Chicago around 1930.

The executive committee of the PNA met in 1894 with S. F. Satalecki, president, seated in center. Others attending were T. M. Helinski, censor; Jan Smulski, director; and editor Frank Jablonski..

The PRCUA Women's Department was established at a convention in 1925. Its first officers in this 1928 photo included Marta Zolinska, president; Maria Osuch, vice-president; Waleria Gorska, financial and corresponding secretary; and Anna Ostrowska, treasurer.

new group divided rather than united the Polish American community. It did not survive.

Other attempts were made to unite all Polish Americans. The Polish League of 1894, established by PRCUA and PNA, expired by 1896 since PNA feared control by the clergy. A Polish Catholic Congress was launched in 1896. At first the PNA was excluded but then was allowed to take part in 1901. Concern about the Polish National Catholic Church drove the PRCUA and PNA further apart with the Polish Catholic Congress dissolving and the PRCUA forming the Federation of Catholic Poles in 1902 which was also short-lived.

Although membership in both the PRCUA and PNA quickly mushroomed (some 200,000 were enrolled in both organizations by 1915), numerous defections and several expulsions–usually members or groups thought to be anarchists–prevented each organization from growing even more rapidly. In 1887, a Chicago Society at St. Adalbert parish left PRCUA to form the Polish Roman Catholic Union under the Care of Our Lady of Czestochowa, Queen of Poland. Societies also left the PRCUA in Milwaukee, Cleveland, and Detroit. PNA also had defections: in Pittsburgh, PNA members formed St. Joseph's Union around

1890 and in Cleveland, the Alliance of Poles left the PNA ranks.

To meet needs not addressed by the PRCUA and PNA, the Polish Falcons were organized in 1887 and the Polish Alma Mater in 1897. Both were Chicago-based groups. The Falcons closely aligned with the PNA and emphasized physical fitness while the Polish Alma Mater was formed as a youth group by the Congregation of the Resurrection to preserve Catholic faith and values. The Polish Falcons moved their national headquarters to Pittsburgh in 1912. Two groups, called nests, are still active in the Chicago area. In 1985, the

Piotr Rostenkowski was president of the PRCUA from 1913 to 1917 and founder of the National Department of the Polish Central Relief Committee.

A PWA group based in Chicago around 1920.

In 1898, Stefania Chmielinska, who went on to form the PWA, hosted the first meeting of women at her mother's house. They formed a society, were joined by several other women's groups, and organized what is today's PWA. Chmielinska was elected PWA's first president in 1900.

49

PNA merged 2,100 members of the Polish Alma Mater into its ranks.

Although there were many heated debates at fraternal meetings, particularly at national conventions, members would return to individual homes where, often, multiple Polish organizations were represented under the same roof. Maria Rokosz, the first president of the Society of the Polish Women's Alliance in America in 1898, was the wife of Stanislaus, national vice-president of PNA in 1899 who was elected national president of PNA in 1901. Michael Osuch, PNA national president in 1887, was married to Mary, who was national vice-president of PRCUA in 1908. Frank Wolowski, husband of Lucja (Lucja was an instructor for the Polish Falcons in the 1870s and seven-term national officer for the PWA), was the first editor, appointed in 1902, of the *Voice of Polish Women,* PWA's official publication. The husband of Stefania Chmielinska, PWA founder, provided dress uniforms for the Polish Falcons.

In a similar vein, when local societies or groups within the PRCUA and PNA could choose the name for its society or group, dramatic shifts in selection came in the periods from 1880-1894 and 1894-1905. There was a more than 400 per cent increase in PNA lodges selecting names of non-Polish saints in the latter period as opposed to the former. Nevertheless, lodges with patriotic secular names were still in the majority of both periods. A review of several hundred names of PWA groups reveals only one that had a male connotation, St. Joseph. All others had the name of a female saint or the word "women." PRCUA societies were generally named to coincide with the parish where they met.

The Polish Falcons of America believed in keeping members physically fit. They often built large gymnasiums such as the one shown above for members organized in "nests." This gymnasium was for members of Chicago Nest 189.

The Polish Alma Mater was organized in Chicago in 1897 as a social group for Polish American youth under the age of 18. Membership was restricted to Roman Catholics of Polish descent. In its early years, the Congregation of the Resurrection provided clerical leadership while instilling pride in the young people to maintain Poland's cultural heritage and language. There was also a strong effort to encourage civic awareness and patriotism and to indoctrinate, as one contemporary observer wrote, "the Poles in the United States with the spirit of America." By the mid-1930s, membership reached 15,000. As the *PNA, PRCUA, and PWA lowered age requirements and started their own sports and youth activities, membership in the Polish Alma Mater rapidly declined. Above, the drum and bugle corps of the Polish Alma Mater pose for the camera.*

POLISH AMERICANS REJOICE AS POLAND IS REBORN

As the threat of war in Europe became more strident, the Polish American community turned its attention to developments affecting Poland. A Polish National Council was formed to assist the Polish cause with the PRCUA providing more than $18,000 for the Council's activities between 1912 and 1918. The PNA at its convention in 1913 appropriated $40,000 to forces fighting for Poland's independence. The PWA also formed a battle fund and collected several thousand dollars.

After hostilities began, a Polish Central Relief Committee was established. Executives of the Polish American fraternals based in Chicago assumed leadership. "Polish Days" were proclaimed with $250,000 raised in 1915 and almost $1,000,000 in 1916. Individually, the PNA, PRCUA, and PWA also made substantial donations during and after the war for humanitarian relief in Poland.

A publication, *Free Poland*, was launched and widely distributed. Polish Americans also purchased some $150 million Liberty War Bonds with fraternals also buying large amounts. Recruits to fight with Polish armies as well as the U.S. Army lined up at PRCUA headquarters after the U.S. entered the war. By war's end, some 23,000 Polish Americans were in the "Blue Army" of Polish General Jozef Haller, with 215,000 Polish Americans serving with U.S. troops. After the war ended, Polish Americans contributed $5 million for Polish immigrants with an additional $3 million for food and clothing.

Other funds were sent directly to Polish families and Polish Government bonds were purchased.

Following World War I, each of the fraternals showed dramatic increases in membership. The PWA rose from 14,500 members in 1914 to 53,000 in 1935; PRCUA grew to 169,000 members in 1931 from 85,000 in 1913; and PNA had 287,000 members in 1930 up from 100,000 in 1913.

Internally, each of the fraternals expanded their focus to include cultural and youth activities. PRCUA's juvenile department grew from an initial count of 1,700 in the 1920s to 45,000 members in 1931. Numerous PRCUA sports teams played in league and tournament competition. Scouting

In 1917, U.S. volunteers were recruited to fight with Polish armies in World War I. In Chicago some 3,000 eventually joined the Polish Army, however, more than twice that amount from Chicago served with the U.S. forces in World War I.

The PNA utilized women recruiters to assist in enlisting volunteers to aid the Polish cause in World War I.

51

became very popular with 26 Boy Scout troops formed in Chicago. By 1941, there were more Girl Scout troops than boys. In 1939, the PRCUA purchased a site near Chicago and established Camp Gieryk for sports and youth activities. It remained open for ten years. The PNA scout movement grew to 50,000 members. At the time, PNA officials strongly objected to the term, "scout," preferring the Polish word *Harcestwo* which implies the preservation of Polish ethnic consciousness. The PNA sponsored a youth jamboree at Riverview Park in Chicago on July 22, 1934. Some 3,000 youngsters involved with PNA youth activities attended.

The PWA concentrated on expanding membership outside the Chicago area after 1918 when half of a total of 272 groups were active in Chicago. By 1938, the fraternal grew to 639 groups with 427 not domiciled in Illinois.

PWA's group 195 Wianek Rezeda *(Garland Rosette) on March 9, 1927. A Garland includes newborns to age 16.*

PNA women's division has prepared Christmas food baskets for the needy since 1930. Maria Czyz, president of the PNA Welfare Association, at right, and division workers pose for a 1942 photo.

Eva Curie, center, stands in front of the portrait of her mother, Nobel Laureate Maria Sklodowska Curie who was an honorary member of the PWA. The painting was dedicated at PWA headquarters in Chicago, February 18, 1940. Dr. Rene Weiler, Consul General of France, spoke at the unveiling of the portrait painted by Walter Krawiec.

After World War I, Polish Americans began to travel to Poland. Shown above are PRCUA officers in New York leading a delegation to Poland in 1927.

In 1928, PWA president, Emilia Napieralska, led the first PWA delegation to Poland after the motherland gained its independence after World War I.

A parade in a Polish American neighborhood commemorates the end of World War I.

Ignace Jan Paderewski often came to Chicago to raise funds to assist the new Polish state in Europe. Here he is photographed at a meeting at PRCUA headquarters where he decorated activists with the medal "Polonia Restituta" for their service on behalf of Polish independence.

America's Polonia Aids War-Torn Poland

It is difficult to comprehend the tragedy that befell Poland during World War II. Germany invaded Poland, September 1, 1939. The Soviet Union attacked Poland from the east 17 days later. Poland, unable to defend itself within two weeks, was subjected to six years of brutal foreign occupation.

At the war's end, Poles who had fought valiantly during the war in Poland, in England, in Italy, in the Normandy invasion, and in other areas, discovered that Poland had been reduced in size by one-third—areas annexed by the Soviet Union during the war—as finalized at a meeting between Franklin D. Roosevelt, Winston Churchill, and Joseph Stalin. Six million Poles perished in the conflict. Warsaw and many other areas were reduced to rubble. The economy was in shambles.

Other details of agreements regarding Poland were revealed after the war. At Yalta, the Allies arranged to set in motion the imposition of a communist-controlled government. Further details confirmed that Russians had slaughtered 14,000 Polish military officers and other professionals in Katyn Forest during the war. Poles throughout the world were not only bitterly disappointed but they firmly resolved to rebuild Poland and began yearning, yet again, for the day they would enjoy an independent government.

Polish Americans knew of the desperate plight of Poland early in the war. In 1940, Joseph L. Kania, PRCUA president, met with Karol Ripa, Polish Council, and placed the Union at Poland's disposal. The goal was to unite Polish Americans to initiate political action on Poland's behalf. Early in 1942, the *Polish Nation*, PRCUA's newspaper, expressed disappointment a Polish American Congress had not yet been established to make the voice of Polish Americans heard in Washington, D.C.

Two years later on May 28, 1944, in Buffalo, New York, some 2,600 representatives of Polish American organizations from 26 states met to form the Polish American Congress. Charles Rozmarek, PNA president, was elected president, Jan Olejniczak, PRCUA president, and Honorata Wolowska, PWA president, were elected other executive officers.

Although urgently sought by the leadership of the newly elected Polish American Congress, a meeting with President Franklin D. Roosevelt did not take place until October 11, 1944. Roosevelt was evasive about Poland's post-war territorial borders. However, a large map of Poland with its pre-war borders was placed behind Roosevelt's desk. Photographs of Roosevelt and the visiting Polish American delegation were released to re-assure Poles that the U.S. recognized the Poland shown on the map. Roosevelt spoke in general positive tones on

After the PWA sold $400,000 in bonds during World War II, the organization was notified that, in its honor, a B-25 bomber was named Polish Women's Alliance of America.

Polish General Wladyslaw Sikorski addresses a crowd at Soldier Field in April 1941 encouraging Polish American support for the Allied effort in World War II.

U.S. support for Poland but avoided commitments concerning Poland's future political integrity.

As details about the wartime agreements about Poland became known, it became increasingly evident that Poland needed immediate economic assistance and that many Poles would not be able to return to Poland.

A Polish Inter-Organizational Council had already been formed in 1936 to assist needy Poles. It evolved into the Polish American Council in 1937 and, working with other agencies, provided some $20 million in aid to Poland by 1948. The Polish American Congress Charitable Foundation worked closely with other organizations and $33 million in aid had been shipped to Poland by 1983.

Poles unable to return to Poland immigrated to other lands. Many came to the United States as the restrictive immigration laws of 1924 were eased with the passage of the Displaced Persons Act of 1948. As communist rule played havoc with Poland's economic, religious, and social life more Poles sought refuge in the United States. These new arrivals came to be called the New Polonia. Often they were from large cities, generally had more schooling than Poles arriving in the early decades of the 20th century, and had lived in a free democratic-identifiable Polish state in the period between the wars. Polish immigrants arriving in the United States before World War I were generally of peasant background. They lived their entire lives before coming to the United States under foreign, and increasingly restrictive, domination. They would become known as Old Polonia.

Many Polish immigrants came directly to Chicago. Adela Lagodzinska, PWA president and deputy chairman of the American Committee for Resettlement of Polish Displaced Persons, a unit of the Polish American Congress, found new homes in Chicago for 15 families (81 persons) from Poland in 1948. Today, the Polish American Association, formerly the Polish Welfare Association, continues to assist thousands arriving from Poland to Chicago with resettlement and assimilation.

A Walter Krawiec cartoon portrays an American eagle providing additional aid (Dalsza Pomoc) to Poland after World War II.

Polish Americans supplied Poland during and after World War II. The drive pictured was probably organized by the PNA as Charles Rozmarek, PNA president, and Albin Szczerbowski, PNA secretary, stand atop a shipment leaving Chicago.

St. James Elementary School students sold Liberty Bonds and helped in other projects to raise funds to purchase an ambulance, shown below, to aid Polish soldiers fighting on various frontiers of World War II. Rev. Edward Przybylski, pastor of St. James, stands before the cross on the ambulance.

Maxine and Patricia Olejnik collect newspapers for resale in order to purchase stamps to support the United States World-War-II effort.

Polish Army Veteran's Post #1 was organized in September 1921. It moved several times before purchasing a permanent home at 1239 North Wood Street.

Women's auxiliaries were formed to assist fund-raising efforts for Polish Army veterans. Shown above is the auxiliary associated with Placowka 39, Stowarzyszenie Weteranow Armii Polskiej, commonly called "SWAP" in the Chicago area.

Patriotic appeals were made to raise funds to support disabled Polish Army veterans living in Chicago after World War I. A wounded soldier implores Niech Zyje Polska (Let Poland Live). Donations supported the Polish Army Post #1 veteran's home.

The Alliance of Polish American Veterans was organized in Chicago after World War I. They merged with other veteran groups to form, in 1931, the Polish Legion of American Veterans. The Chicago group, shown above, was one of the largest in the United States.

As the new millennium dawned, Polish American fraternals based in Chicago faced new challenges and opportunities. As fraternal benefit societies they are strictly governed by state insurance regulations. All have developed new products to meet the needs of members.

The scope of each organization's activities has also expanded. The PNA opened a bank on June 26, 1990 with initial funding of $30 million. In April 2006, Alliance FSB had two locations, in Niles and on Chicago's south side, with assets of $186 million. It is estimated that 80 per cent of the patrons are Polish Americans.

Since 1987, PNA has operated radio station WPNA from studios in Oak Park. News from Poland, historical insights on Poland and Polish Americans, as well as Polish American events are broadcast 13 hours weekly. The station operates on a full-time basis and sells program time.

The PNA publishes a daily Chicago Polish-language newspaper, *Dziennik Związkowy*, Daily Alliance. A typical weekend edition has three sections of 50 large pages and a tabloid-sized insert, *Kalejdoskop*. Each fraternal also publishes a newspaper, all predominantly in English, for members. PRCUA's is *The Polish Nation*. PNA's is *Harmony*, and PWA's is named *The Voice of Polish Women*. Other Polish language and bilingual newspapers and magazines are available in the Chicago area. A conservative estimate of copies of all such publications would easily exceed one million monthly.

In its early years, PRCUA experienced numerous defections and groups splintering to form their own or merge with other societies. In recent years, PRCUA has aggressively and successfully merged with other Polish American fraternals. Polish Alliance of America joined PRCUA in 1968. The Union of Polish Women in America and its 5,000 members merged with PRCUA in 1997. The Alliance of Poles (9,000 members) and Federation of Life Insurance of America (2,800 members) were welcomed to PRCUA in 2005.

As are other fraternals, PRCUA is committed to supporting Polish language and dance schools. The Pope John Paul II Polish Language School, established by PRCUA Society 1605 in Lemont, Illinois, had 90 students in 1991. Today, it has an enrollment of over 700. The Polanie Dance

PRCUA president, Joseph L. Kania (center right), and his family are congratulated by Samuel Cardinal Stritch (center) in 1949 when Kania became a Knight of St. Gregory.

Maria Lorys, editor of Glos Polek *(Voice of Polish Women) for 31 years authored a volume on the history of the PWA. She presents copies to Kazimierz Dziewanowski, Polish Ambassador to the United States.*

*A Walter Krawiec cartoon depicts a benefit ball to help children in Poland (*Bal na pomoc Dziecom w Polsce*).*

group associated with the school has 70 members. It performs at numerous church festivals and has participated in the 2006 International Polish Children's Folk Festival in Poland. PRCUA Society 1605 has also formed a very active Polish Club which observes Polish traditional holidays and sponsors numerous civic events such as Senior Citizens Polish Day. Since 1986, PRCUA has also supported the Northwest Center of Traditional Polish Dancing. Dancing instructors are available to youngsters three and older. Dancers from the center have performed in Poland, Taiwan, Rome, and Peru. PRCUA adult dancers formed Wesoly Lud (Happy People) in 1977. They have often performed in Poland and in numerous Chicago locations. In 1982, the group hosted a Polish Folk Dance Festival in Chicago.

Since 1937 the PRCUA has been the principal patron of the PMA. The museum is open to the public and features permanent exhibits such as the Paderewski Room, Polish artifacts from the World's Fair in 1939, and a massive painting, donated by the PWA, of General Casimir Pulaski at Savannah. A permanent art gallery displays works of Polish and Polish American artists as well as frequent temporary exhibits of other works. Numerous organizations within the Chicago area have utilized the museum's facilities for meetings or programs: Polish Genealogical Society, Polish Military History Society, International Polka Association, Polonus Philatelic Society, Polish Arts Club, and Polish American Historical Association. For more than 30 years the museum has hosted a summer ball, recognizing an individual or organization with its Polish Spirit Award. In the past six years the museum has organized five trips to Poland, has hosted a variety of programs with other museums, and conducted tours of Polish Chicago hosted by Jan Lorys, the museum's director. Since 1999, the museum has hosted a variety of workshop featuring Polish crafts and traditions. "Only space limits our enrollment," says Joann Ozog,

The PMA staff get the youngsters ready for the Lajkonik, *a Polish song and dance, during a Christmas presentation.*

*Joann Ozog teaching a class on Polish paper cut-outs (*wycinanki*) at PRCUA headquarters.*

Adult Wigilia *(Christmas Eve Dinner) at the PMA in 2005. From left, Edyta Targonska, Halina Misterka, archivist; Wallace Ozog, PRCUA president; Joann Ozog; Krystyna Gell, assistant librarian; Malgorzata Kot, PMA librarian; Anna Wolan; Jan Lorys, PMA director; and Rich Kujawa, operations manager.*

coordinator of these programs, which includes palm weaving, Polish Easter egg decoration, Polish Constitution Day art contests, Polish paper cutting, Polish Christmas ornament workshops, and adult and children's Polish Christmas observances.

The PNA dedicated its new home office on June 4, 1977. Just as thousands of motorists passed the massive sign of PRCUA and the PMA as they traveled west on the Kennedy Expressway, now thousands more see the PNA sign as they pass the building on the Edens Expressway. The face of Polonia, Chicago's Polish American community, was definitely changing.

Since 1974, the Polish Constitution Day Parade, originally sponsored by the PNA, has been stepping off in downtown Chicago. The parade culminated at the Kosciuszko Monument in Humboldt Park. In 1978, that monument was moved to a lake front location near the Adler Planetarium. The offices of the PNA newspapers were also relocated a few miles north and west of PNA's Cicero Avenue location.

Since the president of the PNA was also the president of the Polish American Congress, it was often difficult to distinguish activities of the PNA from those of the Polish American Congress. Often Chicago-based and national publications presented a Polish American position as reflected in the comments of the Polish American Congress president. Seldom did readers get a glimpse of the importance of the PNA in the Chicago area. With the prominence of WPNA radio station, Alliance FSB, and PNA headquarters in the Chicago area, Chicagoans today have tangible verification that Polish Americans are a vital and significant factor in contributing to the well-being of the Chicagoland community.

PNA quickly adapted to its new and spacious facilities. Numerous activities have taken place on their grounds. The group has opened its front lawn to its members and the community for Easter Egg hunts attracting some 800 youngsters annually for the past 20 years. The back lawn was used for a reception to honor members of Poland's 2002 Olympic team. All the facilities were overcrowded

PNA employees in front of their new building at 6100 North Cicero Avenue in 1976 when the fraternal moved in after leaving its quarters on Division Street.

Leaders of Chicago's Polish American community meet with President Ronald Reagan, December 21, 1981, following the Polish communist regime's repression of the Solidarity movement. Second from left, Helen Zielinski, PWA president; Joseph A. Drobot, PRCUA president; President Reagan; Aloysius A. Mazewski, Polish American Congress and PNA president; John Cardinal Krol; and George H. W. Bush, vice president.

in 1983 when President Ronald Reagan visited to meet with Polish Americans.

PNA has an active Polish dance program with 11 groups in the Chicago area. The Wici ensemble has 200 members ranging in age from 3 to 35. An annual recital for all the dance schools is held at Ridgewood High School. One consistent complaint is that seating is limited and the affair is always standing room only. PNA regularly invites choreographers from Poland to teach its instructors. PNA's youth program is conducted on a 100-acre site in Yorkville, Illinois in one-week sessions from May through September. Sports and Polish-themed programs are featured. "We have Polish Masses, Polish meals, Polish music, Polish vendors, Polish books, Polish performers," and, explains an organizer, "we even have Polish honey." Other Chicago-area programs for youngsters are basketball, volleyball, and golf tournaments with league play as well as a golf club that meets weekly. PNA sponsors programs for seniors on the north and south side of Chicago. Guest speakers discuss topics of interest at monthly meetings usually with 100 to 200 in attendence. Chicago-based PNA Lodge 911 sponsors an annual "Run for Poland." All proceeds from this event are contributed to Polish or Polish American causes. PNA Chicago Society 1450 is also active in promoting Polish culture and Polish American concerns. It observes Polish Christmas, Polish holiday customs preceding Lent, and hosts the brunch before the Polish Constitution Day Parade at a downtown Chicago hotel. Its membership is composed of prominent Polish American businessmen and other professionals from the Chicago area.

The Chicago Society, other local groups, the PNA, PRCUA, and PWA are justifiably proud of the scholarships they have provided to their members for many years. The Chicago Society awards four $1,000 scholarships annually. PNA has appropriated $1,000,000 for scholarships to be awarded between 2003 and 2007. PRCUA and PWA have also made major commitments to provide scholarships to members.

PNA delegates from across the country meet on PNA grounds in Chicago for the fraternal's quadrennial convention in 1987.

Wladyslaw Reymont won the Nobel Prize for literature in 1924 for his four-volume work, The Peasants. This is considered a masterpiece of Polish literature and was translated into many European and Far Eastern languages. In revealing the strengths and deep-seated traditions of Polish peasants, Reymont also presents a well-balanced account of peasant prejudices and vices. Polish Americans often bring attention to their cultural heritage with displays such as the one above in the Polish Constitution Day Parade.

Although the last major fraternal to organize in Chicago, the PWA was often the first in sponsoring events for the benefit of the Polish American community. Saturday Polish language schools were launched by PWA in 1910 as were summer camps for youth. A PWA adult literacy program was available in 1912. Dance schools and choral groups were active in the 1930s. In April 1957, 83 PWA members traveled to Poland, the first Polish American fraternal to do so since the end of World War II. In 1958, a meeting was held in Poland between Polish American representatives and communist officials which resulted in allowing Caritas, a welfare society directed by the Catholic Church in Poland, to continue benevolent work forbidden during the Stalinist era.

After the PWA purchased a facility in Park Ridge in 1979, they organized Park Ridge Society 819 with 280 members. St. Hedwig's group 821 was organized as the Society for the New Millennium. It was comprised of members of the New Polonia. A very different approach was utilized to attract and keep the interest of these members. Seminars about educational opportunities in the U.S. were conducted. Presentations were made by doctors about U.S. medical practices with specific issues of concern to women. Ballroom dancing was taught. Women learned the art of make-up and were treated to showings of the latest fashions from Poland. A PWA Millennium Banquet, aptly titled, "Forward Together," at a large suburban hotel attracted a crowd of 350. Effective bridges between an Old Polonia organization and New Polonia arrivals were in place.

PWA supports Polish language classes and Polish dance groups such as Rzeszowiacy which perform throughout the Chicago area. The Illinois Arts Council has approved four PWA grants to teach Polish paper cut-outs and other Polish crafts. It has its own debutante ball, as does the PNA, for

Adela Lagodzinska, PWA president from 1947 to 1971, in a Krakowski costume while in Poland on a trip before she was elected an officer in the PWA.

Officers and directors of the PWA in 1985 include: (seated, from left) Monica Sokolowski, treasurer; Helen Wojcik, vice president; Helen Zielinski, president; Julia Stroup, secretary general. Standing, from left, are directors Irene Hossa, Lucyna Migala, Virginia Sikora, Olga Kaszewicz, and Albina Mazewski.

The national headquarters of the PWA moved from Chicago to Park Ridge in 1979 and remained there until 2006, when it moved back to Chicago.

members in the Chicago area to raise scholarship funds. Since 1947, boys have been allowed to join PWA. They take part in many of the cultural and educational activities and, in recent years, have been equal in number to the girls' participation. As adults, males have been elected to office on the local and regional levels, but records, to date, do not reveal any male vying for a PWA national office. PWA has supported Polish programs at Loyola University, a Polish book reading club, and has made arrangements with the Newberry Library to preserve vital PWA records. Internally, it is also taking steps to preserve its extensive collection of Polish and Polish American art works.

Would PRCUA, PNA, PWA members of 1899 smile, frown, or look with dismay at their fraternal if they were transported to 2007? One suspects a broad and wondrous grin indicating satisfaction and approval. There would be high praise for the cooperation the three major fraternals continue to exhibit and the unity of purpose of so many Polish American clubs and organizations. Tears might be shed for the democratic Poland which exists today, thanks in no small measure to the efforts of Polish Americans, an American president, and a Pope from a war-torn and communist-dominated Poland.

Perhaps not all children, grandchildren, and great-grandchildren enrolled in the PRCUA, PNA, and PWA a century ago later enrolled their own children. However, the founders of these venerable fraternals would be pleased to witness how their organizations have blossomed into democratic entities whose ideals we all cherish in the United States and Poland. We celebrate and share our unique Polish culture, history, and traditions with the world community thanks to the foresight, courage, and perseverance of our Polish American fraternal pioneers.

Mrs. Frances Dymek crowns Donna Winiecki Queen of the Debutante Ball at the Sherman House in Chicago in November 1966. Winiecki remained active in the organization and was later elected a PNA national director.

In 1971, PRCUA formed an Adult Culture Group in Chicago which sponsors an annual Cinderella-Prince Charming Ball for teens and young adults. Scholarships and other awards are distributed. Mrs. Regina Ocwieja, PRCUA vice president, center, bottom row, was the organizer of the Adult Culture Group.

PWA District I from Chicago has sponsored a debutante ball since the 1960s at a major downtown hotel to raise scholarship funds.

Our Recipes

Products courtesy of Bobak Sausage Company; photo by Katherine Bish

Polish American families still find time to cook succulent and hearty Polish meals for their loved ones. Polish Americans take pride in their heritage, and there are few things more Polish than a fine dining experience. What follows are 24 family recipes which have been handed down for decades. As you prepare these marvelous dishes, many of our skilled household chefs wanted to encourage you to experiment with their recipe, so as to "make it your own." They further explain, "The basic elements for creating flawless Polish meals is taste and technique. This is the method used by our families. It's the way my mother taught me, the same way her mom taught her. Our kitchen shelves weren't crammed with cookbooks or recipe cards; it was a little of this, a pinch of that."

Agata Jira-Owczarzak

PORK TENDERLOIN WITH WILD MUSHROOMS

INGREDIENTS

2 1/2 lbs. pork tenderloin

2 tbsp. oil

2 garlic cloves, minced

1 onion, chopped

1 lb. wild mushrooms

1/2 cup sour cream

1/2 cup heavy cream

1 tbsp. flour

2 cups water or chicken broth

1 tsp. salt

1 tsp. Vegeta (gourmet seasoning)

1/2 tsp. black pepper

Wash and dry the meat. Pound the tenderloin with a meat mallet or rolling pin. Next, rub the meat with garlic. Then sprinkle with salt, pepper, and Vegeta. Heat 1 tbsp. of oil in a large skillet over medium-high heat. Stir in 1 cup of water or broth, cover and cook for 30 minutes. In a smaller pan, heat oil (1 tbsp.), add onion and wild mushrooms and then cook for 10 minutes. Halfway through the cooking time, add the onion-mushroom mixture to the meat. Pour remaining 1 cup of water or broth over all, then cover and cook together. In a small bowl, combine the flour and creams, stirring with a whisk. Add that mixture to the pan. Next, bring the entire mixture to a boil, and cook at boil for approximately two minutes, until it has slightly thickened. Finally, take out the pork and cut into 1/2-inch slices.

Serve over dumplings or new potatoes or with cwikla (red beets with horseradish).

SERVES 6

I was born in Wadowice, the hometown of Pope John Paul II, and I come from a family of four sisters and one brother. I now live in Chicago with my husband of one year. My Polish heritage is very important to me. In my free time, I work for The Gift from the Heart Foundation, a Polish organization that helps children from Eastern Europe. To keep myself close to my roots, I am a member of the Polish Museum of America.

While growing up in Poland, my grandmother, Jozefa Jira, lived with us. She was the best grandma in the world! It was she who gave me this recipe, which had been handed down to her by her mother. I love to cook and make this dish often for my husband and me. It brings back a taste of home.

At left: Taken in the 1910s or 1920s, this is a picture of my great-aunt, my grandmother's sister, Maria Majcherek, on a day when she is dressed up to attend a wedding. Pictured above is my grandmother, Jozefa Jira, with her favorite pig. She loved this pig because he was different. He was black, while all the rest of the pigs were white.

Some of my family members picking flowers and having fun on a summer's day in the 1920s.

My grandfather, Jozef Jira, and my father, Franciszek Jira, are going to work on the family farm in Poland in the 1950s. This farm is still in my family as my brother, Ireneusz Jira, owns it today.

Above: My three-year-old aunt, Bozena Klopotowska, taking a bath in her family's yard on a warm day in the 1930s. Above right: These are my great-grandparents, Edmund and Bronislawa Jira. He was a military man and she was a countess. This picture was taken in the 1890s when he was home on military leave.

Alicia Dutka

All four of my grandparents were of Polish descent and all four lived in Chicago. My paternal grandparents, Anton Latkowski and Wadislawa Talmanowski Latkowski, were both born near Poznan, Poland. My maternal grandfather, John Wiktor, was born in Wozniki, Poland, while my maternal grandmother, Angela Mikolajczyk Wiktor, was born in Wadowice. Though they did not know each other growing up, my maternal grandparents immigrated to the United States in 1905, settled in Chicago, where they met, married, and reared their children.

Grandmother Wiktor, with eight sons, was a good cook. However, my own mother, Helen Wiktor Latkowski, is a great cook. Even now, at 94 years old, she can prepare a fabulous meal, including this family favorite, "King's Feast." Though it has been over 100 years since my grandparents first arrived, our holiday meals are still influenced by our Polish heritage.

68

KING'S FEAST
(POLISH PORK PATTIES)

INGREDIENTS

PATTIES

1 lb. ground pork

1/2 cup coarse fresh breadcrumbs

1/2 cup milk

1 egg

2 tsp. thyme

1 tsp. salt

1/2 tsp. onion powder

1/2 tsp. garlic powder or garlic salt

1/2 tsp. pepper

COATING

2 cups diced fresh white bread -
    (cut off crust)

1 egg – slightly beaten with water or milk

COOKING

1/4 cup olive oil

1 tbsp. butter

PATTIES: Put the egg, milk, and bread-crumbs into a blender or mini-food processor until blended. Pour over meat, add seasonings and mix well. Wet your hands and shape 1/4-cup-size amounts of the mixture into oval patties.

COATING: Dip patties into egg/milk mixture and then onto diced bread. Be sure to pat the diced bread onto the patties. Brown the patties in a hot skillet on all sides in about 1/4 cup olive oil and 1 tbsp. butter. Put the patties on a trivet in a baking pan or roaster that has about an inch of water. Be certain that the water does not touch the patties. Cover the pan tightly with aluminum foil and bake for 1 hour in an oven preheated to 325 degrees. These patties are great with buttered green beans.

SERVES 6

The wedding day of my parents, Chester and Helen Latkowski, on Thanksgiving Day, November 28, 1935, in Chicago.

This picture was taken in 1948, when I was seven years old, on a day my parents, Chester and Helen Latkowski, my sister, Nola (at left), and I were attending a family wedding at St. Casimir Church in Chicago.

My grandparents, John and Angela Wiktor, on the day of their wedding, in Chicago, in 1910.

A photo of my family while attending the wedding of a relative. In the front, my husband, Robert Dutka, and myself. In the back row, from the left, our sons, Jason, Rob, and Aaron Dutka.

Andrzej Gedlek

For over 20 years I have been an active member of the Polish Highlander Alliance in America. Indeed, from 1984 to 1992, I served as this organization's chief of entertainment, its general secretary from 1993-1996, and its first vice president from 1996 to 1999. In addition, I conceptualized and co-founded Polish Highlander Alliance Radio, where I served as a speaker from 1987 to 1992. While keeping active in Chicago's Highlander community, I also owned, from 1991 to 2000, the popular Polish restaurant, Lucky Man, on the north side of Chicago. Moreover, since 1992, I have been happy to be the co-owner and to serve as an entertainer for the popular radio program "Na Goralska Nute" on WPNA 1490 AM.

COUNTRY-STYLE LAMB

INGREDIENTS

1 - 1 1/2 lbs. lamb

Vegeta (gourmet seasoning)

4-5 cups dry red wine

2 tbsp. flour

2 tbsp. butter

MARINADE

8 cups water

3 bay leaves

5 cloves

5 juniper berries

5 allspice seeds

Salt and pepper to taste

2 large cloves of garlic

1 large onion

MARINADE: Cut onion into thin slices and mince the garlic. Combine all the marinade ingredients and bring them to a boil. Then simmer for about 10 minutes. Finally, let the marinade cool, and once cooled, place it in a bowl.

LAMB: Roll the meat, tie with a string, place in the marinade and refrigerate for at least 12 hours, turning the meat several times. Next, take the meat out of the dish and pat dry. Reserve the marinade. Heat oil or lard in a heavy skillet. Rub the Vegeta into the meat and fry on all sides until evenly browned. Then place the meat into a greased baking dish and bake for about 50 minutes, basting often with the pan drippings. Remove the meat and keep warm. Add 4-5 cups of dry red wine and the drippings from the baking dish to the reserved marinade. Bring the mixture to a boil and simmer for 10 minutes. Mix flour and butter together until it forms a paste. Add the flour/butter paste to the marinade liquid in small pieces, stirring continuously until it thickens. Season with salt and pepper to taste. Pour into a saucier (gravy bowl). Serve over lamb with potatoes and cooked cabbage.

SERVES 4-6

My mother, Janina Gedlek, holding me as a toddler in our village of Bioby Dienojec, Poland, in 1956.

A family picture taken in Poland in 1978. From the left, standing: my sister, Zofia; my brother, Jozef; and my sister, Danta. From the left, sitting: my sister, Malgorzata; my grandfather, Andrzej Maciata; and myself.

In 1996, I happily welcomed the Polish Olympic team to my former restaurant, Lucky Man. These athletes competed at the Atlanta Olympic Games, and among them were gold, silver, and bronze medal winners.

This photo shows Jozef F. Krozel, former president of the Polish Highlanders of America; Edward Moskal, former president of the PNA; another friend and myself in the mid-1990s.

Andrzej Arsenowicz

My father, Anatol, was a master chef. Out of all his five children, he picked me as his first assistant and my culinary career began. I have had a chance to meet masters of cooking like Ryszard Zawadzki and Maciej Kuron. In the 1990s, I wrote a culinary column in the weekly magazine Panorama, hosted a cooking show on TVP3 in Poland and cooked for countless guests and celebrities. Currently in Chicago I host a culinary radio show on 1490 AM and write a column about old Polish culinary customs for SZIKagowianka Magazine. I also founded with my two brothers, Jerzy and Krzysztof, the Old Polish Culinary Academy to preserve our culinary culture and tradition. I hope to pass all my knowledge to my children, Dorota, Marta, and Maciej. Polish and Old Polish Cuisine (nobleman-style cooking) are my greatest passions. I am forever making new and inspiring discoveries with this cuisine. I dedicate this recipe to my father, Anatol, my first culinary professor, who awakened the chef in me.

POLISH HARE WITH SOUR CREAM-CARAMEL SAUCE
WITH FRIED RED BEETS AND POTATO DUMPLINGS

INGREDIENTS

HARE

2 hares, about
    3 lbs. each
¼ lb. bacon
½ cup sour cream
4 tbsp. flour
Salt, white pepper
Caramel (instructions
    herein)

MARINADE

1 ½ cups boiling water
2-3 lemons
1 onion
6 allspice
1 bay leaf
Black pepper

FRIED RED BEETS

2 lbs. red beets
2 onions
1 lemon
¼ cup sour cream
    or mayo
3 tbsp. oil
Salt and pepper to taste

POTATO DUMPLINGS

2 lbs. potatoes
1-2 eggs
Salt
12 oz. flour

HARE: Combine the marinade ingredients. Wash the hare and separate the limbs. Marinate for 1-2 days. After the hare has sufficiently marinated, fry the bacon until soft, saving the rendered fat. Then take the hare out of the marinade; rub with salt, and stuff with the bacon. In a baking dish add the stuffed hare and limbs, pour the fat and marinade over the meat and put into the oven. Bake at 375 ºF. for about 2 hours or until tender. Add more marinade or water during the baking process. When ready, place on a heated serving dish. Thicken the rest of the marinade with the flour, boil, add sour cream, caramel (recipe below) and voila – ready to serve. Pour some sauce over the hare, the rest serve in the saucier (gravy bowl).

CARAMEL: To 3 oz. of sugar caramelized in the skillet, add 1/3 cup of water and bring to boil.

As a side dish you could serve home-made noodles, potato dumplings or cooked potatoes. For a vegetable, I would recommend hot red beets from the skillet, red cabbage or cranberries.

FRIED RED BEETS: Wash and clean the beets. Simmer in salted water until tender or bake in a 375-degree oven covered for about 1 – 1 ½ hours until tender. Let cool. Peel and grate the beets. Finely mince the onion and fry in a skillet until golden. Add beets, freshly squeezed lemon juice, salt and pepper. Heat and serve. Top with sour cream or mayonaise.

POTATO DUMPLINGS: Clean potatoes with a brush under running water. Cook, peel, and mash removing all the lumps. Mix cooled potatoes with the flour, eggs, and salt. Form the dough, place it on a floured board and roll to 1-inch thickness. Cut at an angle into 2- or 3-inch strips. Drop into boiling salted water. Cook until dumplings float to top.

SERVES 4

My daughter, Marta, and my son, Maciej, in Poland in the 1980s.

A friend and myself, cooking for the Prince Ball at the Kokonut Restaurant in Niles, in 2004.

This is a picture of me at age 19, in Poland in the 1960s.

Barbara Mirecki

I am a cook who likes to improvise on set recipes. I learned to cook from my mother, Stanislawa, a post-World-War-II immigrant from Jaroslaw in the Podkarpacie region of Southeastern Poland. She lived in France and Canada before immigrating to the United States. My mother often improvised and added both French and American touches to her cooking at home and as a personal chef. However, it is her refined Polish recipes that I love best. I am committed to preserving and passing on this culinary heritage to the next generation of my family. This effort has already met with success, as one niece, Marta, a professionally trained chef, is proudly carrying on the Mirecki family tradition of love of food; while another niece, Maya, is a whiz at sealing pierogi.

DRIED FRUIT COMPOTE

INGREDIENTS

1-1/2 lbs. mixed dried fruit – apples, apricots, figs, peaches, pears, prunes, etc. – cut into bite-size pieces.

A small handful of dried currants or cranberries

8 cups water

8 whole cloves

2 long pieces of lemon rind, removed with a vegetable peeler

3 whole allspice (optional)

1 cinnamon stick

1/2 cup sugar, or to taste

. . . .

In a small bowl, soak the dried currants/ cranberries in hot water until they are plump. Set aside. Place all remaining ingredients in a 3-quart (or larger) non-aluminum saucepan. Bring to a boil, cover, lower heat and simmer until fruit is soft and liquid is syrupy. This takes about 20 minutes. Add water if the liquid is too thick or too sweet. Next, remove lemon rind and cinnamon stick.

Cool and refrigerate at least 4 hours. Add the currants/cranberries prior to serving. They add color to the final result, but would tint the liquid red if cooked with the other ingredients.

The compote will keep for a week if covered and chilled.

Dried fruit compote makes a good dessert any time of the year, but especially in the fall and winter and it is a traditional dessert on Christmas Eve. For example, it can be served with Christmas cookies, poppy seed cake or spice cake (PIERNIK). For purists, this dish is traditionally made with 12 different fruits, each representing one of the apostles. Note: If you choose to add dried berries (blueberry, strawberry, etc), do not cook them with the other fruit, as they disintegrate quickly. Add them once the other fruit is soft; they will soften as the compote chills.

Since fresh fruit was only available in the summer in Poland, fruit was dried and preserved for use in cooking and eating all year-round. Stewed fruit (kompot) from fresh, dried or home-canned fruit is still the most popular dessert in Poland, served after almost every meal. Dried fruit compote is also nice on its own, on top of waffles or pancakes, or stirred into a favorite hot breakfast cereal. Spoon it over ice cream to create an original dessert. I also like it at room temperature with blue cheese at the end of a meal, especially if there's a dessert wine on the table.

SERVES: 12-16

Both of these photographs were taken in 1956. The photo above shows me, Barbara, as a six-year-old, while the photo below is of my mother, Stanislawa Gliniak Mirecki, at age 39. There is a saying that "you only start looking like your mother in old age," but seeing these two pictures together happily reveals that saying does not apply to me. I resembled her all along!

SPLIT PEA SOUP

Robert Kowalski

I learned this recipe from my father, Robert F. Kowalski, who learned it from his father, Edward Kowalski, an immigrant from Krakow, Poland, who was a great cook and loved to make soup.

My family would always make a "bone-in ham" for Thanksgiving, Christmas, and Easter, because my sister, Sharon, did not care for turkey. During the holidays my father would always say, "Save the bone! I am going to make Polish split pea soup." He was very proud of his heritage. He referred to everything as being Polish, this was Polish, and that was Polish. He would freeze the bone and any leftover ham, so when he had time he would make his Polish split pea soup.

So remember, freeze the bone and any leftover ham, take it out on a cold winter's day and try this recipe. It is the best split pea soup I have ever tasted. A side of Polish rye bread with butter is also a must for this soup!

76

INGREDIENTS

20 qt. soup pot

3 slices bacon, cut in half

5 garlic cloves, cut in medium to large slices

1 large onion

3 celery stalks, cut in 1/2-inch pieces (2 cups)

5 large carrots peeled, cut into 1/2-inch pieces (3-1/2 cups)

6 qts. water (24 cups)

3 – 1 lb. bags of no-soak split peas

1 ham bone

6 cups diced ham, 1-inch pieces

1 cup ham skin with fat, diced

3 bay leaves

5 large potatoes peeled, cut into 1 inch pieces (5 cups)

Salt and pepper to taste

3 tbsp. butter

1 beer

1 tbsp. Vegeta (gourmet seasoning)

My grandfather, Edward Kowalski, on the day of his First Holy Communion, taken in Krakow, Poland, in 1923.

In a 20-quart soup pot, fry bacon until fully cooked. Then remove the bacon and set aside, leaving the bacon grease in the pot. Dice a quarter of the onion and slice all 5 garlic cloves into medium to large pieces. Add to the pot and sauté for about 2 minutes. Next, add 6 quarts of water and 3 bags of split peas, along with the celery, carrots, ham bone, 3 bay leaves, and 3 tbsp. of butter. Cover the pot, and then bring to a boil on medium heat.

In the meantime, cut up the bacon into 1/2-inch pieces, cube the ham and potatoes into 1-inch pieces, and dice the remaining onion.

Once the water is boiling, add the ham, ham skin with fat, bacon, onion, and potatoes. Salt and pepper to taste. Bring back to boil uncovered, stirring occasionally. Once boiling, bring down to a simmer, then cover, stirring frequently so peas do not stick to bottom of pot. Now open and drink beer while waiting for soup to cook. (Optional). Cook for 1 hour or until peas have completely broken down. Add Vegeta during the last 5 minutes, and serve with rye bread and butter. My father would always make a large batch to share with family and friends. This soup freezes well. For smaller servings of soup use 1 bag of split peas, 8 cups of water, and divide the remaining ingredients by thirds.

SERVES 30

The whole Kowalski family on a Sunday picnic in 1942 in Chicago. From the left: My young Aunt Rosemary, Grandmother Alice, my father, Bob (who in the picture happens to be enjoying a big piece of candy as can be seen by his left cheek), Aunt Patricia as a little girl, Grandfather Edward as a young dad, and toddler Aunt Carol.

At left: My younger sister, Linda Kowalski Goltz, in Chicago in 1969. Below left: Grandfather Edward, in 1960, cooking a bass that he also caught, cleaned, and stuffed himself. My grandfather also grew almost all of his own vegetables in a summer garden and harvested mushrooms in his basement all-year round.

My grandfather, Edward Kowalski, as a two-year-old toddler, in Krakow, Poland, in 1912.

77

Mushroom Barley Soup

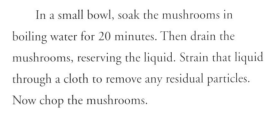

Christine Rasinski

Many years ago my paternal grandmother, Karolina Rasinska, shared this recipe with my mother, Leona Rasinski, a third-generation Polish American. Though they did not know one another in their homeland, both of my paternal grandparents immigrated to America from Poland with the dream of a better life. Karolina emigrated from Pilzno, Poland to Toluca, Illinois, in 1899. In Toluca, she met and married my grandfather, John Rasinski, who had emigrated from Parkosz, Poland as a young man around 1894. They eventually moved to Chicago to raise their family. In my grandmother's house there was always a pot of soup on the stove and bread on the table.

Ingredients

7 oz. dried Polish mushrooms

1 1/2 cups of boiling water

1 medium white onion, chopped

1 or 2 small leeks, chopped, using
  the white part only

3 tbsp. butter

1 medium carrot, diced

1/3 cup barley

6 cups chicken broth

Pepper

Seasoned salt

2 white potatoes, diced

2 bay leaves

1 cup water

3/4 cup sour cream

Above: My parents, Chester J. and Leona A. Rasinski, the youngest son and daughter-in-law of Karolina Rasinska, in 1944, while my father was on military leave. At left: Karolina Rasinska in 1941, reading the Polish daily newspaper on the back porch of the family apartment on Belden Avenue in Chicago.

In a small bowl, soak the mushrooms in boiling water for 20 minutes. Then drain the mushrooms, reserving the liquid. Strain that liquid through a cloth to remove any residual particles. Now chop the mushrooms.

Next, using a stockpot or a Dutch oven, saute the onion and leeks until soft. Then add the carrot and barley, and saute in the butter. Add the mushroom liquid and the chicken broth, and salt and pepper to taste. Allow this mixture to simmer, covered, for 1 hour.

After the hour has passed, add the potatoes, bay leaves, mushrooms and 1 cup of water to the mixture. Stir together, and then leave covered to simmer for another 20 minutes. Discard the bay leaves.

Place the sour cream into a bowl, and slowly add spoonfuls of the hot soup while stirring constantly. When the sour cream has been brought up to the temperature of the soup, add the sour cream mixture into the pot of soup and stir until well mixed. At this point the soup is ready to serve, or to freeze if you wish to serve the soup later. This soup freezes well.

SERVES 4-5 AS A MAIN DISH,
6-8 AS A STARTER

Aunt Eva Rasinska Welnicki, in the middle, dressed in the white dress and hat, with several relatives at the Chicago World's Fair.

Karolina Rasinska with her sons, Joseph and John, in June of 1942. Four of my grandmother's five sons served in the military in World War II.

Five ladies after Mass at St. Hedwig's. My Grandmother Karolina is in the middle of this group of friends and relatives, while her daughter and my Aunt Eva, appear on the right end.

Danuta Szymanska

I was born in 1955 in Brzezinki Stare, Poland. After graduating from Gastronomy school and marrying Marian Szymanski, I moved to Swidnica, in southwestern Poland in 1976. There I worked as a waitress for almost 18 years. In late 2002, I decided to start a new life in the United States. My husband, younger son and I now live in Chicago, while my older son and his wife still live in Poland.

My mother was a very good cook. She taught me how to prepare all sorts of wonderful goodies, including Chicken Roulades, though my mother's did not contain cheese. I added that later. Today, Chicken Roulades are a family favorite. I usually make them on special occasions, and sometimes I prepare them for Sunday dinners. Those Chicken Roulades remind me of my old days in my hometown; they remind me of time spent with my mother.

Chicken Roulades with Cheese and Mushroom Filling

Ingredients

4 chicken breast filets

1 lb. button mushrooms

2 onions

Vegeta (gourmet seasoning)

Pepper

2 tbsp. unsalted butter

1/2 lb. cheese (almost any Polish cheese, Edamski, Krolewski, Gouda or you can use Mozzarella or Swiss)

3 eggs

Breadcrumbs

Cooking Oil

Wash the chicken and dry with a paper towel. Cut pieces in halves, lightly pound and sprinkle with Vegeta and pepper. Next prepare the filling: Clean and cut the mushrooms. Chop the onions. Melt the butter in the skillet, caramelize the onions, add mushrooms, fry about 10 minutes. Add salt and pepper for taste. Cut the cheese into 1-inch strips. On the underside of each chicken breast, place 1 spoon of mushrooms with onions and a piece of cheese. Roll tightly and tie. Scramble the eggs, dip the roulades in the eggs and roll in the breadcrumbs. Preheat the oil in the skillet, place the roulades and brown them on each side, cover, lower the heat and let them cook for about 45 minutes.

When I prepare Chicken Roulades for my family, I often serve them with potatoes or dumplings and a salad.

Serves 8

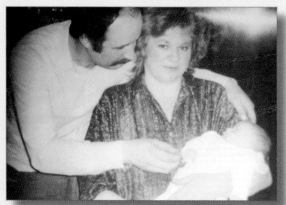

Taken on April 15, 1990, the day of my son Piotr's baptism, in Swidnica, Poland, this picture shows my husband, Marian, and me (Danuta) with our newly baptized son.

A traditional Sunday family dinner in November of 2002, in Swidnica, Poland. From the left: Marian, Danuta, Pawel Szymanski (my older son), Agnieszka Szymanska (my daughter-in-law), and my son, Piotr.

Marian, Danuta, and Piotr Szymanski, in Chicago, on Easter Sunday 2005.

CREAM CAKE

Favorite Pastry of Pope John Paul II

INGREDIENTS

PASTRY

8 oz. wheat flour
8 oz. margarine
3 tbsp. sour cream
A dash of salt

CREAM #1

3 oz. potato flour
3 oz. margarine
*3 oz. sugar (preferably Polish Krysztal made from
    sugar beets)*
5 egg yolks
1 cup of milk (reduced fat)
1/2 oz. vanilla sugar

CREAM #2

2 whole eggs
3 oz. sugar

CREAM #3

8 oz. soft butter

PASTRY: Mix, with a knife, all the ingredients. Then carefully knead the dough. Put into the refrigerator for 24 hours. Next, the dough should be divided into 2 parts and rolled with a rolling pin. Transfer dough to a floured board. Each part should be rolled to the shape of the pan 3 times. Then the rolled dough should be bent into the shape of an envelope and rolled again. Bake in an oven preheated to 450-degrees until golden (for about 10 to 15 minutes). The dough tends to create bubbles as it bakes. After putting the dough into the oven, let it create a bubble, then poke it with a fork to let the air out, and finish baking.

CREAM #1: Mix egg yolks with potato flour in a 1/2 glass of milk. Bring the rest of the milk to a boil with margarine, sugar, and vanilla sugar. Remove from heat, continuously stir and add milk mixed with egg yolks and potato flour. Cook on low heat while mixing until mixture thickens. Let cool.

CREAM #2: Over a double boiler beat eggs and sugar until firm. Remove from heat and continue beating until it cools down.

CREAM #3: Mix 8 oz. of soft butter in the bowl, add cream #1 and cream #2 a little at a time and mix thoroughly.

Spread the cream on 1 sheet of dough, cover with the second one and sprinkle powdered sugar on the top.

SERVES 8

My grandchildren and the children of my oldest daughter, Jolanta Wyrazik Dyjak, vacationing by the Baltic Sea in 2004. From the left: Ania, Lukasz, Natalia and Konrad (in the middle).

Danuta Wyrazik

As long as I can remember, I liked to cook, especially to bake. In Poland, I worked as a chef in the kitchen for a scout camp. I also catered for special events such as christenings, First Holy Communions, and weddings. I came to Chicago in January of 2003, to visit a friend. I liked it so much that I decided to stay. Soon after, my fiancee followed me. We then married in Chicago and began to create our new life in this land. I am still strongly connected with my family in Poland, as my children and grandchildren are still there. Sometimes they come for a visit, but never for long enough.

Both of my daughters like to bake. I hope that my granddaughters will enjoy it as well. My dream is to open my own little pastry shop one day. I like the look on the faces of people enjoying my baking.

The First Holy Communion of my younger daughter, Agnieszka, in May of 1985, in Mielec, Poland. Standing from the left: Marian Wyrazik, my late husband; Alicja Kot, Jozefa Kazimierska, Agnieszka Wyrazik (now Kozik), dressed in white; Mariusz Kot, myself, Jolanta Wyrazik (now Dyjak), my older daughter; and squatting from the left, Janusz Wyrazik, my son, and Marta Mikosz.

The First Holy Communion of my granddaughter, Klaudia Kozik, in Mielec, Poland, in May of 2005. Standing from the left: Bogdan Kozik, my son-in-law, Klaudia, and my children Agnieszka Wyrazik Kozik, and Janusz Wyrazik.

My husband, Czeslaw Wydro, and myself, at our wedding on October 16, 2004, at St. Ladislaus Church in Chicago.

83

Dominika Wilk

Pheasants are not indigenous to the United States, but were successfully introduced from their native Asia in the late nineteenth century. In addition to wild birds, farm-raised birds are available commercially. Generally, farm-raised pheasants do not have the same flavor as wild birds. Young birds can be cooked as you would chicken, but older birds, because they are less tender, require moist heat, such as braising.

Since I can remember, wild game has been a part of my family cuisine. Often my grandmother or mother would prepare incredible dishes using pheasant, quail, venison, and even wild boar. My father was so proud of my mother's cooking that he used to invite his hunting partners for dinner. They would enjoy her great recipes, while exchanging their hunting stories until the late evening hours. Today, I try to continue my family traditions by both hunting and cooking wild game.

Pheasant in Rosemary and Sage Cream Sauce

INGREDIENTS

1 pheasant, cut in quarters
1 cup poultry stock
1 cup cold heavy whipping cream
1 tsp. flour
1 tbsp. chopped fresh sage

MARINADE

1 cup olive oil
4 cloves crushed garlic
1/2 tsp. red sweet pepper
Bunch of fresh rosemary
Bunch of fresh sage
Salt and freshly ground pepper to taste

Combine all of the marinade ingredients and marinate the pheasant pieces overnight. Then remove the pheasant pieces and reserve the marinade.

Next, brown the pheasant pieces in a non-stick skillet over high heat. Add the marinade and the poultry stock, cover and cook over medium heat until the pheasant is done.

Remove the pheasant pieces, rosemary, and sage, and strain the liquid.

Combine the flour with the cold heavy whipping cream, then stir, gradually adding in the cooking juices, until a smooth, creamy sauce is obtained. Adjust the seasoning.

Return the pheasant pieces to the sauce; simmer for 5 to 10 minutes.

Finally, sprinkle with fresh sage and serve.

SERVES 4

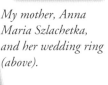

My mother, Anna Maria Szlachetka, and her wedding ring (above).

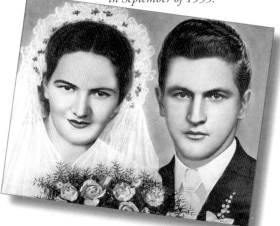

The wedding picture of my parents, Anna Maria Szlachetka-Wilk and Stanislaw Wilk, taken in September of 1955.

From left to right: My mother, Anna Maria Szlachetka, in 1952, standing in the Main Market Square in Krakow, Poland. Next, a photo of my mother, and her sister-in-law, Weronika Szlachetka, taken in 1953. Finally, my mother sewing at our family home in Krakow in 1965. My mother was not only a great cook, but also a wonderful couture dress designer.

Jim Jankowski

My Grandma Jankowski ("Grandma Jan") and Grandma Golubski both loved to cook. I could never leave either of their houses without being served hearty helpings of traditional Polish food. One of my fondest childhood memories is of watching my Grandma Golubski slice homemade noodles with her "special" knife, one where the blade had been worn into a notched curve near the handle. How she managed to move so fast without nipping one of her fingers was an awesome mystery to me as a six year old. The two recipes here pay homage to my grandmothers. "Grandma's Chicken" is Grandma Jan's original recipe, and is still served on the tables of her thirteen grandchildren. The noodles are a traditional, potato-based dough, but the slicing is all Grandma Golubski style.

86

Grandma Jan's Chicken

Ingredients

Chicken

1 chicken, cut up, or specific pieces as desired

Butter

1 small onion, chopped

1 small carrot, chopped

2 tbsp. chopped celery and leaves

Salt and pepper to taste

1 tsp. granulated sugar

3 to 4 tbsp. paprika (Sweet Hungarian is best)

1 cup water or chicken stock

Little Hoofs (Kopytka)

5 potatoes, cooked and mashed

1 egg

Flour

Chicken

Brown chicken on all sides in a small amount of melted butter in a large skillet. Discard excess fat, leaving some pan juices. Add onion, carrot, celery, salt, pepper, sugar, and paprika. Simmer for 30 minutes. Water at this time should not be necessary since the chicken and vegetables will create their own juices. Next, turn all the chicken pieces. Simmer for 30 minutes longer, and then remove chicken to a platter. Now add water or chicken stock to the mixture in the skillet and mix well. Heat until mixture thickens. It can be used as a sauce for chicken, mashed potatoes or noodles.

Little Hoofs (Kopytka)

Mix potatoes with egg and add flour until you have a loose dough that does not stick to your fingers. Roll out the dough on a floured board and cut into thin strips. (Watch fingers!) Bring some salted water to a boil and drop the noodles into it. They are ready when they float to the surface.

Serves 4 to 6

My wife, Carla, and I, on the day of our wedding in 1969.

The Jankowski and Golubski families spending a day at Indiana Dunes in 1949. I am the blond baby who seems to be the center of everyone's attention. Verna Golubski and Harriet Jankowski, my grandmothers, are in the back.

Lidia Filus

I grew up in Siedlce, a town 60 miles east of Warsaw, Poland. In my childhood, I often visited my maternal grandmother, Otollia Pawlik, who lived in the small village of Wolka Wisniewska, which was four miles away from Siedlce. She was my model of a strong, positive, open, and warm woman, as she was a widow who raised seven sons and one daughter on her own. During my visits, she and I would have wonderful talks about the past. Even when I began my studies at Warsaw University, where I received Master's and Doctoral degrees in Mathematics, and later began to work at the Warsaw School of Economics, I would frequently visit my grandmother, as I always had something to learn from her. She and my mother taught me the traditions of my homeland. I took those traditions for granted until I left Poland to teach at universities abroad. In 1982, my husband, Jerzy, and my son, Christopher, and I came to America, where I taught at the University of Kansas for three years. From there we moved to Chicago, where I have been a Professor of Mathematics since 1985. The longer I am away from my homeland, the more I see how important my Polish roots are.

Vegetable Salad

INGREDIENTS

5 carrots

2 parsley roots

1 small celery root (can be replaced
    with 1 potato)

1 lb. green peas (can be replaced by 1 can)

4 hardboiled eggs

1 apple

1/2 - 1 onion

3-4 pickles

1 tbsp. mustard

2-3 tbsp. olive oil

Salt, pepper, and mayonnaise according to taste

Boil together, with skin, the carrots, parsley roots, and celery roots. Then separately boil the green peas. Once those ingredients have been softened (though they should retain some firmness), remove them from the pot and proceed to peel, slice, and/or chop all the ingredients. Then mix in a bowl. Next add a tbsp. of mustard and 2 to 3 tbsp. of olive oil and mix again so that the mustard and oil are evenly distributed. You may also add salt, pepper, and mayonnaise. This dish may be nicely decorated with pieces of pickles, vegetables, and eggs.

SERVES 4-6.

This is a picture of me, taken on the day of my First Holy Communion in May of 1957, in my hometown of Siedlce, Poland. This photo reminds me of my childhood and an important event in my spiritual life.

This photo was taken on the occasion of my baptism in July of 1948. In the top row, from the left, is my mother, Stanislawa Pawlik Plichta, and my father, Edward Plichta. In the bottom row my then nine-year-old brother, Wenanty, is standing, while my godparents are sitting and holding me. This picture is important to me as it is my first family photo.

To the left is a photo of my paternal grandmother, Eleonora Plichta. This photo was taken in 1907 for identity purposes in Warsaw where my grandmother lived at that time. This is the oldest family photo that I have. All of our other older family photos were lost during the Second World War.

The photo to the right was taken during the spring of 1966 in front of my maternal grandmother's house in Wolka Wisniewska, a village close to Siedlce, Poland. The photo memorializes one of the rare visits of my uncle, Father Lucjan Pawlik. My uncle was a Catholic priest in Belarus, and this was his first visit to his home village after he was released from a camp in Siberia. From the left: my mother, Stanislawa Pawlik Plichta; my father, Edward Plichta; my maternal grandmother, Otollia Pawlik; my grandmother's daughter-in-law, granddaughter and great-granddaughter; and my uncle, Father Lucjan Pawlik.

89

Malgorzata Konieczna

Green Tomato Soup is an old peasant recipe. Early in the season (May/June), women pickled the fresh-picked green tomatoes in jars. Then with the coming of the harvest in July and August, those same women would wake up early in the morning, and before they went out to work in the fields, they prepared this tasty soup using the pickled tomatoes. The peasants enjoyed the soup at its best – a few hours after cooking or the following day.

The history of this family recipe goes back to the 19th century. My grandmother, Stefania Rogowska, learned it from her mother and passed it on to me. This plain peasant soup seems quite unique today. It could be served in the best restaurants or at the most elegant of dinners. I receive many compliments whenever I prepare it. I am glad that this recipe is in my family, and I hope that it will live on through our future generations.

GREEN TOMATO SOUP

INGREDIENTS

GREEN TOMATO SALAD

4 1/2 lbs. green
    tomatoes

7 oz. onions

1.7 oz. salt

BRINE

34 fl. oz. water

1/2 cup 10% vinegar

3 1/2 oz. sugar

50 bay seeds

5 bay leaves

10 whole peppercorns

SOUP

1 jar (17 1/2 oz.) green tomato salad

6 medium white potatoes (2 lbs.)

3 medium carrots (1/2 lb.)

2 medium parsley roots (6 oz.)

1/2 medium red onion (4 oz.)

3 oz. leek

5 oz. celery root

1/2 cup chopped green parsley

1/4 cup butter

1/2 cup sour cream

1 tbsp. flour

1 tbsp. salt

GREEN TOMATO SALAD

Chop tomatoes and onions into slices, sprinkle with salt, and place in one container. Leave for 24 hours. The following day, drain the tomatoes and onions from the natural juices and mix with the brine, composed of water, vinegar, sugar, bay seeds, bay leaves, and whole peppers. Cook for approximately 25-30 minutes. Pour the boiled contents into 17 1/2 oz. jars.

SOUP

Add chopped potatoes, carrots, parsley roots, celery root, leek, red onions, and butter to a large pot containing 4 quarts of water and 1 tbsp. of salt. Cook for approximately 25 minutes. Toward the end, add the green tomato salad.

Cook for another 5 minutes. Stir together the sour cream, flour, and 1/2 cup of water. Then add it to the boiling soup for another few minutes. At the very end, add chopped green parsley. Best when served a few hours after cooking or the following day.

SERVES 8

A photo of me on the day of my First Holy Communion, taken in 1967, in Debica, Poland.

My twin daughters, Ania and Iwonka, in Debica, Poland, in 1983, eating soup from the same bowl, just as peasants did long, long ago.

Malgorzata Kot

I was born in the little town of Bogoria, located in the Gory Swietokrzyskie region of Poland. When I was a child, my family – Mom Elzbieta, Dad Czeslaw and my sister, Ania, and I – would prepare galareta *together for family occasions. My father, a sculptor, always carved carrots in the shape of flowers for it, while my mother was acclaimed the best* galareta *maker in the whole family. The memories that I cherish most are those of our family home in Poland and preparations for the holidays. Indeed, I enjoyed cooking, serving, and cleaning dishes with my immediate family even more than celebrating with our extended family. Today I grow all the herbs needed for the Polish cooking that I learned from my mother. With scents and tastes from the past, I hope to create future traditions for my own family. I hope that my husband, Mariusz, and my little sons, Tunio and Tomik, will soon enjoy making our family preparations. Indeed, this wonderful dish will always be on our table.*

JELLIED MEAT (GALARETA)

INGREDIENTS

4 pork hocks

4 pork feet

6 chicken wings

2 chicken thighs

2 bay leaves

5 allspice seeds

5 black peppercorns

5 carrots

6 garlic cloves, crushed

Salt and pepper

OPTIONAL

Hard boiled egg

Fresh parsley

Green peas

Gelatin

Soak meat in cold water for ½ hour. Drain the water. Next, fill a large pot with 2 gallons of fresh cold water. Slowly bring pot of water, with meat, to a boil, skimming foam as it forms. Add 2 bay leaves, 5 allspice seeds, and 5 black peppercorns. Lower heat and simmer uncovered for about 3 1/2 to 4 hours or until the meat feels soft when pierced with a fork and falls off the bone (add more water as needed). Add 5 whole peeled carrots. Continue cooking until carrots are sufficiently soft (10 to 15 minutes). Remove meat and carrots from the stove and set aside to cool. Using a colander strain the broth and skim off grease. Put the semi-clear broth back into the pot.

Cut meat into small pieces and add to pot with 6 cloves of crushed garlic. Bring mixture to a boil for 1 minute. Add salt and pepper to taste. Into the bottom of several small containers or one large bowl, add sliced egg, fresh parsley, green cooked peas, sliced carrots (in our family we cut the carrots in the shape of flowers).

Slowly add hot mixture to the containers. Let cool for 1 hour, and refrigerate overnight when galareta (natural gelatin) will set. (For a firmer texture add gelatin to the mixture (optional).

Separate it from the mold with a knife. Place a plate over it and turn it upside down. Slice and serve cold.

Galareta can be served with bread, lemon, vinegar, or horseradish and chilled Polish vodka.

SERVES 15 +

Our family friend, Julita Siegel, took this picture of my mother, Elzbieta Baran Brudek, and my older son, Artur Grzegorz Kot ("Tunio") in November of 2004 in Chicago.

Taken in 1942, in Bogoria, Poland, this photo shows, from the left, Anna Baran Gorska, my aunt and godmother as a child; my grandmother, Maria Kosowicz Baran; and my uncle, Czeslaw Baran, as a toddler.

My grandmother and grandfather, Maria and Tomasz Jozef Baran, in Poland in 1937.

Christmas 1996, the last Christmas my whole family spent together in Poland. From the left, sitting, Zofia Kot (my mother-in-law), Elzbieta Brudek (my mother); from the left, standing, Mieczyslaw Kot (my father-in-law), myself, Anna Brudek (my sister), Mariusz Kot (my husband), Alicja Kielb (my sister-in-law), and Czeslaw Brudek (my father).

Maria Marton

WALNUT TORTE

INGREDIENTS

All ingredients must be fresh and at room temperature.

CAKE

11 extra large eggs, separated

3/4 cup granulated sugar

1/2 lb. walnuts, finely ground

1 tbsp. cocoa, sifted

3 tbsp. breadcrumbs

1 tsp. vanilla or 1 sachet vanilla sugar

2 tsp. baking powder

COFFEE FROSTING

2 egg yolks

1 cup powdered sugar

3/4 lb. unsalted butter

3 tbsp. instant coffee

1 tbsp. boiling water

1/2 tsp. vanilla

1 tbsp. brandy

3-5 tbsp. currant jelly

Walnuts (enough for garnish)

CAKE: Using an electric mixer, beat the egg yolks and granulated sugar at high speed until thick. Then mix together all the dry ingredients (walnuts, cocoa, breadcrumbs, baking powder, and vanilla sugar). Next, beat the egg whites at high speed. However, do not overbeat. Then gently fold the egg whites and all the dry ingredients into the yolk batter.

Use two round (9-inch) layer cake pans, well-greased and floured, bottom-lined with wax paper. Then bake the cake batter in an oven preheated at 350 degrees for about 30 minutes or more, until a toothpick inserted in the middle of the cake comes out clean.

COFFEE FROSTING: Make the instant coffee and allow to cool. Next, using an electric mixer, combine the egg yolks, butter, brandy and vanilla, and beat until smooth. Then add the cooled coffee to the mixture. Gradually add the powdered sugar to the mix until you have a smooth, thick frosting.

When the 9-inch cake layers and the frosting are prepared, spread the currant jelly on the bottom of the first layer. Then spread frosting on top of that first layer. Next, place the second layer on top of the first. Spread the frosting on the second layer. Finally top the finished cake with walnuts for garnish or other decorations if you desire.

SERVES 12 TO 15

I am from the town of Raclawice in southeastern Poland. In Raclawice I lived on a farm that has belonged to my family for several generations. Though it is very rare for walnuts to grow in Poland due to our cold winters, my family was blessed to have a walnut tree in our yard. This walnut tree is now 50 years old. When this special tree was only three years old, it had to endure a very cold, Polish winter which damaged it greatly. However, my father had faith in the tree's survival and decided not to cut it down. He was right, for within two years the tree had come back to life.

At home in Raclawice, my family and I would pick walnuts straight from this wonderful tree to make Walnut Torte, and eventually we grew to love this delicious dessert so much that Walnut Torte became a family tradition for Christmas Eve dinner. To this very day, this lovely tree still gives walnuts to my family in Poland.

This picture was taken in May of 1979, which was only a few months after I had first arrived in Chicago from Poland. It shows me (at the far right), and two dear friends, both of whom were also from Raclawice, Poland.

This photo shows my hometown of Raclawice, Poland, as it was in December of 1978, the same month I left Poland for America. The townspeople are walking in a funeral procession in remembrance of a well-loved teacher who had taught many children in Raclawice, including...

Mariusz Zaleski

AGED LIQUEUR (NALEWKA)

A nalewka *is a fruit extract infused with alcohol. Its origin dates back to medieval doctors who created their remedies using the same formulas. Hence, the toast* Na Zdrowie *(for health) is still used today while consuming alcoholic beverages. By the 16th century, nalewka had become an important custom among Polish townsmen, gentry, and nobility. No feast was complete without it. Families have proudly kept their own secret recipes for generations, with each competing for the best. It is almost impossible to make the same* nalewka *twice. Quality of materials, light, temperature, and length of maturity make for endless variations.*

I was introduced to nalewka *by my father. He treated me to a dark, wonderfully smelling liquid made from fresh walnuts. I remember a bitter taste, followed by a sophisticated range of smells and tastes that I had never before known. He told me that he would combine various* nalewkas *to complement the taste. To me it had a complete taste, but my father was attempting to create a new* nalewka *that would become a part of my heritage.*

INGREDIENTS

*1 liter of rectified spirits
(92% - 98 % alcohol; 184-196 proof)*

1 liter of white vodka

*3-4 lbs. of cherries (Try best
quality, organic if possible)*

*2-3 cups of sugar (Substitute honey for
sugar for a more complex taste)*

Clean well-ripened, pitted cherries. Place the cherries into a 1-gallon jar with a tight-fitting lid until it is 3/4 full. (You may save the pits). Then mix the spirits and vodka together. Pour the mixture into the 1-gallon jar until it is filled to the top. Place the cherry pits in a separate, 1 quart-size container, and then pour the remaining spirits/vodka mixture into that container until it

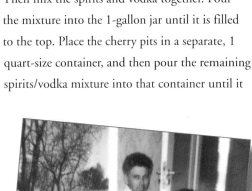

is filled to the top.

Wait 3-6 weeks. After this time, you may create the first extraction from the 1-gallon jar containing the cherries. Drain the liquid, the first extraction, from that jar into a half-gallon bottle. After the extraction is drained, add the sugar to that 1-gallon jar with cherries, and then wait 2-3 weeks for the second extraction.

Using a separate, 1 quart-size container drain the liquid, the second extraction, from the 1-gallon jar. Combine the second extraction with the first-bottle extraction and, if you wish, with the optional extraction made from the cherry pits. Drain this mixture of extractions into bottles and store in a cool place. Mature extractions for at least 6 months (the longer the better).

Enjoy nalewka at room temperature in a very small shot glass.

Do not discard cherries in the mature nalewka. Instead, they can be added to smoothies, or used as garnish on ice cream or baked goods. They can also be used for sauces or to marinate meats.

SERVES YOU AND ALL YOUR FRIENDS

This photo shows a casual gathering of my family during the 1980s, when we all still lived in Poland. I am sitting in front of the table, while my father, Adolf-Adam, my mother, Helena, and my younger brother, Pawel, sit behind the table. This photo is precious to me as it is one of the few photos I have from when we lived in Poland.

This is a photo of my
maternal grandparents,
Antoni and Maria,
taken in Plac Downary,
Poland, in the 1990s.
My grandfather is
wearing his AK (Armia
Krajowa) uniform.

A photo of my father,
Adolf-Adam, taken in the
area of Augustow, Poland,
in the 1960s.

Taken at Midway Airport in the
1990s, my father, Adolf-Adam,
was awaiting an airplane for
New York.

Monika Nowak

GRANDMA STEFCIA'S PLUM-FILLED POTATO DUMPLINGS

My two grandmas were both from the Zaglebie Dabrowskie region of Poland, and both were excellent cooks. Grandma Jasia (Janina Duraj) was famous for her amazing chicken noodle soup and wild mushroom soup with Lazanki, while Grandma Stefcia (Stefania Nowak) had a special way to cheer me up. As a child, when I would catch a cold, she would make her unforgettable plum potato dumplings. This memory of her kindness still stirs my heart. Plum dumplings are a delicious dish, especially for late summer and fall when fresh plums are widely available on the market.

INGREDIENTS

DOUGH

4 cups mashed potatoes

1 1/2 cups flour

1 tbsp. potato flour

2 eggs

1/2 tsp. salt

STUFFING

16 small Italian plums (Wegierki)

1 tsp. sugar

1/3 tsp. ground cinnamon

TOPPING

4 tbsp. butter

2 tbsp. breadcrumbs

1 tbsp. confectioners' sugar

Peel and cook the potatoes. Mash them thoroughly. Wash, drain and pit the plums. Cut every plum in half. Mix the plums with ground cinnamon and sugar. Mix cooled mashed potatoes with the flour, potato flour, salt, and eggs. Quickly knead the dough. If the dough is too sticky, add some flour. Form a thick roll. Cut with a knife into 1 1/2-inch pieces. Place two halves of the plum in the center of a flattened dough circle. Seal the edge and form the ball. Drop gently into a large deep pot of salted boiling water. Cook about 5 minutes at slow boil until they float to the surface. Remove one by one with a slotted spoon. Melt the butter and add the breadcrumbs, then fry. Pour the fried breadcrumbs over the dumplings. Finally, sprinkle with confectioners' sugar.

SERVES 4

My husband, Sławek Sobczak, posed with his family on the day of his First Communion in the 1960s, in Wroclaw, Poland. From left: Wanda Stoklosa (aunt), Robert Knizewski (uncle), and Otylia Sobczak (mother).

My grandma, Janina Duraj; my mom, Krystyna Duraj; and my charming grandpa, Miecio Duraj, in 1947, in Zabkowice Bedzinskie, Poland.

My wonderful Dad, Jerzy Nowak, as a boy in 1939, in Krynica, Poland.

Selected books by my mom, Krystyna Duraj-Nowakowa. She is a scientist who interestingly places my and my father's pictures on the covers of her books to make us smile.

My grandma, Stefania Nowak, with my dad, Jerzy Nowak, in Zegiestow, Poland, in 1938.

99

Olga Balcerowska

Cabbage Rolls

I was born in Kielce, capital of Gory Swietokrzyskie, and lived there until the age of 18 with my parents and younger brother, Kajetan. Seeking adventure and wanting to visit a larger city, I traveled to Chicago. Falling in love with the "Windy City," I decided to stay. However, I am still strongly tied to my Polish origins and traditions.

I remember summer vacations at my grandparents' house – filled with love and fun. After playing at the beach all day, I would help my grandmother pick fresh vegetables from the garden for dinner, but I was too young and busy having fun to pay attention to my Grandma's special recipes. Her passion for cooking led her to open her own restaurant. Longing for my favorite Polish dish, I decided to call home and get the recipe for golabki *(cabbage rolls). Passed from my grandma, to mom, from me to you, I hope you too enjoy one of our family favorites.*

INGREDIENTS

GOLABKI (CABBAGE ROLLS)

1 lb. ground pork

1 cup rice

Salt and pepper to taste

1 cabbage

1 tbsp. Vegeta (gourmet seasoning)

MUSHROOM SAUCE

½ lb. mushrooms

Salt and pepper to taste

1 tbsp. butter or margarine

1 tsp. Worcestershire sauce (optional)

3 1/2 cups of water

2 cubes mushroom broth (Knorr, Winiary, Kucharek etc.)

2 tbsp. flour

Sour cream

Three-year-old Olga (second from the left) ponders future recipes, while baby brother, Kajtek, pokes fun at crying little cousin Lukasz Wisnios. Kasia Wisnios, looking beautiful as always!

GOLABKI (CABBAGE ROLLS): Remove the core of the cabbage (to let the leaves peel off easily) and put the cabbage into a large pot of salted, boiling water. Cover and let stand until leaves are limp, about 10 minutes. Remove leaves; drain. Cook rice for 10 minutes. Mix ground pork, semi-cooked rice, Vegeta, salt and pepper. Place the mixture in each cabbage leaf, roll up, tucking all sides under. Place cabbage rolls seam side down in a Pyrex dish. Pour the salted cabbage cooking liquid over cabbage rolls and place the unused cabbage leaves over the rolls (to prevent burning). Cover with foil and bake at 400 degrees for 90 minutes.

MUSHROOM SAUCE: Wash and slice mushrooms. Put into frying pan and add butter or margarine.

Cover and cook on low heat for 10 minutes, then add salt to taste. In the meantime, boil 3 cups of water and add 2 cubes of mushroom broth. Add salt, pepper, and Worcestershire sauce. Add cooked mushrooms and boil. In a separate cup, mix ½ cup of water with 2 tablespoons of flour. Slowly add mixture to boiling broth. Keep stirring until broth slightly thickens. Pour over cabbage rolls; add sour cream on top. Enjoy.

SERVES 10

Generations of golabki goodness. Grandma Helenka preparing a Christmas dinner.

The Balcerowskis, right after my First Holy Communion celebration. From the left: Dad / Andrzej, Uncle Krzysztof, Brother / Kajetan, Grandma Genowefa, myself, Grandpa Jan, Mom / Dorota, Uncle Zbigniew. Twenty years later my Dad still proudly wears that same suit and mustache.

At four-years-old I was eagerly awaiting Christmas and Santa. I always had my list ready and millions of stories to share with Santa.

Pumpkin Soup with Potato Dumplings

*Tammy Hicks, at right, and
Virginia Krygowski Kielanowicz*

Edward Kielanowicz and Virginia Krygowski Kielanowicz, the parents of my father, Joseph, are both first-generation Polish Americans, with roots in Krosna and Rzeszow, Poland. As a child I lived with my Dad and grandparents in Posen, Illinois. I have so many wonderful memories of my grandparents, especially their celebration of Polish traditions. One of my favorite memories is cooking Polish food with Grandma Virginia. She is the reason why I love cooking and why I uphold our Polish family heritage today. This specific recipe reminds me of how Grandpa Edward would come home with fresh pumpkins from our family farm in Michigan, and how Grandma Virginia and I would talk while we prepared the soup. When I think of this soup, I remember the happiness I felt cooking with Grandma.

Ingredients

Soup

4 cups water

4 cups chicken stock

1 medium-sized pumpkin

1 carrot peeled and grated

2 cups whole milk

Salt and pepper to taste

Dumplings

3 small or 1 large potato(es)

1 cup all-purpose flour

1 cup whole milk (approximate)

Salt and pepper to taste

. . . .

Soup: Slice pumpkin in half and de-seed. Remove skin and cut pumpkin into medium-sized cubes. Place pumpkin in large soup pot and cover with water and chicken stock. Cook over low to medium heat for 40 minutes or until pumpkin is soft. While the pumpkin is cooking in the pot, carefully mash pumpkin pieces. After the pumpkin is cooked, puree the pumpkin for a creamier soup, if desired. Add salt, pepper, and grated carrot.

Dumplings: About 30 minutes into the cooking of the pumpkin, begin the potato dumplings. Peel and grate potatoes. Mix with milk, flour, salt, and pepper into a thick paste. Add the dumplings into the soup.

Before adding the dumplings, first wet the tip of a teaspoon with hot water or the hot soup. Dip the tip of the teaspoon into the potato mixture. Slowly add the teaspoon into the hot soup. Let it roll off the teaspoon. Do not drop too much potato mixture into the soup.

Let the dumplings and soup cook for another 15 – 20 minutes. Then add 2 cups of whole milk and warm the soup. Do not bring to a boil. Serve in a bowl and enjoy on a crisp fall day.

Serves 8

Virginia Krygowski Kielanowicz and her husband, Ed Kielanowicz, in the late 1990s.

Virginia Krygowski Kielanowicz and Edward Kielanowicz in Chicago in the 1940s.

My great-grandmother, Victoria "Buszia" Rzonca Krygowski. Born in 1885, in Jaslo, Rzeszow, Poland, Buszia immigrated to America in 1909. In that same year, she married Antoni Krygowski, who had been born in 1884 in Pagorzyna, Krosna, Poland. Buszia and Antoni eventually settled in Posen, Illinois, where they raised 11 children.

To the right: Edward Kielanowicz and Virginia Krygowski Kielanowicz on Harrison Street in Posen, Illinois, in the 1940s.

103

Violetta Mical

Apple Pastry

INGREDIENTS

2 sticks butter (room temperature)

2 cups flour

1 1/2 tsp. baking powder

2 tbsp. sour cream

2 tsp. vanilla extract

4 egg yolks

1 cup sugar

4 big Macintosh apples

1 small jar cinnamon applesauce

Beat the egg yolks with the sugar. Then add the butter, flour with baking powder, sour cream, and vanilla extract to the mixture. Knead the dough and put it in the fridge for about 40 minutes.

Peel and cut the apples. Cook them in a covered pan for about 10 minutes, and then add cinnamon applesauce. Let cool.

Put 2/3 of the dough into the greased baking pan and spread the apples on top of the dough. Using the remaining dough, form 1-inch strips to create a plaid pattern on top of the apples. Bake at 375 degrees for about 45 minutes.

SERVES 10

I was born in the town of Blazowa, located in the Podkarpacie region of Poland. And though I now live in America, I still feel a very strong connection to my Polish roots, especially to Blazowa. In fact, right here in Downers Grove, Illinois, I have a home filled with things that remind me of my hometown.

One such bridge between the continents and cultures is szarlotka (apple pie), a recipe that I received from my Grandma Bronia Plesniak. I bake szarlotka for every occasion. All of my friends, family, and co-workers love it so much that they are now baking it for themselves. As I have made szarlotka over the years, my grandma's original recipe has evolved. I now add more butter and eggs, and I have replaced some of the apples with applesauce, but I think my grandma would approve of me trying new things. I hope that my children, Mateusz and Paula, will continue the tradition in the future.

By 1971, when I was seven years old, my mother, Maria Gawrys, and I had moved to the city of Iwonicz Zdroj. This picture shows my mom and me taking a break from a summer stroll to spend some time with a friendly bear. (The bear worked with the photographer to attract customers).

Modern women of the 1930s. This picture captures, from the left, my young grandmother, Bronislawa Plesniak, her friend, Cecylia, and her sister-in-law, Zofia Cag.

104

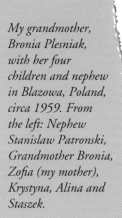

My grandmother, Bronia Plesniak, with her four children and nephew in Blazowa, Poland, circa 1959. From the left: Nephew Stanislaw Patronski, Grandmother Bronia, Zofia (my mother), Krystyna, Alina and Staszek.

A lazy Sunday afternoon in the backyard of my grandparents' farm in the village of Blazowa, circa 1948. From the left: Aunt Paulina Czapla, Uncles Franciszek and Jozef Plesniak, and my Grandfather Wiktor Plesniak.

Violetta Woznicka

As a child growing up in Konin, a city located in the Wielkopolska region of central Poland, I always liked helping my Grandmother Stefania in the kitchen. She was the person who taught me my first culinary lessons. I remember the joy of making little flat breads from the leftover pasta dough on Grandma's wood burning stove. Later, my mother guided me through the culinary world, while my sister always shared her new recipes with me. It is good to know that they are just a phone call away if I ever have any cooking questions.

I always enjoyed baking, so it's no wonder that my favorite recipes, such as this one, were among many of the necessary and precious things that I brought with me to the United States. Far away from my native country, they made this new place feel like home; keeping memories alive, bringing comfort and joy.

Cheesecake

Ingredients

1 lb. white farmer's cheese (can be substituted with Philadelphia cream cheese)

3/4 cup sugar

5 eggs, separated

1 stick unsalted butter

1 tbsp. flour

1/2 tbsp. potato starch

1/2 tsp. baking powder

1 cup raisins

Grind the farmer's cheese (no need to do this with Philadelphia cream cheese). Whip together the sugar, egg yolks, and butter. Then add the cheese and continue mixing. Next, add the flour, egg whites, baking powder, potato starch, and raisins. Finally, bake for 1 hour 15 minutes at 325 degrees.

Serves 8-12

My grandfather and grandmother, Roman and Stefania, on the deck of a boat on the Warta River in Konin, Poland, in the 1930s.

This is a picture of my sister, Agnieszka, who is my best friend, and myself (standing), while playing in our uncle's garden in Konin, Poland, in the mid-1970s.

My parents on their wedding day, stand in the courtyard next to my Grandma Stefania's house in Konin, Poland. My Grandpa Roman, stands to the far left, with two family friends, while my mother, Jadwiga, and my father, Andrzej, appear arm in arm. I love this picture because it was taken in the courtyard of my grandparents' house where I grew up as a child,

From the left: My Grandma Stefania, my Grandpa Roman and my Great-Aunt Maria, taking a stroll in Konin, Poland, in the 1930s.

Polish Coffee Cake

Wallace Ozog

I grew up on the west side of Detroit near the Dearborn, Michigan border. My parents raised 13 children and most of us were involved in Polish community events. As one of the charter members of a local society of the Polish Roman Catholic Union of America, I was committed to raise funds for our various projects.

Our parents indeed helped us out in our community efforts. However, as they became older they were not able to bake the "good old fashion pies and cakes." Thus, I took up the challenge of carrying out the tradition of making Polish coffee cake for our various bake sales to raise funds for the PRCUA society programs. When I moved to Chicago, I continued the baking of my mother's "Babka," called THE Polish coffee cake.

INGREDIENTS

1/2 cup butter (one stick)
1/2 cup granulated sugar
1 1/2 cups 2% milk
1 level tsp. salt
4 extra large whole eggs
6 cups flour
2 packages active dry yeast
1 1/2 cups dark raisins (Optional)
1/2 tsp. vanilla
1/2 tsp. almond extract

TOPPING

3 tbsp. flour
4 tbsp. sugar
2 tbsp. butter or margarine

Place the sugar and butter in a large bowl. Next, scald the milk and mix it with the sugar and butter. When this mixture becomes warm, add the active dry yeast and mix. Using a separate bowl, beat the 4 eggs with a fork for a few seconds and then add the salt. Do not make this mixture foam.

Now place about 2-1/2 cups of flour into the sugar, butter, and milk mixture, stirring constantly. Add the eggs and salt and mix. Next, add 1/2 tsp. of vanilla and 1/2 tsp. of almond extract for taste. In addition, this would be a good time to add the dark raisins if you have chosen to include them. Now continuously stir the mixture while gradually adding the balance of the flour. Do this until the consistency is tacky.

Knead the ingredients for a few minutes. Cover and let rise for at least an hour. It should more than double in size. After the mixture has risen, remove and place on a flat surface. Knead and size to the pans being used. This recipe makes a babka pan size and a small rectangular 9 x 5 (interior measurements) pan.

To prepare the topping, mix the sugar and flour. Blend these ingredients by hand with the butter or margarine until the dry mixture adheres to the margarine. Sprinkle mixture over the cake dough.

Next, surface the pans with margarine, and let the dough rise for at least another hour. Then place in the oven at 300 degrees for 50 minutes if it is a gas oven and an hour if it is electric. When removing the babka, the bottom should be light brown, and the dough should spring back when you touch it with your finger.

Cool for at least 3 hours.

You can substitute whole milk for 2%, but it makes the babka heavier. Damp weather makes the ingredients rise quicker.

SERVES 8 TO 10

Taken outside of the Ozog family home on St. Lawrence Street in Detroit, Michigan, this photo shows me holding my younger brother, Eugene, in his stroller, while my sister, Joan, takes a break from pushing the stroller.

The Ozog family. In the first row, from the left: Thaddeus, Joseph, my father; Dorothy, Maryanna, my mother; Ann, and Frank. In the second row, from the left: John, Stella, Joan, Joe, and Eugene. In the back row, from the left: Anthony, myself, Lottie, and Stanley.

My sister, Lottie, holding me in the back of our family house in Detroit on a Holy Communion Sunday.

The family of Wallace and Joann Ozog. From the left: Christopher, my son; myself, Joann, my wife; Tina, my daughter-in-law; Michael and Mark, my sons.

Wojciech & Ellen Wierzewski

Ellen was born in Scotland to a Scottish mother, Kitty; and a Polish father, Stanley, a World-War-II veteran who fought for Poland's freedom. After Kitty and Stanley passed away at a young age, Ellen was raised in Poland, where she would later work as a journalist in Warsaw. After arriving in the United States in 1979 to join her husband, Wojciech, she worked for the Polish Cultural Center, which is the Copernicus Foundation in Chicago. Wojciech was born in Krakow, the ancient capital of Poland. He studied at one of Europe's oldest institutions, the Jagiellonian University, and received his Ph.D. from Warsaw University, where he taught Polish literature and film. At the same time, he was one of Poland's more renowned film critics. Over the years he has published many books on the topic of cinema, and has taught at Indiana University and DePaul School of New Learning. Since 1985, he has served as editor-in-chief of Zgoda. This recipe is totally Ellen's invention. She loves to cook instinctively and according to her own philosophy, which is that dried wild mushrooms, fresh dill, and basil are the secrets to great cooking!

Meatballs in Dill Sauce

Ingredients

3 lbs. of ground pork or beef

1 large onion, finely chopped

Salt and pepper or Vegeta (gourmet seasoning)

2 oz. dried wild mushrooms or

2 lbs. of fresh mushrooms

2 qts. water

4 oz. half and half

2 tbsp. flour

Mix together the meat, finely chopped onion, and the salt and pepper. Form the meatballs from that mixture. Next using a large pot, cook the mushrooms in boiling water for 30 minutes. Then add 2-3 cubes of chicken or beef bouillon. Next, place the meatballs in the pot and cook together with the mushrooms (on low heat) for 90 minutes. Finally, add 4 oz. of half and half mixed with two tbsp. of flour, and then mix to thicken the sauce. Serve with mashed potatoes or buckwheat (Kasza Gryczana).

Serves 8

Above: Ellen, in 1953, on the day of her First Holy Communion.

To the right: The future Ph.D. Wojciech, in Krakow in 1945, wearing a vest and hat embroidered by his mother.

A photo of Ellen's Catholic kindergarten, taken in Warsaw in 1950. Having arrived from Scotland, Ellen learned to speak Polish in this class. Ellen is the little girl who is turning toward the camera, with her back partially facing the photographer.

EASTER MEAL
(SWIECONKA GORALSKA)

Zofia Grele

INGREDIENTS

4 hard boiled eggs

1/2 lb. Polish smoked sausage

4 slices of Polish rye bread

2 tsp. horseradish

2 cups buttermilk

Salt and pepper according to taste

Slice eggs, sausage, and bread into small pieces, and place in a bowl. Then add horseradish followed by salt and pepper. Finally, pour the buttermilk into the bowl and mix together.

SERVES 4

I was born in the southern region of Poland called Podhale, more specifically Szaflary, while my husband is from Sadkowa Gora, Poland. To this day we maintain our Polish roots by keeping our Polish traditions alive. Our children were brought up going to Polish school to learn the language and history of their culture. We celebrate each holiday as we would have in Poland. On these occasions, my daughters observe while I prepare special Polish dishes. My hope is that they will one day cook like their Mom and carry on with their heritage. This dish, Swieconka Goralska, is just one of the many Polish dishes that my family enjoys.

Swieconka Goralska is a traditional Polish Easter dish. Prior to being served to the family at Easter morning breakfast, all the ingredients are blessed on Holy Saturday by the local parish priest.

In 1962, I celebrated my First Holy Communion in Szaflary, Poland. This photo was taken outside of the church.

In 1968, my husband's family photo was taken in Sadkowa Gora, Poland. From left, my husband, John, his mother, Zofia; Yolanta, and Malgorzata. In the back row are his older brother, Marian, and his father, Adam Grele.

In 1999, we all traveled to the Vatican to have our parish church's mosaic of Our Lady of Czestochowa be blessed by the late Pope John Paul II. This picture shows my family in St. Peter's Square.

In 1986, my oldest brother, Jozef, a priest from Szaflary, Poland, had a private audience with Pope John Paul II.

113

Wesolych Swiat Bozego Narodzenia

That is the way to say "Merry Christmas" in Polish. Among Poles, wherever they are, the most beloved and beautiful of all traditional festivities is that of Christmas Eve. It is then that the *Wigilia*, or Christmas Eve Dinner is served. It is a solemnly celebrated occasion and arouses deep feelings of kinship among family members.

For days in advance, Poles prepare the traditional foods and everyone anxiously awaits the moment when the first star, known as the *Gwiazdka*, appears in the eastern sky. For that is when the feast to commemorate the birth of the Christ Child begins.

There is always a thin layer of hay under the white tablecloth in memory of the God Child in the manger. Before sitting down at the table, everyone breaks the traditional wafer or *Oplatek*, and exchanges good wishes for health, wealth and happiness in the New Year. This is such a deeply moving moment that often tears of love and joy are evoked from family members breaking this symbolic bread. The *Oplatek* is a thin, unleavened wafer similar to the altar bread in the Roman Catholic Church. It is stamped with the figures of the God Child, the blessed Mary, and the holy angels. The wafer is known as the bread of love and is often sent by mail to absent members of the family.

The dinner itself differs from other evening meals in that the number of courses is fixed at seven, nine, or eleven. According to myth, in no case must there be an odd number of people at the table, otherwise it is said that some of the feasters would not live to see another Christmas. A lighted candle in the windows symbolizes the hope that the God Child, in the form of a stranger, may come to share the *Wigilia* and an extra place is set at the table for the unexpected guest. This belief stems from the ancient Polish adage, "A guest in the home is God in the home."

The *Wigilia* is a meatless meal, no doubt the result of a long-time Church mandate that a strict fast and abstinence be observed on this day before Christmas. Although the Church laws have been revised and permit meat to be eaten on this day, the traditional meal remains meatless. Items that would normally be included in a traditional *Wigilia* menu include mushroom soup, boiled potatoes, pickled herring (*sledzie*), fried fish, pierogi, beans and sauerkraut (*groch i kapusta*), a dried fruit compote, assorted pastries (*babka, placek*), nuts, and candies.

After the meal the members of the family sing Polish Christmas carols (*koledy*) while the children wait impatiently around the Christmas tree (*choinka*) for the gifts to be exchanged.

Photo by Stanley Wlodkowski
Courtesy of White Eagle Restaurant

115

Aside from the beautiful *Wigilia*, the Polish people have a number of other traditions that they practice throughout the Christmas season. Polish Christmas carols are numerous and beautiful, especially when sung in Polish parishes at the Christmas Eve Mass. This Mass is called the *Pasterka*, which means the Shepherds' Watch, and there is a popular belief in Poland that while the congregation is praying, peace descends on the snow-clad, sleeping earth and that during that holy night, the humble companions of men–the domestic animals–assume voices. But only the innocent of heart may hear them.

Christmas Day itself is spent in rest, prayer, and visits to various members of the family. In Poland, from Christmas Day until the Twelfth Night, boys trudge from village to village with an illuminated star and a ranting King Herod among them to sing carols. Sometimes, they penetrate the towns in expectation of more generous gifts. In some districts, the boys carry on puppet shows called *szopki*. These are built like a little house with two towers, open in the front where a small crib is set.

During the Christmas season, the theaters give special performances. On the feast of the Epiphany, the priest and the organist visit parish homes, bless them and write over their doors the initials of the three wise men–KMB (Kasper, Melchior, and Balthazar)–in the belief that this will spare the homes from misfortune.

The Christmas season closes on February 2, known as Candlemas Day. On that day, people carry candles to church and have them blessed for use in their homes during storms, sickness, and death.

Wesolych Swiat, Bozego Narodzenia i Szczesliwego Nowego Roku!

Youngster enjoying making Christmas ornaments.

Oplatek *in the Polish American community suggests the ceremony of sharing a wafer at an event before Christmas. A business meeting of a Polish American group in December, a gathering at a Polish social event in December, or even a banquet will have all sharing the* Oplatek *and extending wishes for the New Year. An overwhelming majority of Polish Americans continue this centuries-old tradition on Christmas Eve before the evening meal. Here Halina Misterka shares the* Oplatek *with her parents, Janina and Kazimierz Konieczny.*

Several variations of the celebration of the Feast of St. Nicholas were observed in Poland–usually on December 6–and in the United States. The above American adaptation is based on observances in the Krakow area where, on the eve of St. Nicholas Day, a man was dressed as a bishop in a mitre with a long coat holding a stick resembling a crosier. He would go from house to house listening to children recite their catechism and prayers, He praises some and gently rebukes others. When he leaves he distributes holy pictures and pierniki, cookies made with honey and spices.

In 1987, the first Polish Spirit Award was presented by the PMA to Aloysius A. Mazewski. In announcing the award, Edward G. Dykla, chairman of the board of directors for the PMA, explained that the award would be given annually at the museum's summer ball, "to an American who embodies the Polish spirit in the most significant way."

In his acceptance of the first such award, Mazewski, president of the Polish American Congress and PNA, said, "I am convinced that (this award) will unify Polonia, so we can blend the Polish spirit with the American spirit."

A congratulatory message from President Ronald Reagan was sent to the ball. It read, in part, "As president of the Polish American Congress you've worked tirelessly in wide-ranging efforts with our colleagues in behalf of Polish Americans and the gift of self continues to inspire Polish Americans with the faith and love of liberty inherent in their Polish and American heritages."

POLISH SPIRIT AWARD

1988–Bishop Alfred Abramowicz
1989–Legion of Young Polish Women
1990–I.George and Joan Kosinski
1991–Chester and Stella Sawko
1992–Congressman Dan Rostenkowski
1993–PeKaO Trading Corporation
1994–Justice Mary Ann McMorrow
1995–Polish American Medical Society
1996–Adam Cardinal Maida
1997–Matt Rodriguez
1998–Polish Womens Alliance
1999–LOT Polish Airlines
2000–Chicago Society PNA
2001–Polish Roman Catholic Union
    of America
2002–Stanley and Barbara Stawski
2003–Donald V. and Joan Versen, Sr.
2004–Chet and Dolores Schafer
2005–Walter L. Sojka
2006–Polish Highlanders of
    North America

The PMA presented its Polish Spirit Award to Walter L Sojka in 2005. From left: Robert Bielinda, PMA board member; Maria Ciesla, PMA president; Sojka; and Wallace Ozog, chairman of the board, PMA.

On behalf of Chicago Society PNA, Romuald Matuszcak, president, accepts the PMA's 2000 Polish Spirit Award as, from left, Richard Ciesla, past president of Chicago Society PNA; Wallace Ozog; Matuszcak; Joan Kosinski, PMA president; I. George Kosinski; and Jan Lorys, director PMA look on.

Jefferson Award Winner Reflects Polish Spirit

Chicago's NBC Channel 5 recognized Joann Ozog, activities director and volunteer coordinator for the PMA, with its Jefferson Award, April 27, 2004. The award aims to "celebrate heroes... who work with little acclaim... in their communities... who change lives for the better."

In making the presentation NBC stated that Ozog "has dedicated herself to enriching the lives of Chicago-based Polish Americans by introducing them to Polish customs and traditions... by educating and introducing the public to Polish traditions... (such as) the Christmas Eve meal, the Polish St. Nicholas, the annual Polish Heritage Month Art Contest, Easter palm weaving and workshops and Easter Egg decorating."

NBC also acknowledged Ozog's two-year fund-raising efforts in raising more than $100,000 for the PMA.

The PRCUA established a museum and archives in 1935. The collection rapidly expanded with donated exhibits from the Polish pavilion at the New York World's Fair in 1939, the Paderewski permanent exhibits which opened in 1941, and the purchase of the Kosciuszko letters and other memorabilia in 1945. The deaths of the founder of the museum, Joseph Kania in 1953 and the museum's first curator, Miecislaus Haiman in 1949, both of whom had worked tirelessly for the institution's growing and favorable reputation, revealed that continued growth would require efforts of the broader Polish American community. Accordingly, the name of the Archives and Museum of the PRCUA was changed to PMA. The administration would now include representatives of all major Polish American organizations. The museum sponsors major historical, art, and other exhibits and programs. Since 1987, the museum has also attracted media coverage with its observance of Pulaski Day in March attended by numerous federal, state, and city officials along with other dignitaries.

At the museum there were classes organized for students to learn Polish arts and crafts.

PNA formed a library and museum committee in 1891 and opened a library in Chicago at their headquarters with about 6,000 titles and a budget of $1,000. They built up this collection and encouraged local lodges to launch libraries and reading rooms. By 1930, some 114 PNA libraries and 36 reading rooms throughout the country with 45,000 volumes were available to the public. Chicago's PNA library transferred a large portion of its collection to Alliance College in Pennsylvania which, unfortunately, was destroyed in a fire in 1931. Nevertheless, the collection in Chicago grew to more than 25,000 titles by 1956, photo above. Josephine Rzewska was the PNA librarian for many years. After the PNA moved to its new headquarters in 1976, the library and other Polish American historical artifacts were donated to the PMA.

The auditorium of the PRCUA, before 1937, was the site of many dances for PRCUA members and guests. In 1937, the hall was converted, and serves until the present day as the main exhibit area for the PMA.

When the PRCUA opened its national headquarters in 1913, at Augusta Boulevard and Milwaukee Avenue in Chicago, it had a circulating library of 4,000 volumes. That library grew to 18,000 titles by 1935 and new facilities, above, were designed to accommodate the collection and its many patrons. In 1937, the Archives and Museum of the PRCUA was formally dedicated. Mieczyslaw Haiman was appointed curator for all the artifacts including the library collection.

The Historic Museum of Krakow lent the PMA a collection of its szopki for an exhibit. These Christmas nativity scenes are intricate and elaborate presentations, each of which utilizes as many architectural features as possible of St. Mary's Cathedral in Krakow. Szopki are extremely popular in Poland and the exhibit of the szopkas at the museum here resulted in record attendance.

A meeting in the Great Hall in today's PMA which features Stanislaw Batowski's painting of Pulaski at Savannah in the background.

The PMA sponsored a float in the Polish Constitution Day Parade to commemorate the 25th anniversary of the Papacy of John Paul II in 2003.

Leaders of the Polish American community greet U.S. Senator Dick Durbin at the PMA. From left, Maria Ciesla, president, PMA; Virginia Sikora, president, PWA; Frank Spula, president, PNA; Paul Odrobina, vice president, PNA; Senator Durbin; Wallace Ozog, president, PRCUA; Anna Sokolowski, vice president, PRCUA; Kasimierz Musielak, treasurer, PNA; and Joyce Szarowicz, secretary-treasurer, PRCUA,

PRCUA Vice President Stella Nowak, standing eighth from right, organized the Ladies Auxiliary of the PMA in 1971. The first officers are shown seated, from left, Barbara Pawlowska, secretary: Jane Peckwas, vice-president; Clara Winiecki, president; and Dolores Molek, treasurer.

The paintiing, Pulaski at Savannah, by Stanislaw Batowski of Lwow, Poland, was first exhibited in Chicago in 1933 at the Century of Progress World's Fair. It was then on display at the Chicago Art Institute before it was purchased by the PWA, which presented it to the PMA in 1939. The painting is the focus of attention when the Polish American community celebrates Pulaski Day, an official state holiday in Illinois since September 9, 1973, the first Monday in March. On this date prominent state and local officials, religious dignitaries, and invited guests gather for a program at the PMA. The Council of Educators in Polonia also awards scholarships to Pulaski Day Essay Contest winners.

At right: Governor of Illinois Daniel Walker, while at the PMA, signs the bill designated Pulaski Day in Illinois. Present at the signing, from left, are Rev. Donald C. Bilinski, OFM, curator, PMA; Joseph L. Osajda, PRCUA president; Aloysius A. Mazewski, PNA president; State Senator Nobert Kosinski; Joseph W. Zurawski, PMA president; Rev. Edwin Karlowicz, CR, PRCUA chaplain; and State Representative Leroy Lemke.

121

Poles clung tenaciously to the Polish language during the period of and after the partitions of Poland (1772-1918). They resisted efforts of Germany, Austria and Russia to impose foreign languages on the Polish population. Although it was Jan Kochanowski who crystallized Polish literary language in the 16th century, Adam Mickiewicz is credited with preserving the unity of literary Polish during the 19th century. However, the novelist Henryk Sienkiewicz, writing in the late nineteenth century and early 20th century, probably did more than anyone to preserve the Polish language for Poles in all social and economic classes with his immensely popular novels that were avidly read in Poland and in the United States.

Many Poles arriving in the United States during the industrialization of America (1880-1920) did not receive extensive formal schooling. Nevertheless, they cherished their Polish language and continued to read Polish newspapers, magazines, and novels.

Numerous Polish language publications appeared in Chicago after the influx of Polish immigrants. By the 1920s and 1930s three Polish language daily newspapers were published with combined circulation reaching 100,000.

Since the end of World War II, Poles settling in Chicago have been better educated than Poles who arrived before World War I. These newer arrivals also prefer to speak and read Polish. Three Polish language daily newspapers are still published in Chicago today. Numerous other publications are also available at bookstores in the Chicago area that serve the Polish American community.

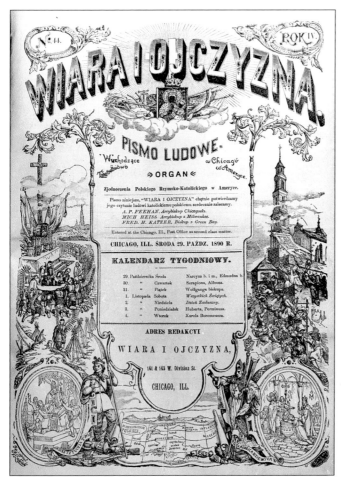

Wiara I Ojczyzna *(Faith and Fatherland)*, *the official organ of the PRCUA, was launched in 1887. It also was a "Peoples' Newspaper"* (Pismo Ludowe) *and within its masthead had a portrait of Our Lady of Czestochowa, the highly revered Patroness of Poland. Other Polish images were also on the page as well as a calendar listing of saints' feast days for the week.* Wiara I Ojcyzna *was replaced in 1888 by* Narod Polski *(Polish Nation) which remains the official organ of PRCUA until the present day.*

Chicago's first Polish language newspaper, Gazeta Polska Chicago, *1873 to 1913, was published by Wladyslaw Dyniewicz. Within the masthead the phrase* Boze Zbaw Polske *implores the "Almighty to save Poland." The phrase,* Pismo Ludowe Dla Polonii w Ameryce, *can be translated as "Peoples' Newspaper for Poles in America." Dyniewicz frequently serialized numerous Polish literary classics in the newspapers. Since these were eagerly awaited and read, he also printed them as books. His editorials were fervently patriotic and generally supported the PNA.*

The editorial offices of Zgoda (Harmony) are shown in Chicago in the early 1900s. Zgoda, originally published in Milwaukee in 1881, was the first PNA newspaper. It was moved to New York and then to Chicago in 1888 where it continues to be published to the present day.

Setting type in the Dziennik Zwiazkowy (Daily Alliance) press room around 1920 was labor intensive and physically demanding work. The linotype machine shown above cast each line as a separate unit in lead. A 500-word story could easily weigh several pounds.

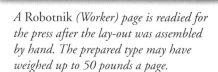

A Robotnik (Worker) page is readied for the press after the lay-out was assembled by hand. The prepared type may have weighed up to 50 pounds a page.

A flat bed press at Alliance Printers and Publishers in 1946 shows printers preparing what appears to be an ad. These were usually set up before the news is typed for inclusion in the Dziennik Zwiazkowy (Daily Alliance).

Wladyslaw Dyniewicz, publisher of Chicago's first Polish language newspaper, also wrote Polish language literary texts, grammar guides, and compiled a Polish-English dictionary for use in elementary schools. Dyniewicz was born in Poland and came to Chicago in 1867. This photo is believed to have been taken, January 17, 1913, on the occasion of his fiftieth wedding anniversary. Dyniewicz died in 1928.

The Polish Socialist Alliance published a socialist weekly newspaper Robotnik *(Worker) in Chicago around 1900. The paper was launched in New York in 1896, transferred to Chicago for a few years, and then moved to Detroit without ever achieving a wide readership. Editorially, it took socialist positions.*

Dziennik Chicagoski (Polish Daily News) was published by the Congregation of the Resurrection from 1890 to 1971. It was launched to combat anti-clerical sentiment which was forcefully presented in several newspapers at the time. However, its editorial scope also rallied readers to demand independence for Poland and it supported progress and advancement of Chicago's Polish American community. The Dziennik Chicagowski which is published today has no historic ties to Dziennik Chicagoski.

Alliance Printers and Publishers dedicated the building at 1201 North Milwaukee Avenue, October 31, 1942, where they published the Zgoda, Dziennik Zwiazkowy, and other official publications of the PNA. In 1976, when the PNA moved its national headquarters to offices at 6100 North Cicero Avenue, this facility was no longer used by the PNA.

Delivery trucks load Dziennik Zwiazkowy *on North Greenview Avenue and Division Street in the 1940s. The print shop of the newspaper is to the left and the national headquarters of the PNA appears at right. Daily editions of the newspaper had 12 to 16 pages. Several special weekend sections doubled the newspaper with holiday editions often totalling 50 or more pages.*

Dziennik Zjednoczenia *(Union Daily News) was published from 1921 to 1939 to supplement the weekly official organ of the PRCUA,* Narod Polski *(Polish Nation). The sign on the PRCUA headquarters at 984 North Milwaukee Avenue emphasizes in English the word, "Polish," even though it is not part of the official newspaper title.*

A growing number and large variety of Polish language publications are available today. These include many that are printed and published in the Chicago area as well as in Poland.

PNA president, John Tomaszko, seated in center, meets with PNA's Harcestwo (Scout) leaders in 1933 at the PNA offices in Chicago.

PRCUA established Camp Gieryk just south of Chicago in 1939. Originally occupying 27 acres, it was expanded to 100 acres to accommodate numerous youth and Scout activities which took place for about ten years. Shown below are Girl Scout "Cory" (Daughters) departing for Camp Gieryk.

PNA president, Aloysius A. Mazewski, fifth from left standing, enjoys a day at Yorkville, the PNA youth camp which has been operational since the 1930s.

PRCUA Boy Scouts organized an impromptu band at Camp Gieryk.

PRCUA Girl Scouts were known as "Cory" (Daughters). They were taught Polish arts and craft skills in group sessions.

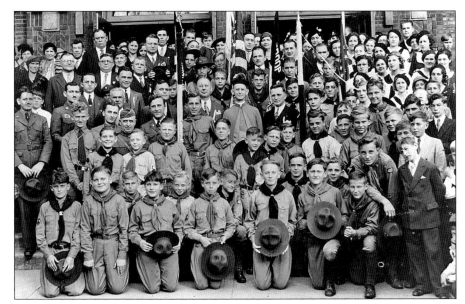

PRCUA Boy and Girls Scouts would frequently dress in uniform and attend Masses on Polish Holidays at churches throughout Chicago.

Swimming and playful hazing were routine at PRCUA's Camp Gieryk.

Trying to keep the old ways was difficult in this new country.

Alleys were often the first playgrounds of Polish American youngsters of immigrant parents. This alley, as it appeared in November 1918, was on Chicago's south side between Brandon and Burley avenues, looking north from 85th Street.

The notation that accompanied this photo: "Our main wall in our residence in our home at 94 Cleaver Street 18 May 1901," shows religious photos above the PNA emblem which is surrounded by photos of family members. A typical scene in many Polish homes.

The Olejnik family on a Sunday outing with their Model-T Ford. The Model-T was affordable to many families living near the Chicago's South Works steel plants.

A typical scene in many early
Polish immigrant neighborhoods.
A horse and buggy bring fruit and
vegetables to waiting customers.

At the washtub May 18, 1901. An old method that was soon to be replaced
by modern conveniences.

Prepared and ready
to attend the May 3
Polish Constitution
Day Parade in 1907.

A Polish American family on
Cleaver Street, April 1903.

A Polish American family outing May 7, 1903. The Poles were always attacted to the open spaces of Chicago parks and beaches.

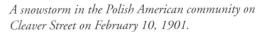

Chicago's famed "L" tracks over Madison Street in November 1902.

A snowstorm in the Polish American community on Cleaver Street on February 10, 1901.

Joseph Olejnik was proud of the Chicago-style bungalow he owned at 8505 Baltimore Avenue. Unfortunately, like many others, he lost his residence during the Depression of the 1930s.

Perhaps the most joyous and anticipated event in the lives of Polish Americans is a wedding. In Poland, weddings often were celebrated for three days or more with numerous customs and centuries-old traditions bringing together family, friends–the entire village–in prayer, in feasting, in song and dance to usher the bride and groom into their new life together.

As Poles adapted to their new land, usually in urban centers such as Chicago, practical considerations made it difficult to duplicate the elaborate weddings they experienced in Poland.

Nevertheless, Polish Americans spent considerable effort in preparing for a *wesele* (the wedding experience) and *slub* (official church ceremony) to make the day a most memorable one. Before leaving for church on the day of the wedding, parents extend a blessing (*blogoslawienstwo*) to the bride and groom at home. A *goral* tradition, still practiced in some urban areas, has a *kapela*, group of singers with instruments, serenade the bride at her home and take her to church. They wait outside to

The wedding card was a family treasure for all generations.

Polish Americans celebrate a wedding in 1919.

continue serenading the newly married couple after they exit the church.

A generation ago, the *slub* included a High Mass celebrated in church. Today, often only the marriage ceremony is observed in church. After the exchange of vows at the main altar, the bride prays, and places a bouquet of flowers, before the altar or statue of the Blessed Virgin.

After the *slub*, the couple, in years past, would have a long session at a photographer's studio, and then return to the home of the bride's mother. The newlyweds are greeted by the mother of the bride with bread, salt, honey, or wine as a reminder that they will need sustenance in their new life.

The wedding reception, often at ballrooms such as Oaza, Wonderland, or Pulaski Hall 50 or more years ago and today at the White Eagle, Jolly Inn, or a major hotel, is marked by seemingly endless feasting, drinking, and dancing. As the bride and groom enter the hall, a well-known Polish American band is in full swing. A few minutes later, after greeting all guests, the bride and groom often will lead the invited to their tables for the meal which features Polish foods in abundance. After a greeting and prayer, said by the same priest who officiated at the church ceremony, a toast is offered, and the traditional *Sto Lat* ("May they live a hundred years") is sung by all to the newlyweds. During the meal, guests may start clinking their glasses with silverware or calling out *Gorzko, Gorzko* (Bitter, Bitter). They stop only when the bride and groom kiss.

Non-stop and very lively dancing ensues after dinner until, before midnight, the bride is encircled by guests on the dance floor, her veil is removed (*oczepiny*)–sometimes by the mother, other times by the eldest sister, or perhaps the maid of honor–and she receives a *chusta*, a small cap, or an apron (as photo below) signifying she is now a married woman.

After the party ends, the bride and groom invite family members the following day for *poprawiny* (making better) where the merrymaking continues.

Oczepiny, *after the bridal veil is removed, the bride receives an apron.*

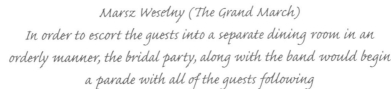

Marsz Weselny (The Grand March)
In order to escort the guests into a separate dining room in an orderly manner, the bridal party, along with the band would begin a parade with all of the guests following

*Extending a blessing (*blogoslawienstwo*).*

A Highlander wedding was organized in Chicago, September 22, 1920, through the efforts of the PNA Freedom Eagle Society.

Oczepiny (Removal of the Veil)

Bride and Groom would sit opposite each other. The mother or maid of honor would remove the veil and often the groom would place his boutonniere in the bride's hair. Then an apron (with toy babies) was placed on the bride. This was meant to signify leaving maidenhood and taking on the responsibilities of wife, homemaker, and mother (This was considered a beautiful transition to family life). The bridal party and all the guests would then join hands in a circle.

The wedding of Josephine Nowak and Edmund Czonowski, photo above, was treated to a Kocia Muzyka (Cat's Music), a Polish adaptation of charivari. The newlywed couple from Immaculate Conception Church, in background above right, on Chicago's south side was paraded down the street accompanied by the wedding party with others blowing horns and beating drums. Often the bride was presented with a baby carriage. Other weddings in the Polish American community were more formal affairs with some celebrations lasting two days. At left is a wedding at St. Stanislas Bishop and Martyr Church in 1963.

The wedding, right, of first-generation Polish Americans, Alyce Nicpon and Ted Przybylo, on August 25, 1943. Ted started the popular White Eagle Restaurant.

The tradition of wedding gowns with long, flowing trains has given way to more contemporary styles. This is the wedding of Alex and Florence Kolpak in 1947.

133

While the Wojciechow-ski Funeral Home was located at 2129 West Webster Street, funerals often originated at the home of the deceased, followed by a parade down the street to St. Hedwig's Church for the Requiem Mass.

The entrance gate to St. Adalbert's Cemetery around 1900 in Niles. Some 21 acres were purchased in 1872 for the cemetery. The Congregation of the Resurrection provided the cemetery's early administrators. They were also organizers of parishes for Polish American communities and officiated at many funerals in the cemetery. To date, there have been about 300,000 burials at the cemetery with a majority, if not most, from families in the Polish American community.

As St. Adalbert Cemetery was located in Niles, a funeral trip in the early days was virtually an all day affair. To serve the Polish population, two other Polish cemeteries were established on the southeast and southwest sides: Holy Cross in Calumet City (1893), and Resurrection in Justice (1904). In addition, some older parishes had individual graveyards. Resurrection Cemetery is also noted for the legend of "Resurrection Mary," a ghostly character in Chicago lore who is supposed to haunt its premises.

Sixteen-year-old Mary Prochot's funeral at the Prochot's home at 47th and South Loomis.

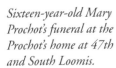

The funeral of Casimir Zychlinski, PNA president from 1912 until his death on August 28, 1927, attracted thousands of mourners. Zychlinski was also one of the founders of the Polish Falcons of America and was known as the Father of the Falcons.

Grave sites, such as this one at St. Adalbert's Cemetery, were often decorated every week by family members with exquisite floral arrangements, wreaths, flags, and banners. Cemetery officials no longer allow such extensive decorations at grave sites which, today, are all grass covered.

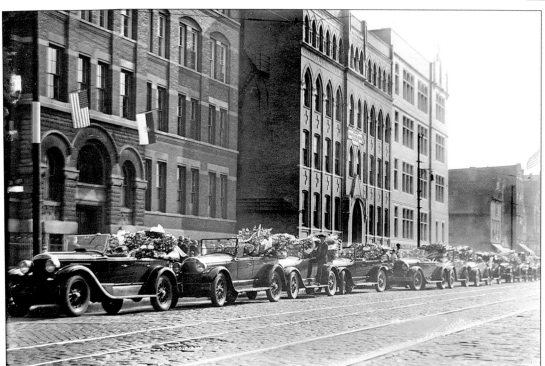

A long funeral procession drove down Division Street past the headquarters of the Polish National Alliance where Zychlinski was president.

Polish Steel

By 1898, the steel industry, known as South Works on Chicago's South Side, had expanded from 74.5 acres to 260 with one of the most modern mills in the industry. Some 3,500 men were producing 960,000 tons of steel annually. Poles were the largest immigrant group working in the South Chicago mills. In 1910, Polish Americans accounted for 24.2 per cent of all steel workers in the Midwest.

Most Polish Americans working at the mills were unskilled. Often they had to bribe a foreman who would hire on a daily basis from groups who gathered at the main gate in the mornings and afternoons.

Steel workers suffered low wages and long hours. Blast furnace workers had to work 84-hour weekly shifts (6:00 a.m. to 6:00 p.m.) often staying on the job 24 hours when shifts changed. The general hourly rate was 21 cents per hour in 1900, it dropped to 20.2 cents in 1905, and went up to 23.7 cents in 1910.

As the steel industry continued to consolidate into giant firms such as U.S. Steel, unions began to organize. A major strike in 1919 against U.S. Steel was not successful. However, unions continued to attract workers and were able to wrangle benefits from management for their members.

South Works would become a ghost town. In the early 1970s some 12,000 were employed at the plants. By 1985, the work force fell to 900. U.S. Steel South Works closed its plant and its 575-acre-site in April 1992.

The main gate at the Illinois Steel Company in August 1902.

Many Polish immigrants lived in an area known as the "bush," located near Lake Michigan and the South Works steel plants. Small scruffy plants grew in the sandy soil making it possible for some residents to raise livestock from the time of their arrival in Chicago to the 1960s.

An employment office at the Illinois Steel Company is shown accepting applicants. Mill employees and plant security are identified at left. The sign in the center is printed in multiple languages informing applicants that the plant hires workers who are concerned with safety.

St. Michael's Church, which served the many Polish immigrants who began arriving in the area in 1892, is visible in the center of this circa-1970s image. The U.S. Steel South Works is in the background. Russell Square Park appears in the foreground.

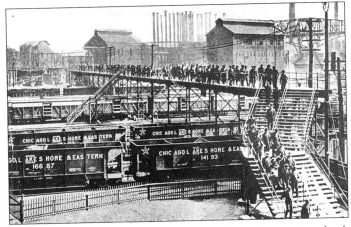

A lunch hour at the South Works in 1910 had a major impact on local traffic and business.

Blast furnaces at South Works in 1885. Lake boats on the Calumet River brought iron ore and coal to the mill.

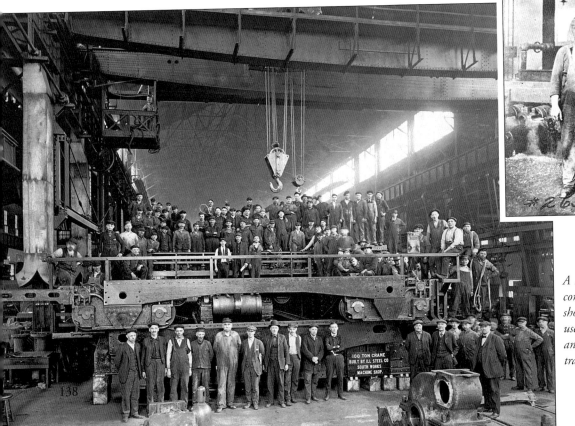

Safety was a constant concern in the mill. A mask was designed to protect mill workers.

A 100-ton crane was constructed by the machine shop at South Works. It was used to manufacture tools and parts which were then transported to the mill site.

138

The Dolatowski family opened a cigar and candy store in 1918 at 8409 Burley Avenue on Chicago's south side. Frank Dolatowski and his godfather, Frank Mularski, are shown above in the store.

Kurnik's Tavern, located at 13200 Houston Street in the Hegewisch neighborhood, was a "stand up" establishment serving the Polish American community. It was across the street from St. Florian Catholic Church which also served Polish Americans.

Bond rallies during World War I were common in many neighborhoods. Members of the Hegewisch Red Cross Auxiliary and other residents took part in the rally at 133rd and Baltimore during World War I.

Polish Americans and others were becoming more aware of the cohesiveness of the Polish American community even when it was not the most populous ethnic group in a specific area. The packing industry had been located on Chicago's south side since 1865. The surrounding area, known as the Back of the Yards, began to attract Poles in 1877 as other ethnic groups were leaving.

Poles were used as strikebreakers in 1884 when Irish and German workers walked out. Polish American fraternal groups and other Polish American societies helped to firmly establish Poles in the area, besides opening St. Joseph Parish in 1887.

The Amalgamated Meat Cutters began to organize the stockyard workers in earnest in 1900 using bilingual organizers and forming ethnic locals. Poles flocked to join because living and working conditions were horrific. Although the economy prospered with World War I, conditions became bleak after the war. However, immigrants owned more than 60 per cent of the homes in the area even though they comprised only 50 per cent of the population.

Dangerous and unhealthy conditions persisted. By 1921 the tuberculosis rate of Poles and other East Europeans in the Back of the Yards was the highest in Chicago. Packinghouse workers found some relief during the Woodrow Wilson administration which set up an arbitration board to resolve differences and settle disputes. The Amalgamated Meat Cutters were recognized as the official representative of packinghouse workers. A basic eight-hour day, wage increases, and overtime pay were secured in 1918. Further increases followed in 1920 and union membership mushroomed. In 1921, the major packers notified the government they would not abide by wartime agreements. Workers agreed to reduce wages but balked when management asked for continued reductions.

A strike was voted for November 15, 1921. On November 18, further cuts were proposed by Swift, one of the largest meatpackers, and supported by the other packers. A strike was called for December 5, 1921. Fierce rioting erupted as workers were driven back by Chicago police. About 150 were injured. Some 8,000 strikebreakers were called in

Chicago had several small stockyards scattered throughout the city before 1850. After the Civil War, the stockyards were consolidated on Chicago's south side. By 1900, when the yards occupied 475 acres, many of the 25,000 employed at the yards were from Polish American communities. By 1921, some 40,000 were employed. When the yards closed on July 30, 1971, the boundaries were Pershing, Ashland, 47th Street, and Halsted.

but the union remained optimistic. On January 9, 1922, Armour management announced, "There is no matter of dispute between the management and workers." The strike was over.

Former workers found their jobs were no longer available to them. Non-strikers and strikebreakers had taken and would keep their former jobs.

Dominic A. Pacyga, who has studied Polish American neighborhoods, writes:

"The Poles… in the Back of the Yards had, by 1921, passed the first crucial test of settling into a community… adapting to a population…. From predominantly rural areas in Eastern Europe to the unfamiliar industrial environment of America this had been successfully accomplished…. Many of the stockyard Poles came from the High Tatra mountains…. (They) shared a long cultural tradition that embraced the notion of the extended family and fostered a deep feeling of community…. Much

of the leadership of community came from the Polish Catholic Church… and pastors who… organized the Guardian Angel Nursery and Home for Working Women in the Back of the Yards in the early 1900s… this helped to preserve the Polishness of the people. Proliferation of ethnic institutions continued…. Neighborhood libraries carried books in the Polish language…. Polish banks, commercial clubs and even theatres had been permanently established by World War I…. What may have been described as a conglomeration of Poles… had by 1921 become a stable community with a network of interlacing institutions and a high degree of self-awareness."

"Whiskey Row" was an area near the stockyards at 42nd and Ashland Avenue. Dominic Pacyga, an historian who did considerable research on this area, was quoted on a television documentary featuring Whiskey Row. "When the bell rang at 12:00, men would run out to Whiskey Row, which was the major street just to the west of the stockyards… they would get a beer, and a shot, and then they could have a free lunch. So there'd be huge steam tables in these taverns in which they'd come in…. there you had your pickled hogs feet and your eggs and your Polish sausage and your ham or whatever." Strictly ethnic taverns existed on nearby side streets. When asked about the fate of a drunken German who wandered into a Polish tavern as a newspaper article reported, Pacyga responded, "The newspaper article stated that something magical happened. A bottle had come to life. It hit the German on the head and dragged him out and left him in the sewer…. then jumped back up on the bar…. there were various witnesses who said this is exactly what happened…. the bottom line of the article was, 'Drink in your own bars.'"

A one-stop family shoe shopping destination for the Polish American community in the Back of the Yards neighborhood: Florsheim shoes were adult shoes for special occasions; Red Cross Shoes featured women's fashions; youngsters were fitted at Tiny Tot Shoes.

Lottie Kwiatkowsk, on right, sits on the roof of the Libby plant near Chicago's stockyards. Libby was a meat packer in the 1940s when the photo was taken. As the stockyards curtailed activities, Libby began processing canned fruits and vegetables.

In the 1970s, Sacred Heart Church hosted a Polish Highlander Alliance (Zwiazek Podhlan w Polnocnej Ameryce) Convention. The observance on parish grounds reads Witamy Gosci *(Welcome Guests). Many consider Sacred Heart the mother church for the* gonali *(highlanders) in Chicago.*

The first building of St. Joseph School parish in the Back of the Yards neighborhood was built in 1888 and served as a church and school until a new church was built in 1914. School enrollment in the original building reached over 1,000 students during the 1920s and 1930s. For 112 years the school was administered under the auspices of the Felician Sisters from 1888 to 2000 when they had to withdraw from the school due to a lack of sisters to continue the work.

Polish Americans in their traditional Highlander garb at Sacred Heart Church. The icon is the patron of Poland, Our Lady of Czestochowa, sometimes referred to as the Black Madonna. Tradition holds that St. Luke was the original artist of the painting. Brought to Poland in 1382, the holy picture suffered an attack in 1430 which resulted in deep slashes on the face of the Virgin Mary. Between 1632 and 1648, a basilica was built in Czestochowa where the icon remains on display until the present day. In 1655, the shrine withstood an attack by the Swedes. The following year, King John Casimir made a solemn vow proclaiming the Mother of God to be the "Queen of the Polish Crown" and the shrine at Jasna Gora (Bright Mountain) to be the Mount of Victory, a spiritual capital of Poland.

A PNA society, the Hussars, around 1915, pose in uniform in the Back of the Yards area at 4859 South Ada Street. A dance hall is on the left. The Podborny tavern was later operated, in the 1920s, by Joseph Kwiatkowski.

Polish American parish groups united for numerous causes in the Back of the Yards neighborhood.

Watra Church Goods was founded in the depths of the Depression by John and Irene Skupien. Its humble beginnings in 1935 were that of a local card and gift shop. The business has since grown to a full-service religious goods and articles store. The original store (above) was located at 22nd and California. In 1986, it was moved by then owners Jim and Janine Kucera to 4201 South Archer Avenue. This facility has over 30,000 square feet of showroom space, making it the largest religious goods stores in the nation. Watra has further expanded to open a location in Florida.

Watra is currently owned by the Peter and Karin (granddaughter of John and Irene) McCauley.

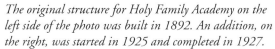

In 1912, Holy Trinity High School, above, began operations in the former Kosciuszko School on Division Street near Cleaver Avenue. After the new school building opened in 1927, at left, this building was used as a residence for the brothers teaching at the school.

St. Stanislaus Kostka High School began teaching girls in 1914 to prepare them to work in the business world. Courses continued to be expanded until the late 1930s when students could graduate after completing a four-year curriculum. The building was operational until 1959. Below is a class at St. Stanisalus Kostka in 1898.

The original structure for Holy Family Academy on the left side of the photo was built in 1892. An addition, on the right, was started in 1925 and completed in 1927.

St. Stanislaus College students in session around 1910 (at left above). In 1909, completion of a a six-year course would lead to a bachelor's degree. The curriculum was based on a European model and classes were taught in English, Polish, German, and Latin. After 1915, the curriculum was adjusted to courses taught in traditional American high schools. Above is the assembly hall at St. Stanislaus College as shown in the school's 1900 yearbook.

St. Stanislaus College moved, in 1899, to the building below, originally built as an orphanage in 1890. The school was renamed Weber High School and remained at this Division Street location until 1950 when it moved to 5252 West Palmer Avenue.

After Weber moved, Gordon Technical High School, photo right, conducted classes here and at a nearby location on Haddon Avenue until a new school was opened at Addison Street and California Avenue in 1961.

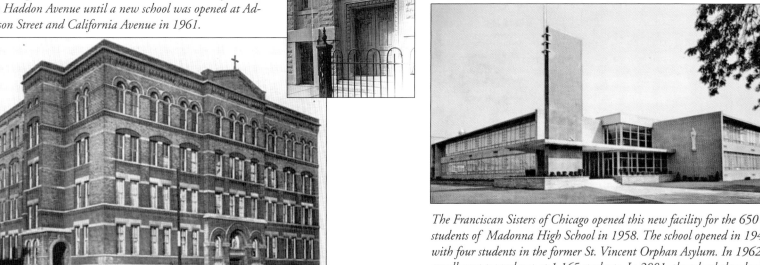

The Franciscan Sisters of Chicago opened this new facility for the 650 students of Madonna High School in 1958. The school opened in 1949 with four students in the former St. Vincent Orphan Asylum. In 1962 enrollment topped out at 1,165 students. In 2001, the school closed when there were only 240 students attending.

A class at Gordon Technical High School in the 1950s shows students learning office skills.

A new Weber High School opened in September 1950 at 5252 West Palmer Avenue. Rapidly increasing enrollment required an addition that was built in 1962. Enrollment peaked in 1969 with close to 1,400 in attendance and a graduating class of 325. Although the school closed in 1999, a very active Weber Alumni Association continues to meet monthly.

President Ronald Reagan visited Gordon Technical High School, October 10, 1985. He was greeted by Carl Zielinski, student body president; Rev. Henry Blaski, CR, principal; and Bill Jepsen. The president was presented with a school jacket and cap.

Gordon Technical High School was a branch of Weber High School while the school was located on Division Street. After Weber opened new facilities in 1950, Gordon Technical built separate facilities at Addison and California. Weber closed in 1999. Gordon Tech continues in operation with an enrollment of 625 students.

A sewing class in the 1950s at Resurrection High School. Sewing is no longer taught at the school and this same room serves as the computer technology room.

It may have been "only" practice for a theatrical presentation at the new Weber High School. However, Edwin Hebda appears to let it be known that young ladies are more than welcome at the all-boys school. Ken Nawrocki, in background, seems ready to tell Hebda to follow the script.

A class at Kelly High School designs Polish paper-craft items. It was estimated that more than 90 per cent of all students at the school were Polish Americans in the late 1940s.

The Polish Arts Club conducted literary contests with students submitting essays, short stories, and poetry in both the English and Polish languages.

Karol Cardinal Wojtyla and Bishop Alfred Abramowicz, seated center, meet with teachers of the Maria Konopnicka Polish Saturday School at Five Holy Martyrs Church. The school was organized in 1974 with 78 students. In 1975, the enrollment was 150 which increased to 220 in 1976 when this photo was taken.

A Walter Krawiec cartoon illustration from the 1950s encourages parents to have their children learn the Polish language.

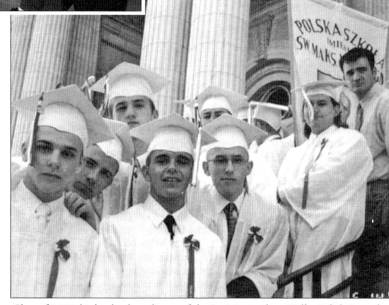

Class of 2000 high school graduates of the St. Maximilian Kolbe Polish Saturday School from St. Constance Church where some 600 students were in attendance at the time. Polish Saturday schools began in Chicago in 1952 with two schools and an enrollment of 39 students. In 2007, there were 35 schools in the Chicagoland area teaching Polish to 17,000 students in grades 1 through 11. Graduation ceremonies for several schools were held at St. Mary of the Angels (above).

Sisters of the Holy Family of Nazareth Arrive in Chicago

"Mother Foundress [Frances Siedliska, of the Sisters of the Holy Family of Nazareth] and her little company departed from Rome on the 17th day of June and arrived in New York on July 4th. Two days later Reverend V. Barzynski, superior of Polish Missions and Reverend J. Radziejewski, met the Sisters in Chicago and conducted them to their quarters on Belden Ave., in the vicinity of St. Josephat's Church and School. 'First of all,'–writes the Venerable Foundress–'we visited the church located on the second floor of the building; it was merely a large room in which three wooden altars were erected; there were few pews; indescribable poverty was found. The Tabernacle was of plain wood, a small vigil lamp indicated the Holy Presence.'

The parishioners came to seek acquaintance with the Sisters and supplied them with various articles and food. The women seeing the Sisters, cried with joy, and greeted them as 'the good Sisters from our native land.' The Sisters' home was poorly furnished–they had neither beds nor tables. They found here ten orphans–the oldest boy, 10 years of age, was quite ill, the youngest girl of about a year and a half. Mother Siedliska energetically began the work at once. The following days were spent in organizing their home, meeting the children, and parishioners. Mother Siedliska would present each with a medal, religious card or rosary.

God wished to test the love and courage of Mother Foundress and her Sisters, for scarcely a month passed when the little community lost one of its members.

After making a retreat during which Mother Frances prepared her Sisters for school work, classes were opened on September 9, 1885, on which day two hundred children were registered."

Archbishop Vincent Sardi as quoted in Golden Jubilee (commemorating the)
Work of the Sisters of the Holy Family of Nazareth in America, [1935]

The Congregation of the Sisters of the Holy Family of Nazareth were invited to teach at St. Josephat School. Shown above are the first students of the school which opened in 1885.

St. John Cantius School opened in 1903 and remained in session until 1967.

St. Hedwig's School had 800 students in 1901. Classes were always overcrowded and by 1914 enrollment at the school reached 1,882. Another story was added and, in 1921, a three-story annex was built for St. Hedwig's. Within four years, enrollment was 2,651 children being taught by 39 Sisters of the Holy Family of Nazareth. After the Kennedy Expressway was constructed within the boundaries of the parish, school enrollment dropped dramatically to 362 by 1978.

149

Sports

Since its earliest days, sports have been embraced by Chicago's Polish American community. Indeed, it was Oscar Bielaski, son of a Polish immigrant who died in the Civil War as a captain in the Union Army, who joined the Chicago White Stockings and helped them win their first-ever National League pennant in 1876.

White Eagles Turners Hall was opened in Chicago's first Polish American parish, St. Stanislaus Kostka. Their White Eagles Football team went undefeated in 1900, 1901, 1902, and 1903.

Bowling also became popular with Polish Americans when Barney Filipowski rolled a 300 game in 1908. Universal Bowling Alleys and Billiard Hall, opened in the heart of the Polish American community at North and Milwaukee avenues in 1910, quickly becoming the largest and most modern facility of its kind in America.

In 1912, the Polish Alma Mater Bowling League was launched to prepare youth for membership in the PRCUA. Likewise, the Polish Falcons organized with support from the PNA. The Falcons strove for its members to be physically fit as well as good gymnasts.

By the 1930s, the PRCUA and PNA appointed their own sports and youth directors to coordinate and promote thousands of youth and adult sporting activities. There were hundreds, perhaps thousands, of bowling teams as well as basketball, baseball, softball, volleyball, golf, duckpins, and other sports events in which PRCUA and PNA members participated.

Recent arrivals from Poland have continued the tradition by organizing soccer leagues along with auto, yacht, tennis, golf, and ski clubs.

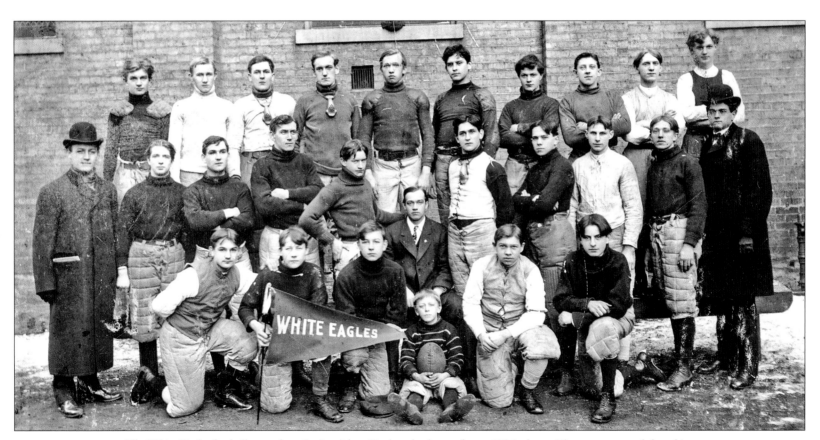

The White Eagles football team from St. Stanislaus Kostka school poses for an 1899 photo. The team was undefeated in 1900, 1901, 1902, and 1903. The White eagles often confused opponents by calling its signals in Polish.

National Polish-American Sports Hall of Fame Members from Chicago:

Oscar Bielaski - 1876 Chicago White Stockings

Ziggy Czabowski - 1948 Chicago Rockets, 1949 Chicago Hornets

Mike Ditka - 1982-92 Head Coach, Chicago Bears

Moe Drabowsky - 1956-60 Chicago Cubs

Jim Grabowski - 1971 Chicago Bears

Ted Kluszewski - 1959-60 Chicago White Sox

Mike Krzyzewski - Head Basketball Coach, Duke University (1981-2007)

Eddie Lopat - 1944-48 Chicago White Sox

Johnny Lujack - 1948-51 Chicago Bears

Greg Luzinski - 1981-84 Chicago White Sox

Ted Marchibroda - 1957 Chicago Cardinals

Joe Niekro - 1967-69 Chicago Cubs

Ed Olczyk - 1984-87 Chicago Black Hawks

Bill Osmanski - 1939-43, 46-47 Chicago Bears

Tom Paciorek - 1982-85 Chicago White Sox

Ron Reed - 1984 Chicago White Sox

Al Simmons - 1933-35 Chicago White Sox

Bill Skowron - 1964-67 Chicago White Sox

Bob Toski - 1954 World Championship of Golf winner at Tam O'Shanter

Frank Tripucka - 1950-1953 Chicago Cardinals

Tony Zale - 1947 Defeated Rocky Marciano at Chicago Stadium for Middleweight Championship

Richie Zisk - 1977 Chicago White Sox

The 1906 White Eagles softball team that played for St. Stanislaus Kostka parish.

The St. Stanislaus Kostka's White Eagles basketball team, organized by the Polish Falcons of America, is pictured in a 1907 photo.

151

Scoutmasters from Poland were hosted to a White Sox baseball game at Comiskey Park, July 21, 1936. Toney Piet greets Leszek Gorski (left) and Larry Rosenthal welcomes Joseph Kret.

PRCUA sponsored a variety of sports tournaments such as this 1948 basketball tourney.

PRCUA Circuit 54 Ladies Bowling League, representing several Chicago-area societies, sponsored a team in the Herald-American tournament, April 1, 1940. Members were, from left, Harriet Olewinski, Jean Pryka, Marie Bulkowski, Victoria Stanislawski, and Florence Szadkowski.

Girls were active in the PRCUA sports programs and entered several teams in the 1940 tournament.

An enthusiastic crowd didn't give the players any bench space during a timeout at this PRCUA tournament in 1941.

Henry C. Kamienski, a PRCUA member, swam on the University of Michigan varsity swim team. After graduation he served as sports director at Chopin Park in Chicago.

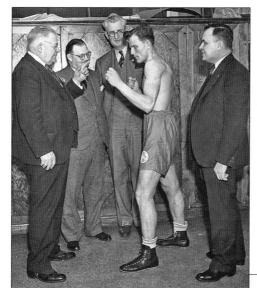

PRCUA director Stanley Adamkiewicz, left, gives Joe Matula, Golden Gloves novice champ some pointers while Dr. M. Badzmierowski, PRCUA chief medical examiner, PRCUA treasurer, Jan Olejniczak, and Joseph Barc, PRCUA editor, look on.

Josephine and Edward Wilkowski display trophies and medals they won at the 1940 PRCUA Annual Track and Field Meet in Chicago's Kosciuszko Park. Each won four first place medals or trophies.

Chicago-style 16-inch softball was a favorite pastime in the Polish American community. Action shown was from a game in 1941.

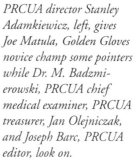

Young ladies relax after a game of tennis around 1920.

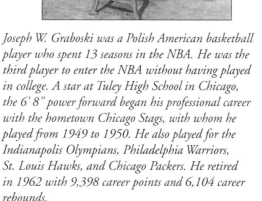

Joseph W. Graboski was a Polish American basketball player who spent 13 seasons in the NBA. He was the third player to enter the NBA without having played in college. A star at Tuley High School in Chicago, the 6' 8" power forward began his professional career with the hometown Chicago Stags, with whom he played from 1949 to 1950. He also played for the Indianapolis Olympians, Philadelphia Warriors, St. Louis Hawks, and Chicago Packers. He retired in 1962 with 9,398 career points and 6,104 career rebounds.

Chicago Mayor, Edward T. Kelly (second from right), congratulates Stan "Cookie" Wojcik, co-captain of Weber High School football team, which played before 80,000 spectators at Soldier Field in the 1944 Prep Bowl.

A heated football rivalry developed between Weber High School and Gordon Tech High in the 1950s. At that time both schools were building new facilities and continuing to attract the majority of their students from among Polish Americans. The Red Horde's (Weber) clash with the Rams (Gordon) had great fan support especially when they played at Soldier Field. The games came to be called "The Polish Rose Bowl."

Everyone was a winner when high school football teams from the Polish American community clashed in Soldier Field for benefit games. Weber High School and Holy Trinity High School football captains decorate nurses Theresa Grembla, left, and Teresa Koziol from St. Mary of Nazareth Hospital before a benefit game for the hospital.

154

After graduating from Weber High School, Bill "Moose" Skowron went to Purdue University to play football. However, his .500 baseball batting average cut short his football career and gave way to a fast-blossoming baseball career from 1954 to 1967 with the New York Yankees, Chicago White Sox, and Los Angeles Dodgers. A six-time All-Star, Skowron had an impressive .519 slugging percentage in eight post-season world series. After his playing days, Skowron returned to Chicago and today is a community representative of the White Sox.

Chet Ostrowski, a Weber High School graduate, played football first at the University of Notre Dame, and then later, for the Washington Redskins, for which he appeared in 68 games between the years 1954 and 1959.

Ted Kluszewski played for the Chicago White Sox in the 1959 World Series. He batted in a record ten runs, hit three home runs, and was tied for series high batting average at .391. A popular player throughout the league, Big "Klu" also came to be known as the Mayor of Rush Streeet.

Joe Krupa holds one of the trophies he won as a member of Weber High School's Red Horde in the 1950s. After earning All-American honors at Purdue University and playing in the 1955 East-West Shrine Game, Krupa went on to play 110 games for the Pittsburgh Steelers, between 1956-1964, and was selected for the 1963 Pro Bowl.

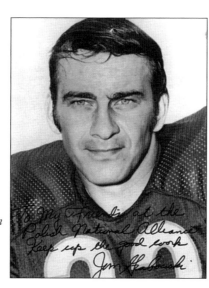

Jim Grabowski, graduate of Taft High School, went on to the University of Illinois, where he was the Big Ten's leading rusher with 2,878 yards from 1963 to 1965. Named the MVP for the 1964 Rose Bowl, Grabowski gained 125 yards to lead the Illini to a victory over the Washington Huskies. Drafted by the Green Bay Packers in 1966, Grabowski earned two Super Bowl rings before finishing his career with the Chicago Bears in 1971.

Jim Les attended Notre Dame High School in Niles. After being named the Missouri Valley Conference Player of the Year in 1986, while at Bradley University, he was drafted by the Atlanta Hawks that same year. In the 1990-91 season, he led the league with a .461 3-point field goal percentage. In all, he played in the NBA for seven seasons, with a total of four teams. He returned to Bradley to serve as head basketball coach in 2003. By 2006, he had his Bradley Braves in the NCAA Sweet Sixteen bracket. Jim Les has been inducted into the Francis Pomeroy Naismith Hall of Fame as the best basketball player under six feet tall.

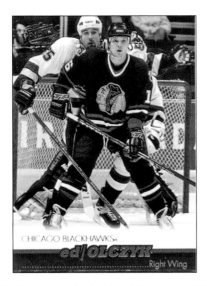

Eddie Olczyk was drafted by his hometown Chicago Blackhawks in the 1984 NHL Entry Draft, first round, third overall. After being traded a number of times, Olczyk finished his career with the Blackhawks. In 2003, he became head coach for the NHL Pittsburgh Penguins. He played 1,031 NHL games and produced 342 goals and 452 assists for a total of 794 points. Olczyk is currently the game analyst for the Chicago Blackhawks television broadcasts.

Mike Krzyzewski, better known as "Coach K," was born in Chicago in 1947. He attended St. Helen Elementary and Weber High School, where he was elected class president and twice was the high scorer in the Catholic High School Basketball League. After attending and later returning to coach at the U.S. Military Academy, he accepted a position as head basketball coach at Duke University in 1981. Coach K has won numerous basketball championships at Duke and was named national coach of the year in 1986, 1989, 1991, 1992, 1997, 1999, 2000, and 2001, and was inducted into the basketball Hall of Fame in 2001. He is also active in numerous community service organizations such as the Emily Krzyzewski Family Life Center named in honor of his mother. Photo right: A Chicago street was named "Honorary Coach K Way." The Weber High School Alumni Association organized the April 20, 2005 program and dedication ceremonies to honor Mike Krzyzewski. Coach K and Rev. Frank Rog, CR, chaplain of the Weber High School Alumni Association and one of Krzyzewski's teachers at Weber, stand beneath one of the Coack K street signs with the building of the former Weber High School in the background.

Polish American fraternals were represented at Cellular Field during Polish American Night. From left, Robert Gonny, Polish Falcons of America; Anna Sokolowski, PRCUA; A.J. Pierzynski, White Sox; Richard Piasecki, PNA; Bill "Moose" Skowrow; Sharon Zago, PWA; and Paul Odrobina, PNA.

The Polish American community was recognized by the Chicago White Sox on May 24, 2006, as some 1,500 were able to purchase tickets to watch the White Sox defeat the Oakand A's, 3-2.

The Music of Polish Chicago

Although Poles arriving in Chicago in massive waves of immigration from 1880 to 1920 had little formal education, probably all could sing more than a few songs.

As parishes were established, choirs formed in these congregations, and formal singing societies were organized. Anthony Malleck was the organist at Holy Trinity Parish from 1880 to 1916. He and his brother, Konstanty, started the Polish Singers Alliance more than 100 years ago. A Chicago chapter, Number 15, *Chor* (Chorus) *Filareci Duda* is still active today. Anthony Malleck edited the journal of the Polish Singers Alliance from 1886 to 1903. He also published choir music, including patriotic songs, in 17 song books.

Ignace Jan Paderewski frequently gave well-attended concerts in Chicago when he was helping to raise funds for the establishment of a free Poland after World War I. He would return after the start of World War II to again raise funds in assisting Poland which was then occupied by Germany and the Soviet Union.

Jerzy Bojanowski came to Chicago in 1933 as guest conductor for the Chicago World's Fair. He would remain in Chicago to promote friendship and cultural relations between Poland and the United States. He served as guest conductor of the Chicago Park District Orchestra from 1937 to 1944 and conducted Poland's famous opera *Halka* by Stanislaw Moniuszko for its Chicago premier.

Poland's folk ensembles formed after World War II, and *Maszowsze* and *Slask* were well-received when they first appeared in Chicago. The Warsaw Philharmonic has played several times in Chicago's Orchestra Hall; however, as the *Chicago Tribune* critic commented after its 1997 performance, "Polish music was notably absent." A more favorable impression was left by the eight Orchestra Hall performances of Marta Ptaszynska's work, *Inverted Mountain*, commissioned by the Chicago Symphony Orchestra in 2001. Also, Chicago's recently-formed Paderewski Symphony Orchestra has presented over 90 concerts highlighting the music of Polish composers Wieniawski, Karlowicz, Lutoslawski, Szynamowski, Gorecki, and Kilar. It has performed in Orchestra Hall and has received a Certificate of Excellence from the City of Chicago, Cook Country, and Poland's Cultural Ministry.

A choir composed of members of the PWA Group 108 celebrating its 10th anniversary in 1923.

Choirs were very popular among Polish Americans. Chor Wolnosc (*Choir of Freedom*) is featured in a 1920 photo.

The Ladies Choir at Holy Trinity Church celebrating its 10th anniversary in 1915. The choir was organized in 1905 when a cornerstone was laid for a new larger church which was dedicated October 6, 1906.

Marisha Data began her radio broadcasting career as a singer on the "Polish Barn Dance" program in 1935. She had her own daily program for 15 years until 1972. In 1974, she was inducted into the International Polka Hall of Fame. One observer assessed her programming with these words: "The quality of Polish used by Marisha Data in her programs left much to be desired, but it obviously served her listeners, who spoke a combination of country Polish and street Polish."

B.J. Zalewski published and sold music from this store around 1900. The Polish Orchestra and Band also met at this site.

Agnes Nering won well-deserved fame as a concert singer and brilliant teacher. She graduated from Holy Family Academy and, in 1909, from Chicago Musical College, earning the school's highest award. Nering then studied and sang in Europe and returned to Chicago to establish her School of Vocal Art and Dancing. It was reported that Nering "always (performed) to overflowing audiences." Nering died in 1922 at age 46.

Jan Kiepura, world-famous Polish tenor who sang a series of operatic roles with the Chicago Civic Opera during the 1930s, visits PNA headquarters in Chicago in 1940.

"JESZCZE NIE ZGINEŁA".

A Walter Krawiec cartoon takes as its theme the first line of Poland's national anthem, Jeszcze nie zginela, ([Poland] is not yet lost). It strongly suggests that Chicago's Polish American community keeps alive the spirit and songs (piesn) of Poland.

Witold Malcuzynski made several appearances in the Chicago area after World War II. In a performance in Orchestra Hall in 1947, he played an all-Chopin concert. The Chicago Tribune commented, "Malcuzynski is to our taste, one ideal interpreter of Chopin."

Kilbasa I Kapuscina (Mr. Sausage and Mrs Cabbage) was recorded in Chicago by W. M. Mossakowski.

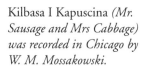

The W.J. Sajewski Music Store was founded in 1897 and had several locations serving Polish Americans for over 80 years.

Young Richard and John Stanislawski get ready to embark on their musical endeavors.

Anthony Kowalkowski had a popular orchestra which performed at numerous affairs in the Polish American community. Anthony's nephew and namesake, Anthony Kowalkowski, carries on the musical legacy and is very popular today.

Thaddeus Kozuch graduated from Chicago Musical College in 1936. He won a contest sponsored by the Adult Education Council in 1939 as the most outstanding pianist in the Chicago area. He performed a solo recital in Orchestra Hall in 1940 and went on to play with the Chicago Symphony Orchestra, Grant Park Orchestra, Illinois Symphony, and at the National Museum in Krakow, Poland. He began a long teaching career in 1951 at DePaul University and was chairman of the Kosciuszko Foundation Chicago Chopin Competition for many years.

In 1965, the Lira Ensemble was co-founded by Lucyna Migala, who continues until today as its artistic director and general manager. The Emsemble consists of five groups: The Lira Singers, The Lira Chamber Chorus, The Lira Chamber Orchestra, the Lira Children's Chorus (Dzieci), and The Lira Dancers. The Ensemble is based at Loyola University in Chicago as artist-in-residence. The groups perform regularly before large audiences locally, throughout the United States, and in Poland. Not only do they feature a variety of Polish music and dance, they also continue to receive critical acclaim and offer audiences a deeper appreciation of Polish culture and music. The Lira Singers include (clockwise from extreme left) Judith Partipilo Murth, Anita Switzer, Susan Smentek, Linda Sue Gurtatowski, Eva Kowacz-Fair, Beata Migdal, Lisa Lulis, Diane Busko Bryks, and Valerie Glowinski.

The Polka

Chicago's most noteworthy, or to some in Chicago's Polish American community, unworthy, contribution to music is the polka. Although it continues to be immensely popular, many of the newer arrivals from Poland do not share in the enthusiasm for this type of music and dance.

Professor Victor Greene's book, *A Passion for Polka*, analyzes the influence of the polka on the American scene. He documents the Chicago contribution to this style of music by pointing out that in 1875 the richness of Polish folk music (the music of the overwhelming majority of newcomers from Poland to Chicago before 1920) was catalogued in some 38 volumes. This music was the basis for such dances as the *mazurek*, *oberek*, *kujawiak*, polka, and

waltz. Regional differences were also noted in the music of the *gorali* (highlanders) and *wiejska* (rural or peasant).

As Polish immigrants poured into Chicago, Wladyslaw Sajewski found he could not keep up with the constant demand he was receiving for sheet music and recordings of Polish music. Frank Przybylski prepared albums for Polish dancing: volume one was published in 1912 with volume eleven appearing in 1934. Przybylski made some recordings based on the rural style in 1915. However, Jan Wanat made over 100 cuts for Victor from 1917 through 1933, which included more typical polkas and waltzes as they were being performed in other ethnic communities.

After the Depression years, polka music made a resurgence, particularly in the Chicago area, with the emergence of L'il Wally (Jagiello). His songs were reminiscent of the rural style, a little slower but bouncier than other polka music played by various ethnic groups. As one observer explained, "you may not know how to dance, but you'll start tapping your foot to the tune and pretty soon you're up and dancing, you can't help it." He sang mostly in Polish but his English version of "No Beer in Heaven" became a popular hit with many outside the Polish American community. Jagiello started his own label and released some 150 albums. He often was a guest artist on The Lawrence Welk Show, and, in 1984, Jagiello and his orchestra were invited and played for John Paul II in the Vatican. He also co-wrote the Chicago White Sox fight song, *Let's Go, Go, Go White Sox*.

Until today, most agree that L'il Wally's Chicago-style polka dominates the polka recording industry. It is estimated there were some 50 Polka

L'il Wally Jagiello was one of the most popular polka musicians in America. With his Chicago-style polka, he launched his own recording company and sold millions of albums. He and Frank Yankovic were the first two members inducted into the International Polka Association Hall of Fame in 1969.

Casey "Fingers" Siewierski performed with his concertina at a wedding when he was 11 years old. With his brothers, he began playing on Division Street during the Depression, then joined L'il Wally, and eventually formed his own band. In 1948, Carousel Polka became a smash hit and Siewierski was in demand as a performer and recorder of the 700 songs he composed. He was inducted into the International Polka Association Hall of Fame in 1981.

clubs on Division Street, known as "Polish Broadway," from the late 1940s through the 1970s. Antonia Blazonczyk began drawing large audiences to her polka club, Pulaski Village, in 1948, and after that site burned, continued with polka music at her Club Antoinette. The Baby Doll on Chicago's south side also attracted large crowds. Eddie Zima, Steve Adamczyk, Johnny Bomba, and Eddie Blazonczyk made frequent appearances at these clubs. The Ampol Aires perhaps had the largest single recording when they sold 150,000 copies of *I Wish I Was Single Again*. They also drew over 4,000 to the Aragon Ballroom in 1955.

With the changing demographics of Polish Americans in Chicago, polka music sought new venues. Polka masses were frequently heard and often became major productions such as "Joe Pat" Paterek and his Orchestra performing a mass in honor of John Paul II at St. Francis of Assisi Church accompanied by a choir and featuring Alice Schafer as soloist.

An International Polka Association was formed and houses its museum at 4608 South Archer Avenue. The Association has established a Hall of Fame and annually elects new members during a three-day festival held in the Chicago area toward the end of summer.

A quick survey reveals that polka music was heard about 23 hours a week on Chicago area radio stations in 2005. Eddie Blazonczyk's "Versatones," were invited to play in Chicago's Grant Park for the Spirit of Music Festival in 2006 and Lenny Gomolka and his polka band were planning a second tour of Poland for 2007. Although some recent arrivals to Chicago from Poland openly express their dislike for the polka, a Chicago dance director, who has frequently taken Polish American dance troupes to Poland for the past several years, explains that when the troupe performs a polka, the Polish people "can't get enough of the polka and we always have to do it over."

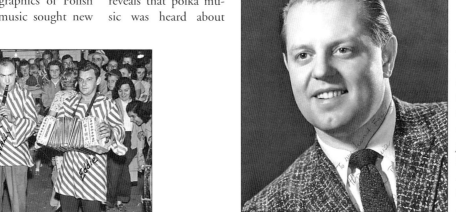

Bob Lewandowski arrived in Chicago in 1953 and would enjoy a long career in radio and television until he retired in 1995. For more than 30 years, he was on the radio 40 hours a month. His television program, The Bob Lewandowski Show, *was telecast for more than 20 years. For two years, his* Polka-Go-Round *was telecast on the ABC-TV network.*

Eddie Zima, at right in above photo, and his orchestra at the St. James Carnival, which had two stages for live musical entertainment in 1950. Carnivals were extremely popular. They were sponsored by many parishes, often lasting for two weeks, with thousands attending.

Eddie Zima, with concertina in photo left, was born in Chicago and began playing the concertina when he was six. His recording of Circus Polka *introduced his style of music to a large audience. Considered the godfather of Chicago-style polka, he inspired L'il Wally Jagiello, who often sang with Zima's band at picnics. Zima's orchestra also formed the nucleus of the very popular Ampol Aires. Zima was inducted into the International Polka Association Hall of Fame in 1972.*

Bruno "Juniorek" Zielinski was one of the stars of the Siekierka family broadcasts for decades on Polish-language radio in Chicago. These humorous tales about a Polish peasant family adapting to urban life had a large audience. He was also organizer of the Grunwald Hour in 1930 and, in 1957, brought Its Polka Time to 29 stations broadcast by ABC-TV.

Joe Durlak and his orchestra were popular in the 1940s. Durlak, also a vocal artist, popularized I'm a Polka Go-Getter and Whose Girl Are You.

Chet Schafer was a popular polka DJ broadcasting for many years from WTAQ in LaGrange, Illinois. He also launched a Chicago Polka recording company which has produced 85 polka albums. He writes about polka music for several publications and is editor of the I. P. A. News (International Polka Association). He was inducted into the International Polka Association Hall of Fame in 1976.

Numerous groups tried to attract attention to their style of polka music such as "Chicago's Milwaukee Avenue" which produced this album featuring John Krawisz, accordion; Joey Czmiel, trumpet, second from left; Greg Hilton, trumpet; Jerry Jendreas, clarinet-sax; and Timmy Okrzesnik, drums.

Pulaski Hall is shown in the 1950s at 17th and Ashland Avenue. Once the site of the White Eagle Brewery, it became a popular polka dance hall. It burned in the 1960s. The bust of Pulaski, seen above the entrance, was saved and is currently at Highlander Hall on Archer Avenue.

In 1950s, the Ampol Aires were composed of Andy Dziagwa, Wally Glowicki, Roman Truskolaski, Frank Barwig, Dick Ziembicki, Tom Kula, and Rudy Sienkowski. They were members of the Eddie Zima orchestra but broke away from Eddie. The band then went on to gain popularity by playing on such favorites as the Lee Edwards Polka Radio Show, the Ron Terry TV Show, and the Chet Gulinski Radio Show. The popular Ampol Aires continue to cut records and entertain around Chicagoland.

Polish Dancing

Early Polish immigrants cherished music and song. Well over 100 years ago, Chicago's fraternals began "Saturday schools," teaching children the Polish language, culture, and traditions. In 1914, the PWA commissioned a march which was regularly performed at all PWA functions. Polish American Catholic elementary schools frequently staged performances, almost always featuring *Krakowiak* dancers. The dances, appreciated for their zest and exuberance, probably had little relationship to the "same" dance as performed in Poland. Costumes definitely reflected an American adaptation, rather than an authentic replica of Polish design and style.

Following World War II, the fraternals and other Polish American organizations became more concerned with Polish folk dancing as it developed and was performed in Poland throughout history. The *Polonaise* and *Mazur* performed at

balls and banquets in Chicago's Polish American community became mirror images of what could be seen in Poland. Folk dance groups from Poland often visited Chicago and Polish American dancers frequently went to Poland to learn authentic Polish folk dancing and costuming.

Today, Chicago's Polish American folk dance groups are in demand for performances throughout the Chicago area and beyond. Among the dancers who have entertained appreciative audiences around the world are: Lechici Folk Dancers, Wesoly Lud Polish Folk Dance Ensemble, Wici Song and Dance Company, Lajkonik Polish Song and Dance Group, Polonia Polish Folk and Dance Ensemble, and Polonez Dancers.

As Micheline "Misia" Jaminski. founder of the Wesoly Lud dance group explains, "Especially in Chicago, folk dancing has become a lifeline and a teacher to the next generations–the variety of dances, the kaleidoscope of costumes, the multitude of songs that accompany the dancers–all add to the character of the Polish spirit. As future generations of Polish Americans become absorbed in Chicago's urban setting, Polish folk dancing will be that lively accent and flavoring of the Motherland that sets us apart from other ethnic groups."

PWA dancers in their goralski *(highlander) attire in June 1958.*

A Polish American dance group in 1936 performing at an event sponsored by the PWA. The PWA was instrumental in introducing and developing many early Polish dance groups.

165

PWA president Adela Lagodzinska, extreme right, and Helen Zielinski, PWA vice-president, extreme left, congratulate the dance contest winners at a PWA youth conference in the 1960s.

In 1991, the Lajkonik Polish Song and Dance Group of Holy Trinity Polish Mission and PNA was organized by Ewa and Marek Kus. The current artistic director and choreographer is Halina Misterka.

The Lechici Folk Dancers of the Polish Youth Association was launched in 1965 by Czeslaw Orzel-Orlicz and Eleonora Lewandowska. Past choreographers include Eugeniusz Raciborski, Konstanty Siemaszko, and Tadeusz Wiecek. The present artistic director and choreographer is Konrad Wiecek.

WICI

Wici Song and Dance Company was formed in 1983. It evolved from the Rzeszowiacy Song and Dance Ensemble which was founded in 1972). Wici is the representative dance ensemble of the PNA. Magdalena Solarz is the artistic director and choreographer.

There are also dance schools and dance groups that are specific to a particular region as in the case of the Siumni Polish Highlander Folkloric Ensemble (Zdislaw Miernicki and Marek Ogorek, Directors) and Polaniorze (Anna Watcha and Marcin Gasienica-Byrcyn, Directors) – both members of the Polish Highlander Alliance.

Since 1977 the Wesoly Lud Polish Folk Dance Ensemble has been the representative dance ensemble of the PRCUA. Micheline (founder) and Richard Jaminski are the group's artistic directors and choreographers.

Kilinski's Ice Cream Parlor at the corner of Thomas and Milwaukee avenues in 1911.

A view of Milwaukee Avenue looking northwest from Ashland Avenue.

The Greenbaum Tannery employed numerous Polish Americans in Chicago as the company grew to be the world's largest manufacturer of women's gloves.

The Horn & Bevier Co, a manufacturing plant located at North and Oakley streets in 1885 employed many Polish Americans over the years.

Men arriving from Poland were already proficient in wood carving. As a result they found employment opportunities in Chicago's frame manufacturing plants in the late 19th and early 20th centuries.

The first horse-drawn rail cars in Chicago made their debut in 1886. One of the major lines was the Milwaukee Avenue pictured above. It bisected the Polish American community on the city's northwest side from the loop area to the city boundaries serving them transport to work, to shop, for entertainment destinations, and almost to St. Adalbert's in Niles to decorate graves of loved ones on Sunday. Once the world's most extensive city rail system, Chicago ran its last streetcar, June 21, 1958.

Continental Clothing was an imposing sight at the intersection of Milwaukee and Ashland avenues during the mid 20th century.

An 1891 list of businesses in South Chicago along Commercial Avenue near 92nd Street included 45 saloons, 40 clothing stores, 24 food stores, nine hardwares, five druggists and numerous other mercantiles. The view is of Commercial Avenue looking south from 87th.

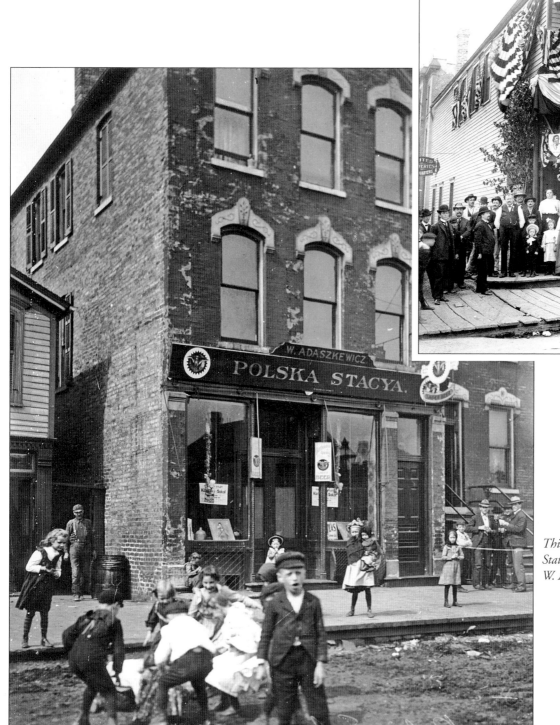

Wladyslaw Klinski's Inn at Noble and Division streets was also headquarters of the Kosciuszko Guards.

This Polska Stacya (Polish Station) was operated by W. Adaszkewicz in 1903.

Anton Smarzewski is generally credited as the first, and most influential, permanent Polish immigrant to settle in Chicago in 1851. He added "Schermann" to his name and store signage to attract German immigrants who were well established in the area. He ran a variety of businesses. Through his travel bureau, Smarzewski assisted in bringing many Poles to the Chicago area.

W. Slominski had a Badge and Bannerworks store at 1025 North Milwaukee Avenue near Noble Street which he opened in 1872. This photo was taken around 1900.

The southwest corner of Ogden and Milwaukee avenues, a shopping area for Polish Americans in the early decades of the 20th century.

John "The Swede" Czaplewski in his bar at 8857 Commercial Avenue. The establishment advertised having "a nationally famous collection of curios" on the wall.

The Wm. Mayer Company, which employed a number of Polish Americans, shipped 400 x-ray machines to dentists in Poland in 1946.

In 1946. Michael Krowka had rose gardens in Park Ridge, near Higgins and Mannheim Road. His company shipped 10,000 to 15,000 roses daily.

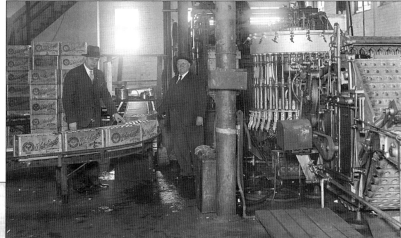

White Eagle Brewery opened for business at 1709 South Ashland Avenue in 1897. It rapidly expanded and moved, in 1907, to larger quarters at 38th Street and South Racine, the site of the former Illinois Brewing and Malting Company. A bottling plant and garage were immediately added. Popular brands included White Eagle Lager, Chopin Malt, and Chevalier. Operations closed in 1950 and the buildings were eventually demolished.

Pulaski Coal Company was one of the largest coal companies in Chicago at 3025 West 26th Street. It had 17 cement silos, serving 15,000 customers in the 1930s, selling 60,000 tons of coal annually.

One of the first and largest financial institutions serving Polish Americans was Northwestern Trust and Savings Bank. It was often called "Bank Polski" in the early years after it opened in 1906. It moved to the corner of Milwaukee and Division Street in 1920, a few years before this photo was probably taken. Alliance Publishers, associated with the Polish National Alliance, purchased the building in 1942.

In 1898, members of the parish of All Saints Polish National Catholic Church formed the Savings Bank of the People of All Saints. The name was changed in 1911 and again in 1938 to Liberty Savings and Loan Association (above photo) before it adopted its current name, in 1990, Liberty Bank for Savings. All Saints Cathedral of the Polish National Catholic Church is visible in the background on the left.

Northwestern Trust and Savings Bank as it appeared at 152-54 North Milwaukee Avenue.

Malec Funeral Home, the busiest funeral home in the Chicago archdiocese handling more than 500 funerals annually around the 1960s, opened in 1935. "At that time many families could not afford a funeral," explains Adrian Malec, son of founder Ben Malec, "so a basic fee of $100 was charged for everything: embalming, casket, wake reception, mass in church, and burial. My dad handled 100 funerals that first year with very little profit." After a new home with six chapels was built in 1941 at 834 North Ashland Avenue, business rapidly increased. Adrian Malec also relates that Mayor Richard J. Daley proved to be a stimulus to future business. "Often the mayor would come to pay respects in one chapel and he would stop in all six. Years later, people kept coming back recalling when the mayor paid his respects to a deceased family member or friend." Today, Malec and Sons is located at 6000 North Milwaukee Avenue.

Joseph Wojciechowski in front of his funeral home. Joseph Wojciechowski and his brother, John, opened a funeral business on Belden and Lorel avenues in 1905. Often they embalmed at the home of the deceased before placing the body in the living room for viewing. After a few years, they moved to 2129 West Webster (photo left) where the busines operated until 1992. Third-generation Joseph and Mark Wojciechowski carry on the business as Colonial-Wojciechowski Funeral Homes from locations on Milwaukee Avenue and in Niles.

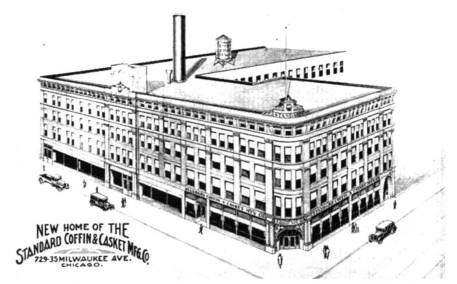

Standard Coffin and Casket Manufacturing was located at 729-735 North Milwaukee Avenue. Organized by a group of Polish American businessmen in 1898 to serve the Polish American community, it was incorporated in 1903. During the 1930s, the business was under the administration of Joseph Magdziarz, president; Martin Wojczynski, vice-president and treasurer; and Roman Grochowina, secretary. Grochowina noted that "due to the wonderful support of the Poles, the corporation's capitalization was increased to $300,000 from its initial capitalization of $25,000." This helped to make the company one of the largest coffin and casket manufacturers in the state at that time.

Workers take a break at an unidentified sausage factory around 1902.

Joseph P. Slotkowski operated a sausage business in South Chicago. He personally delivered his products (photo above). After World War I, he moved to the Pilsen area and opened the Joseph P. Slotkowski Sausage company at 18th and Damen. The firm did a thriving business and was purchased by Leon's Sausage Company in 1992. That company is now owned by Amy (granddaughter of Leon Tiahnybik) and Richard "Chico" Kurzawski. Chico was a member of Weber High School's 1964 Prep Bowl Champions and was named Prep Player of the Year by the Chicago Sun-Times and the Junior Chamber of Commerce.

Bacik's had a very successful deli and sausage business for more than 20 years at 2976 North Milwaukee Avenue until it closed in 1996. Shown above is Adam Stachanczyk preparing Polish sausage for smoking at the shop.

Hams and other cuts of meat were available for purchase in bulk quantities in Polish American communities around 1910. Many families cut up these meats to make sausages at their homes.

WHITE EAGLE

The White Eagle Restaurant has occupied, since 1966, the most cherished commercial location in Niles–right across the street from the entrance to St. Adalbert's Cemetery. Capitalizing and enhancing on previous business establishments which date back almost a century, such as the Silver Leaf Tavern, Helen and Mikes, and Trombas, Ted Przybylo and his family have built what many have called the world's largest Polish American restaurant at 6839 North Milwaukee Avenue. It would be difficult to contradict that reputation as more than 7,000 wedding receptions, 2,000 anniversary observances, 9,000 funeral luncheons, 3,000 banquets, and numerous other dining affairs have taken place at the White Eagle restaurant.

Meals are usually served family style featuring Polish dishes such as barley soup, *pierogi, kielbasa,* and *kolaczki.* A retail shop has been opened in the restaurant where diners can purchase extra helpings of their favorite entrees to enjoy at home.

Ted Przybylo, who had successful restaurant and catering ventures in Chicago, worked diligently with his family in establishing the popularity of the White Eagle. In 1988, the Chamber of Commerce in the Village of Niles recognized Przybylo as its "Citizen of the Year." Today the White Eagle remains a family-owned business with Andrew Przybylo and Vivian Przybylo Kolpak, general managers; Ted Przybylo, Jr., the executive chef; and Alice Przybylo Pawlicki and Vicki Przybylo Pindras, dining room managers.

Ted Przybylo, who purchased Ted's Tap, a tavern in Chicago, in 1937 when he was 21 years old, also had an extensive catering business when he returned to Chicago after World War II. He opened the Glass Bar at 1059 North Western Avenue in 1946, was the exclusive caterer for Congress Hall in 1959, and added a third catering service in 1960 at Bell Hall.

Ted S. Przybylo with his brother, Chester (seated), who operated a pharmacy at Western and Augusta.

In 1947, Ted Przybylo opened The Andrew House, three large banquet and dining rooms at 2441 West Division Street where many Polish American wedding receptions and other affairs took place for the following 20 years.

In 1980, Ted, left, greets President Jimmy Carter at the White Eagle in Niles. In the background is Hilary Czaplicki, PNA censor, and, at the right, is Aloysius A. Maze-wski, PNA president. Pope John Paul II has also dined at the White Eagle as well as other political leaders and celebrities establishing the White Eagle as one of the most popular restaurants in the Polish American community.

BOBAK'S

From the humble beginnings of a husband and wife making sausage in their basement, Bobak's has grown into a multi-million dollar operation that produces 1,000,000 pounds of meat product per week and employs over 500 in four Chicagoland locations. However, to this very day, Bobak's remains a family business committed to the production of authentic Polish sausage.

It all started with Frank Bobak, who lived in the Polish mountain resort town of Zakopane, where he made his living as a shepherd. In 1962, Frank Bobak immigrated to Chicago, where he found employment as a butcher. In his free time, he and his wife, Angeline, would make traditional Polish sausage in their basement.

In 1967, Frank turned his hobby into a business. Experiencing sustained success for 40 years, the now incorporated Bobak Sausage Company owns an internationally known wholesale sausage-making business, while simultaneously operating multiple delis and the Bobak Restaurant Buffet.

Throughout its history, Bobak's has consistently garnered public acclaim, received multiple industry awards and has been named at the top of many media "Best of" lists.

By remaining dedicated to quality, customer service, and community, the Bobak family has retained the loyalty of the Polish American community, while every day introducing non-Poles to the delectable nature of true Polish sausage.

Left to right are Walter Bobak, Stanley Gwizdz, Frank Bobak with Frank's wife, Angeline, kneeling. From the beginning, Frank insisted on authenticity in sausage production methods. Bobak's still use real wood and wood chips to smoke the meat.

Frank and Angeline attend one of the many Highlander functions in the Back of the Yards neighborhood.

The Bobak location at 5275 Archer Avenue (below left) has seen considerable expansion since its beginning in 1989. A small deli was quickly added to the meat processing facilty. In 1997, its success demanded a larger retail store (seen below). In 1998, Frank remodeled and opened the popular Bobak Restaurant Buffet. In 1999, the business expanded its capabilities with an additional 60,000 square-foot manufacturing/distribution facilty.

179

Robert Kennedy was the guest speaker at the Polish Constitution Day Parade, May 7, 1961. He and Frances Dymek, PNA vice president, lay the wreath at the base of the Kosciuszko monument after the parade.

A crowd gathers at the Kosciuszko Monument in Humboldt Park in the 1930s after the May 3 Polish Constitution Day Parade.

The Polish clergy in Chicago were eager to showcase their impact on the development of Catholicism in Chicago after plans were announced for a Eucharistic Congress in Chicago in 1926. A Polish section committee of some 152 members was formed to organize activities during the Congress. After the arrival of the Papal delegate to the Congress, his early meeting with the Polish clergy convinced them that the Pope was very concerned about the growth of the Polish Catholic community in Chicago. Polish clergy proudly discussed the 52 ethnic Polish churches which had been established in Chicago and were now administered by 148 Polish priests, with 950 sisters teaching 50,000 students in parish schools. The Polish section committee also made plans to host three visiting bishops from Poland along with 30 other visiting clergy from Poland with extensive tours of Polish areas of the city and an elaborate banquet at the Palmer House for 600 guests. A summary of Polish activities at the Eucharistic Congress, attended by some 250,000, including 125,000 at a Mass in Soldier Field, was published in a 200-page souvenir book by the Polish clergy after the Congress concluded.

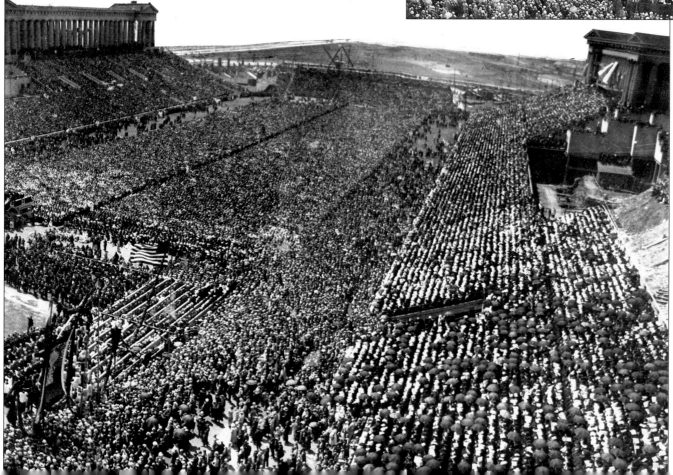

Polish Day festivals were sponsored by the Polish Day Association to share cultural pride and to raise funds for worthy causes. Prominent personalities, such as Madame Helena Paderewski (third from left), wife of the world-famous pianist, Ignace Paderewski, is shown at one of these festivals at Riverview Park, circa 1918, helping to raise funds to restore an independent Poland.

Today's Memorial Day was known as Decoration Day on May 30, 1924, when this Polish American committee met to announce their commitment to build a monument for American pilots killed in action during World War I.

July 22, 1933 was designated as the official Polish Day at the Chicago World's Fair. Some 50 floats, a chorus of 100, and 300 dancers culminated the festivities with a large crowd at Soldier Field.

The St. Stanislaus Kostka choir at a parish picnic around 1900. Notice the prominent display of the American flag as it was usually displayed when any society associated with the church was photographed.

Naming Pulaski Road

Chicago Mayor Edward Kelly reportedly asked PWA president, Emilia Napieralska, "And what can I do for you?" Napieralska responded, "Rename Crawford Avenue in honor of Count Casimir Pulaski, Revolutionary War hero." The street was so named in 1933. Heated legal battles to revert to the previous name of the street continued for 19 years until 1952 when the Illinois Supreme Court ruled in favor of keeping the street named Pulaski.

Pulaski Park was created in 1912 in honor of Casimir Pulaski. The park was a 3.8-acre parcel in West Town, a crowded, predominantly Polish neighborhood of factories and workers' housing. To make way for the park, the West Park Commission displaced 1,200 people, demolished some buildings, and moved others to nearby locations. In 1914, the West Park Commission designed the three-story brick fieldhouse (above) to emulate Eastern-European architecture familiar to the immigrant community. It was one of the most elaborate park buildings of that era.

Polish Americans enjoy celebrating anniversaries. On a personal level, a silver, 25th, or golden 50th, wedding anniversary usually brings together hundreds of relatives and friends. Parishes, fraternal groups, and other social groups among Polish Americans often celebrate a major anniversary with a banquet such as the diamond jubilee observance PRCUA celebrated at Stevens (today's Conrad Hilton) Hotel in 1948.

183

Chicago's Polish Constitution Day Parade is the world's largest Polish parade outside of Poland. The first such parade, in 1892, supported the cause of Poland regaining its independence, a theme for many of the parades until Poland became an independent nation in 1918. More recent parades focus on Polish contributions to American democracy: the 2007 parade celebrated the Polish workers at Jamestown in 1608 who were granted the right to vote after they established the economic viability of the English colony.

The significance of the Polish Constitution of May 3, 1791 to Poland and Polish Americans is keenly analyzed in an essay by Carl L. Bucki. He states that both nations have shared a common devotion to the cause of liberty and freedom. Thomas Jefferson, penned the phrase "We hold these truths to be self evident that all men are created equal" in proclaiming our Declaration of Independence. Those words were an accurate reflection of similiar thoughts in a book in Jefferson's library by the Polish philosopher, Wawrzyniec Goslicki.

Each nation, within a generation of these words appearing in print, would ratify a written constitution: the United States in 1787, Poland in 1791. Both constitutions proclaimed democracy and limited the powers of the executive by establishing three branches of government. Each also assured religious freedom and affirmed personal rights. Rev. Hugo Kollataj, founder of Poland's Commission of Education, began working on the Polish constitution in 1788. He was joined by Ignacy Potocki, Stanislaw Malachowski, Julian Ursyn Niemciewicz, and others who had very

With the PNA headquarters in the background, youngsters prepare to watch the May 3 Polish Constitution Day Parade in 1905.

A group of Gray Ladies, affiliated with St. Mary of Nazareth Hospital, (on left), march on August Boulevard in the Polish Constitution Day Parade in the early 1940s. Nurses from the hospital are on the right. Gray Ladies were American Red Cross volunteers who provided many non-medical services from 1918 until the late 1960s. Almost 50,000 women served nationwide during World War II.

similar backgrounds to those who drafted the United States constitution.

Bucki suggests that "we honor the Polish Constitution of 1791 not so much for what it achieved as for what is represents... a symbol of the Polish people and for their struggle for liberty, justice, and honor."

In 1791, Karl Marx would write with admiration, "This (Polish) constitution looms up against the background of Russian, Prussian, and Austrian barbarism as the only work of liberty which Eastern Europe has ever created independently and it emerged exclusively from the privileged class, from the nobility. The history of the world has never seen another example of such nobility of the nobility."

Although Poland was subject to 120 years of foreign domination and later ruthless communist subjugation, President John F. Kennedy, in 1962, expressed the spirit of the Polish Constitution of 1791 when he said, "The people of Poland (possess) the driving force of liberty, (they believe) that freedom will triumph in the end. I subscribe to that same belief." Freedom did triumph in Poland where, today, a democratic government rules.

Polish Americans share their sense of pride in our nation's and in Poland's democratic heritage by their strong allegiance and support of the Polish Constitution Day Parade in Chicago. Their Polish spirit is further reflected in numerous cultural expressions of Polish dress, dance, music, and song on display throughout the parade.

Maya Piergies on the PWA float in a Polish Constitution Day Parade.

The Polish Constitution Day Parade marching on Chicago's State Street in 1960.

Reflecting the pride of the Polish American community during the 1982 Polish Constitution Day parade are, from left, Helen Hodana, Mieczyslaw Jewula, and Betty Hodana.

Today's Polish American Association was founded as the Polish Welfare Association in 1922 by the Chicago Society of the Polish National Alliance. Its mission was to help stem problems recent arrivals from Poland were encountering while settling in Chicago. Julius F. Smietanka, its first president, emphasized the need for professionalism in serving the Polish American community. By 1926, the organization accomplished that goal when it was granted membership in the Council of Social Agencies.

Although involved in handling 59 cases in juvenile court and 89 cases in other courts, the administrator of the agency, in 1927, noted that 1,000 other cases in the Polish American community were in need of services.

Since 1948, assistance has been provided to Polish immigrants immediately upon arrival from Poland. In 1977, new offices opened on the city's northwest side and, three years later, on Chicago's southwest side.

From a severely depleted budget of $2,000 during the Depression year of 1933, the Polish American Association recorded a 2005 budget of $4.3 million. It employs 92 full-time and 75 part-time bilingual staff and works with 40 volunteers. Through its programs and services, it responds to 3,000 clients monthly seeking services. In 2005, the Polish American Association served 12,000 unduplicated clients.

PAA is the only not-for-profit human services agency that serves Polish immigrants.

P.A.A. Programs and Services

Education and Employment Services
- English-as-a-second language and citizenship classes
- Literacy tutoring
- Vocational training for Certified Nursing Assistants and Physical Rehabilitation Aide
- Office skills training
- Computer literacy classes
- Job development and placement
- Career Counseling
- Computer lab

Social Services
- Crisis intervention
- Individual and family counseling
- Women's services
- After-school program for youth
- Teen counseling
- Senior program
- Day center for homeless men and emergency homeless outreach service
- Intensive outpatient substance abuse treatment
- Homemaker program
- Health outreach and screening
- AllKids applications
- Food pantry
- Clothing closet
- Energy assistance

Immigration Services
- Immigration application processing
- Photographs
- Document translation
- Citizenship information and application filing

Dedication of the PWA building, located at 1303 North Ashland, in January 1955.

The PWA/PAA headquarters on the north side at 3834 North Cicero, purchased in 1985.

PAA Honorary Director and Past Chair John J. Pikarski, Jr., at left, representing the Sovereign Military Order of Malta, presents the check in support of the PAA homeless shelter to PAA Board Chairman Thaddeus J. Makarewicz in 1996.

Polish Welfare Association's south side office at the Rectory of Five Holy Martyrs Church at 4327 South Richmond in 1994.

On March 4, 1996 (Pulaski Day), Polish Welfare Association became Polish American Association. The PAA proudly participated in the 1996 Polish Constitution Day Parade, the first parade under the new name.

The Legion of Young Polish Women was established in 1939 as a humanitarian and cultural organization to assist Poles throughout the world. During World War II they raised funds to aid residents in occupied Poland and to assist Polish refugees. During the communist rule of Poland the group sent medical equipment and supplies to hospitals in Poland. In the Chicago area, they have helped to establish the Chair of Polish Literature at the University of Chicago and developed a Polish collection at the library of the University of Illinois/Chicago campus. The Legion also provides scholarhsips for students interested in Polish studies. They have supported the Polish Museum of America in numerous ways including assistance with the publication of a collection of Kosciuszko letters and providing a major grant to air condition the Paderewski Room. One of their major fund-raisers is the White and Red Ball which is held at a major downtown Chicago hotel. The Legion, often recognized for its work in the Polish American community, received the Award of Merit from the Advocates Society and the Polish Spirit Award from the PMA.

The Legion raised funds in 1940 to purchase an ambulance for use by the Polish Army in England.

The founding members in 1939 of the Legion of Young Polish Women.

The White and Red Ball, sponsored by the Legion of Young Polish Women, is a debutante presentation which attracts a large crowd. The Polonaise, Bialy Mazur and other Polish dances are performed.

Officers and members of the Legion of Young Polish Women join together to observe St. John's Festival in 1999.

The White and Red Ball debutantes in 2006 with the Queen, in center wearing red, crowned at the 2005 White and Red Ball.

The first White and Red Ball debutante tea was held in 1944 preceding the first ball at which debutantes were presented in 1945.

The Polish Women's Civic Club, originally an auxiliary of the Chicago Society, assisted immigrants with assimilation issues, such as language difficulties and settlement in their new communities. The club received its own charter in 1933 and established itself as the Polish Women's Civic Club. During World War II, the club sent clothing and medical supplies to Poland. After the war, settlement assistance was provided for newly arriving immigrants from Poland to the Chicago area. In recent years, the Polish Women's Civic Club has raised substantial funds for scholarships it awards to college students in the Polish American community.

The installation ceremonies of the Polish Women's Civic Club are elegant affairs such as this 1946 installation of the administration of Mrs Frank Trochim, president. The event was held at the presitgious Edgewater Beach Hotel.

Recent recipients of scholarships awarded by the Polish Women's Civic Club include Theresa Brzezinski, Virginia Wolski, Alicia Dutka, and Gloria Lomacki. On the left are club president, Camille Kopielski, and scholarship chair, Eunice Warda.

Installation of new officers at the Drake Oak-brook Hotel in 2006. From left to right are Paul Konrad, WGN meteorologist; Camille Kopielski, president; Alicia Dutka, second vice president; Carmen Czerunski, secretary; Barbara Marquart, fourth vice president; Teresa Shawski, treasurer.

Photo below: Former presidents joined with the current president of the Polish-American Medical Society during the 60th anniversary celebration of the Physician's Ball in 2006 at the Drake Hotel. From left, Dr. Marek Gawrysz (1997-2001), Dr. Anna Szpindor (2001-2005), Dr. Joseph Mazurek (1993-1997), Dr. Walter Cebulski (1974-1990), Dr. Barbara Roniker (1990-1993), and Dr. Bronislaw Orawiec (2005-present). Active in community affairs, the Polish-American Medical Society offers free flu shots, cholesterol screening, asthma screening (photo left), and promotes awareness of health concerns with programs such as the Polish American Breast Cancer Awareness Month.

The insignia of the 100th Bomb Group of the 8th Air Army of the US Army Air Corps which flew 107 B-17 bombers on its mission to fly supplies over Poland on September 18, 1944 to assist Poles in the Warsaw Uprising.

On September 16, 2004, at the Chicago Cultural Center, the Warsaw Committee of the Chicago Sister Cities International Program organized a celebration of the 60th anniversary of the Warsaw Uprising in 1944. At left are the honored veterans of the uprising living in the Chicago area.

The Polonus Philatelic Society was launched in Chicago by Chester Mikucki. It was instrumental in having U.S. postal stamps issued on Poland as a captive nation, on Paderewski, Copernicus, and Poland's Millennium of Christianity. The group sponsors a major Polish philatelic exhibit annually in the Chicago area and publishes Polonus Bulletin *which has international circulation.*

FIFTEENTH
ANNUAL CONVENTION
Polish Medical and Dental Association
of America

TENTH
ANNUAL CONVENTION
Polish-American National Bar
Association

CONGRESS HOTEL
CHICAGO
August 6 to 9, 1947

The Polish Dental Society of Chicago was established in 1908. The Polish Medical Society was founded in 1915. Both groups joined with others to form the Polish Medical and Dental Association of America which conducted its affairs from Chicago where many of the groups' national conventions met, sometimes in conjunction with the Polish American Bar Association.

The Polish Lawyers Association was organized in 1931 "to maintain the honor and dignity of the profession of law; to promote social amity among its members; to establish proper relationship with the public; to promote the reform of law; and to facilitate the administration of justice." (Constitution of the Polish Lawyers Association). The group changed its name in 1946 to Advocates Society. Shown above is the society's 1948 installation of officers which took place at the PWA, 1309 North Ashland Avenue, as Chief Justice Edward S. Scheffler (far left) of the Municipal Court administers the oath of office to attorneys (from left): Stanley Wendell, vice president; Adam J. Penar, historian; S. Charles Bubacz, new president; Harry Biedka, member board of governors, Charles Kaleta, vice president; Anthony J. Kogut, secretary; and Edward M. Koza, treasurer.

Roman Loza, extreme left, holds his painting, Gazda, which won first place at the art exhibition sponsored by the Polish Arts Club in 1969. Thaddeus Pawlak, second from left, was the chairman of the exhibition, with (left to right) Janina Bobrowska, Regina Jakubowska, Mimi Kasprowick, Walter Krawiec, and Alfons Kaplinski, president of the Polish Arts Club also present for the award presentation. The Polish Arts Club art exhibitions have been a major Chicago-area annual attraction since they were launched in 1926.

Mr. and Mrs Walter Poranski, center front row, owners of Poray, Inc., entertained members of the Polish Arts Club in 1964 at their estate in Lake Wauconda. Guests included Adele Lagodzinska, PWA president, Judge and Mrs Thaddeus Adesko, Rev. Stanislaus Lisewski, CSC, Mr. and Mrs. B. F. Males, Robert Lewandowski, Walter Krawiec, and Jane Palczynska.

On August 3, 1926, the largest crowd of the year —some 3,500–flocked to Ravinia Park for a concert featuring Polish music, Dr. M. J. Kostrezewski introduced Ina Bourakaya from Poland, presented her with a loving cup, and spoke of the "glory shed by her on Polish art." The Chicago Symphony Orchestra played selections by Paderewski, Borowski, a composer from Chicago, and Wagner's Polonia Overture. Bourakaya, seated in costume in the center, sang works by Kossobudzki, Moszkowski, Zielinski, and Wieniawski. Thaddeus J. Slesinski, founder and executive director of the Polish Arts Club which sponsored the concert, is standing on the extreme left.

OUR RECIPES

Products courtesy of Oak Mill Bakery; photo by Katherine Bish

As part of the Polish experience, the food industry plays an integral role. With numerous bakeries, family markets, sandwich shops, wholesale outlets, and businesses importing Polish goods, Poles and non-Poles enjoy a horn of plenty. With the advent of the latest enterprising immigrant arrivals, a choice selection of trendy and varied restaurants have burst on the Polish American scene. Highlander chalets, all-you-can-eat international buffets, haute cuisine, first-class European-style bakeries, old-world delis–there is a venue to seduce every palate. Moreover, these new enterprises are proud to present and promote authentic Polish cuisine.

Andy's Deli . . . Polish Pork Chops

Halina and
Andy Kolasa.

INGREDIENTS

2 – 8 oz. pork chops with the bone

Salt and pepper

1/4 cup wheat flour (Tortowa)

1/4 cup vegetable oil

2 tbsp. melted butter

2 cups sliced mushrooms

. . . .

Season the pork chops with salt and pepper and coat with wheat flour. Heat oil in a large sauté pan and sauté the pork chops for 5 minutes on each side. Meanwhile, heat the 2 tbsp. of melted butter in a sauté pan, and then sauté the mushrooms for 8 minutes. To serve, place the pork chops on a plate and top with the sautéed mushrooms. Mashed or whole potatoes, sprinkled with chopped parsley, serve as a great accompaniment to these pork chops.

SERVES 1-2

Entering Andy's Deli and Mikolajczyk Sausage Shop, Inc, owned by Halina and Robert "Andy" Kolasa, is like walking into "Little Warsaw." Clerks and customers banter in Polish, savory sausages hang along the wall, and deli cases display authentic Polish hams and imported cheeses. In 1918, Mike Mikolajczyk opened his homemade sausage business at Wicker Park/Division Street. Andy Kolasa purchased the business in the 1980s and expanded the operation to include a combination deli, supermarket, café, and take-out store at 5442 Milwaukee Avenue. "We are now," comments Andy "the largest producer of a variety of authentic Polish sausages in the Chicago area. In addition, to stay on the cutting edge of developing new specialty meat foods we constantly research international markets and new technology." On the wholesale end, Andy sells 150 products to stores all over the U.S. Andy's manager is the efficient and affable Damian Gorgon. "At first customers were mainly of Polish heritage. Now, more non-Poles visit because of our competitive pricing, homemade cakes, and full-service restaurant. Also when they try our sorrel soup, salmon marinated with dill, or a delicately prepared borscht they discover that Polish cooking is not only comfort food and country cooking but also can be quite sophisticated."

196

Polish Highlander Restaurant . . . Sauerkraut Rib Soup

INGREDIENTS

1 gallon water

1 lb. smoked ribs

1 lb. sauerkraut

1 lb. potatoes

3 cloves of garlic, minced

1 carrot

1 onion

1 tbsp. Vegeta

Salt and pepper

Bring the water to a boil, and then add the ribs and simmer for about 30 minutes. In the meantime, boil the potatoes.

When the meat is tender, remove it from the pot. Add the sauerkraut and the rest of the ingredients to the cooking liquid. Then cook the mixture on low heat for about 40 minutes. Serve in a bowl with the potatoes and ribs.

SERVES 10-12

Valleys of swift rivers and mountain ridges at the foot of the Tatra Mountains – a world heritage of nature and unique Highlander folklore seduces visitors from all over Europe. It was the love of this picturesque mecca and a proud Polish Highlander tradition that formed the basis of this fraternal, the Polish Highlander Alliance of America, founded on November 6, 1929. In 1983, under President Jozef Gil, the organization opened this restaurant and banquet hall to the public. Known for its old-school food, fine dining, and service, the Highlander chalet at 4808 South Archer near South Lawndale hosts banquets accommodating 130 to 350 guests. Preserving their Highlander traditions, the sharing of the Oplatek is a memorable Christmas highlight, and Easter draws the young for basket-decoration contests, egg painting, and specially prepared meatless dishes and pastries for parents.

Krystyna Wiszowata, chef; Bernadeta Mazur, waitress; Maria Remiasz, manager; and Krystyna Kondys, cook.

The Jolly Inn ... Cheese Blintzes

BATTER

2 eggs

1 1/2 cups flour

1 tbsp. cooking oil

1 cup milk

1/2 cup water

Salt to taste

FILLING

1 lb. Farmer's cheese

2 egg yolks

3 tbsp. sugar

1-3 tbsp. raisins

1 tbsp. finely chopped, candied orange peel

A pinch of vanilla sugar

Sour Cream (optional as garnish)

Jolly Inn Restaurant and Banquet Hall has proudly served the Chicagoland area for over 20 years. Its owners, Ewa and Stanislaw Chwala, opened their first Chicago-area restaurant, Staropolska, in 1984. After a few years of excellent service, they moved their operation to a new location, which was called Jolly Club. At this site, they opened the Jolly Inn Restaurant and Banquet Hall, which has come to be known as both a spectacular special occasion destination and a home for delicious everyday dining.

In 2007, Ewa and Stanislaw brought the taste of royalty to their patrons when they opened Jolly Inn A' La Carte, a beautiful establishment offering four-star cuisine in a very elegant setting. Thus, Jolly Inn can serve, under the same roof, those who cherish a traditional taste as well as seekers of new culinary thrills. All will find a dish to please their taste buds at the Jolly Inn.

The cheese blintzes, pictured, are one of the 24 hot dishes offered at their well-known smorgasbord. Jolly Inn is famous throughout Chicago for not only its great homemade-style food, but also for its two delivery trucks which cater delicious meals to corporate parties and home entertainment events.

From the left: Mariola Zawada, restaurant manager; Maria Obracaj, head chef; and Agnieszka Judasz, general banquet manager.

CREPE BATTER: Break the eggs into sifted flour, add cooking oil and salt, pour in milk and mix in a blender until the batter is smooth. Add water gradually, depending on how thick the batter is. Cover the batter with a towel and leave for 30 to 60 minutes. Then fry crepes on both sides until they are a light golden color on a non-stick frying pan (or on a regular frying pan greased with a piece of fatback). When frying, the crepes should spread over the entire surface of the frying pan.

FILLING: Grind the cheese. Then add sugar, vanilla sugar, and egg yolks to the grinded cheese and mix into a smooth mass. Next add raisins and orange peel and mix.

Spread the mixture on the crepes, roll up or fold into triangles. Then fry the crepes lightly, sprinkle with powdered sugar and top with sour cream if desired. Many customers prefer these blintzes with cherry preserves.

SERVES 6

200

Kasia's Polish Deli ... Potato & Cheese Pierogi

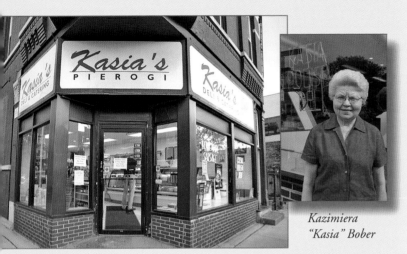

Kazimiera
"Kasia" Bober

Kazimiera Bober, better known as Kasia of Kasia's Deli, first opened her doors in December 1982 as a two-person operation. Living proof of the "American Dream," Kasia immigrated to the United States from Poland in the 1970s. After years of working odd jobs and of financial struggles, she opened her deli and offered home cooking to the neighborhood. Cooking at night, she sold her taste-tempting ethnic cuisine during the day. Now the next generation pursues that same American dream. From its fresh deli sandwiches to homemade soups and salads, Kasia's Takeout Deli/Sausage shop serves up 26 kinds of salad daily, many with a Polish flair reflecting the Bober's ethnic background. In addition, she offers 18 soups from Ukrainian borscht to chicken noodle, and 16 types of pierogis. The staff makes everything fresh daily, working from homemade recipes passed down from Bober's mother in Poland.

On the catering side, some of Kasia's prominent customers include; the City of Chicago, the Governor of the State of Illinois, United Airlines, LOT Polish Airlines, and the Consulate of the Republic of Poland. Dignitaries such as President Clinton and Mayor Richard J. Daley have sampled Kasia's award-winning pierogi. Customers know Bober personally and call her Kas for short. At age 70, she still works at the deli every day.

INGREDIENTS

DOUGH

3 cups all purpose flour

3 whole eggs

1 cup water (more if required)

1 tbsp. butter or oil

FILLING

3 potatoes

3 tbsp. unsalted butter

1 large onion, diced

3 tbsp. Baker's Cheese

1 tbsp. salt

1 tbsp. pepper

DOUGH: Combine flour, half of the water, butter (oil), and eggs in a large bowl. Stir vigorously to incorporate the eggs. Slowly stir in the remaining water until a dough begins to form. Continue lifting and stretching the dough until smooth and somewhat sticky inside, about 3 minutes. Do not overwork. When the dough is ready, cover, set aside, and prepare filling.

FILLING: Cook peeled potatoes in slightly salted water. Mash while hot and let chill. In a skillet, brown onion in butter. Then mix together potatoes, cheese, sautéed onion, salt and pepper.

PIEROGI: Go back to the dough, forming into balls 1 1/2 to 2 inches in diameter. Lightly flour. Roll out with a rolling pin into a 3-3 1/2-inch round approximately 1/8 inch in thickness. Hold the dough in one hand, and place a spoonful of filling into the center. Fold in half to enclose, and pinch the edges securely together. Be sure there are no openings along the edges or the filling will boil out. Boil a large pot of salted water while continuing to fill the remaining pierogi until all ingredients run out. Gently lower pierogi into rapidly boiling water 3-5 at a time and cook for a few minutes until they float to the surface. Remove with a slotted spoon and continue until all are prepared. Serve fresh with melted butter, or sauté in butter until lightly browned.

SERVES 8

From the left: Magda Mirga and Sylwia Czarkowska, Kasia's Deli staff members.

203

Lutnia Continental Café . . . Tenderloin of Venison

One of the few Chicago establishments offering haute-Polish cuisine, Lutnia is located at 5532 West Belmont near Central Avenue. Named after a famous 1930 Warsaw restaurant, Lutnia celebrates Polish and Eastern European favorites. "Our signature dishes include," says Manager Monika Chmielewska, "goose with sauerkraut and pears, roast boar with juniper, and Polish Woods venison with a spicy hunters gravy. For the American palate, popular choices include the chicken breast and a nicely spiced goulash in a giant potato pancake."

The owners, Mr. and Mrs. Mark Pieprzyk from Krakow, have hosted the First Lady of Poland, Jolanta Kwasniewska, as well as Polish actors, singers, and notables. Lutnia (the Lute) features a classical pianist, tableside flambé service, elegant mirrors, and original works from a noted Krakow artist.

"The cuisine compares to the best fine dining experience in Krakow," says the soft-spoken, Warsaw-trained chef, Kamil Narkiewicz. "In addition, our Christmas szopka, (colorful, illuminated Krakowian creche scenes) draw Polish Americans singing kolendas (carols) every Christmas." "We are also a great place," concludes Monika, "to come for a birthday, First Holy Communion, graduation, and a family wedding."

Milan Wrubel, waiter, and Ania Miller, hostess.

INGREDIENTS

VENISON
2 – 5 oz. venison steaks about 3/4-inch thick

2 tbsp. butter

MARINADE
1/2 cup oil

Hint of rosemary and garlic to taste

Red wine, enough to cover tenderloins

SAUCE
4 tbsp. butter

1/2 cup red wine

1/2 onion

1 beef bouillon, rehydrated with 1/2 cup water

1/2 cup chopped fresh mushrooms or 1/2 cup dry Polish mushrooms, preboiled for one hour

3 stalks celery, finely chopped

2 garlic cloves, chopped fine

1 carrot, finely chopped

1 tbsp. fresh rosemary, finely chopped

1 tbsp. fresh thyme, finely chopped

Allspice and salt and pepper to taste

2 tbsp. flour

Marinade tenderloin overnight. Brown on low heat with butter till cooking preference is attained (rare, well done, etc). With 2 tbsp. butter fry all vegetables, garlic, mushrooms, and spices until vegetables are translucent. Add wine and rehydrated beef bouillon and cook down 50%. Take remaining 2 tbsp. butter and mix with 2 tbsp. flour. Add to sauce in small amounts using fingertips. Whisk for 2 minutes until mixture reaches gravy consistency. Serve with Polish-style beets and potato dumplings.

SERVES 2

Oak Mill Bakery . . . St. Martin's Croissants

INGREDIENTS

DOUGH

2 1/2 lbs. flour

6 eggs

9 oz. Polish butter, melted

2 tbsp. sugar

2 oz. yeast

8 oz. milk

FILLING

12 oz. powdered sugar

7 oz. almonds or nuts

3 1/2 oz. white poppy seed – if not available
use blue poppy seed

30% cream (approximately 1/2 cup)

FONDANT GLAZE

1 1/2 cups powdered sugar

1-3 tsp. lemon extract

Dissolve yeast in ¼ cup warm milk, set aside. Mix together eggs and sugar until dissolved. Add melted butter, milk, and yeast mixture. Slowly add flour until incorporated. Kneed the dough into a ball. Set in cloth-covered bowl and let rise until doubled in size. Blanche almonds/nuts and poppy seed. Grind them with sugar and small amounts of cream until you get a smooth paste. Roll raised dough with a rolling pin, cut into triangles and put filling onto each of them. Form the croissants and leave them in a warm place to rise again. Put into a preheated oven and bake at 350 degrees until golden brown. After croissants cool, glaze with fondant glaze and sprinkle with toasted almonds.

SERVES 8

When only high-quality, unique cakes, pastries, sweet tables, and chocolate are in demand, they all come to the grande dame of Chicago's Oak Mill Bakery, Bogna Iwanowska-Solak, at right. In her Des Plaines corporate headquarters, a visitor finds 100 baking books in three languages next to a plaque that reads, "The Best Man For a Job is a Woman." Stranded in Chicago in 1981 (because of martial law in Poland), this former importer from Poznan boldly bought, in 1986, what became her flagship bakery in Niles. The accomplished and hospitable businesswoman now manages locations in Niles, Arlington Heights, Harwood Heights, West Belmont, and South Harlem. What are her bestsellers? "At Easter it is rum babka, mazurkas, and elaborately decorated Easter blessing baskets." Christmas favorites include the exquisitely decorated Yule log, spiced honey cake, gingerbread houses, and blue poppy seed strudel ("It is illegal to import white poppy seed in large quantity."). What is Bogna's greatest challenge? "Constant vigilance on quality ingredients to meet the ever-increasing customer and corporate demand."

St. Martin's Croissant is a special delicacy for Poznan inhabitants. Its origins go back to the legend about the Poznan confectioner who once dreamt about St. Martin entering the town on a white horse. In the confectioner's dream the horse stumbled and lost its splendid golden horseshoe. The confectioner believed his dream prophetic and the following morning he baked horseshoe-shaped croissants, adding almonds, white poppy seed, nuts, and raisins. Then he gave baked croissants to the poor. In memory of that distant event, on the 11th of November, St. Martin's Day, the confectioners of Poznan have always baked croissants. Poznan locals pride themselves on their centuries-old tradition, and rejoice in the city streets during grand festivals organized on that day.

Red Apple Restaurant . . . Stuffed Peppers

INGREDIENTS

4 medium green bell peppers

1 lb. ground beef, lean

1/4 cup finely chopped onion

1 1/2 cups cooked rice

1 tsp. seasoned salt

1/2 tsp. black pepper

Mix ground beef, onion, rice, and seasonings well. Cut tops off of peppers and hollow out any seeds. Stuff peppers with equal portions of ground beef mixture. Place stuffed peppers in a baking pan.

Cover and bake for 1 to 1 1/2 hours at 350 degrees until ground beef is cooked through and pepper is tender. Serve with tomato gravy.

SERVES 6 – 8

Janina,
head chef

Her law training and the "gift of the gab" shine through as Anna Hebal, the vivacious owner of the Red Apple, an all-you-can-eat international buffet, sits down for coffee in a front booth at 6474 North Milwaukee. "We first opened a produce store and the name 'red apple' was a natural," intones the savvy owner. "It is the king of fruits and evokes images of harvests and prosperity." Raised in Katowicz, Poland, and marooned in Chicago in 1981 "with tanks at the Polish border and all flights cancelled," she waitressed at a Greek restaurant in Morton Grove. With her husband, Ferdynand, they expanded the produce shop to a deli. In 1989, the transition was made to the Red Apple Restaurant at 3121 North Milwaukee. The following year witnessed the opening of 6474 North Milwaukee and ironically was a location where Anna had first waitressed. "The Chicago Tribune jump started us with an article that said, 'Look how much you can eat for $4.00 at the Red Apple.'" The buffet brims with creamy cheese pierogis, savory apple fritters, crisped potato pancakes, and much more. The secret of their success? "Staff loyalty and head chef, Janina, who prepares everything fresh daily. "There is nothing that unites people," Anna philosophizes, "like love of food, family, and faith." Red Apple is a great place to practice that maxim.

208

Retro Café . . . . Roast Duck with Apples

Retro Restaurant and Café is an exciting new addition to the local Polonian culinary scene. Opening in 2005 in the heart of the Polish neighborhood at 3246 North Central, it offers a wide variety of traditional Polish dishes as well as a large selection of alcoholic drinks. Upon entering Retro Café, with its exposed brick walls, tasteful artwork, and warm lighting, one feels transported to a stylish eatery in old Krakow, the native city of the owner, Zbigniew Gancarz, seated at right in photo.

Zbigniew shares managment duties with his mother, a vibrant woman who worked in the restaurant business for many years in Poland. When asked for the secret behind Retro Café's success, Zbigniew simply answers, "tasty food and a team of friendly staff." He recommends trying every dish in his establishment. especially the trout, beef stew with potato pancake, and of course, the roasted duck should not be overlooked.

210

INGREDIENTS
1 - 4-5 lb. duck
Salt
Marjoram (optional)
1 clove of garlic, mashed
2 to 2 1/2 lbs. apples
1 tbsp. water

Wash a 4-5 pound duck and pat dry. Rub inside and out with salt, marjoram (optional), and one bud mashed garlic. Place in covered container and let stand at room temperature one hour.

Peel, core, and cut into quarters 2-2 1/2 pounds apples or enough to fill the duck's cavity. Sew up. Place duck on rack in roasting pan and roast in pre-heated 450 degree oven for 10 minutes. Reduce to 350 degrees and roast 80 minutes to 2 hours or until fork tender.

Sprinkle with about one tbsp. water at start of roasting and puncture with fork at intervals to release fat. Baste occasionally with pan drippings. Serve with mashed or boiled potatoes. Stewed red or white cabbage or braised beets are typical accompaniments.

SERVES 6-8

Sami Swoi Restaurant . . . Trout with Almonds

INGREDIENTS

1 – 8-oz trout, cavity
    cleaned
2 tbsp. flour
1 5-6-inch sprig of dill
2 tbsp. butter
1/4 cup olive oil
1 tbsp. almonds

MARINADE

1/4 cup oil
1 tbsp. lemon juice
White pepper to taste
1 to 2 tbsp. Vegeta
(gourmet seasoning)

Lay trout in shallow pan. Combine marinade and pour over trout. Let stand one hour, turning once. Discard marinade.

Dredge fish in flour. Stuff trout with butter and dill sprig. Fry in hot oil until golden brown, turning once. Garnish with almonds.

SERVES 1

The hip and handsome owner of Sami Swoi Restaurant, Tomasz Debicki, is a good fit with the trendy bar and restaurant he opened three years ago. An informal setting, excellent food priced to please, "and the waitresses," according to patrons, "are the best looking in the Polonia community." "My first job," says the engaging owner, "when I came here from Wkockawek 14 years ago, was a busboy/waiter in a Polish Club in Miami Beach." In the ensuing years the dream took root to establish his own restaurant serving lots of Hungarian potato pancake which continues to be the eatery's bestseller. The faithful, both American and Polish, congregate to enjoy Sami Swoi's extensive lunch and dinner menu.

Tomasz explains that the restaurant name, Sami Swoi, means "Among Our Own" and was resurrected from a black and white 1967 movie very popular in Poland. The movie is the story of two quarreling families after the end of the Second World War. The bad blood runs deep until the families reunite through a Romeo-and Juliet-like marriage between the patriarchs' son and daughter. Scenes from this all-time favorite, photo above, and many other films grace the Sami Swoi walls.

Tomasz Debicki

Szalas Restaurant

... HIGHLANDER-STYLE POTATO PANCAKES WITH GOULASH

INGREDIENTS

POTATO PANCAKES
2 potatoes
1/2 tsp. salt
Pinch of pepper
1 tsp. flour
1 egg
1/4 cup oil

GOULASH
8 oz. cubed pork
1 cup water
1/4 of a red pepper
2 mushrooms (washed)
1 onion
1 tsp. salt
1/2 tsp. pepper
1 tsp. of Maggie seasoning
3 pieces of allspice
1 bay leaf
Mozzarella cheese (optional)
Green onion (optional)

Strong ties to traditional ethnic culture is a hallmark of the Polish Highlanders, and such dedication is well shown in the chalet-style restaurant called Szalas. Its stunning interior, designed according to custom, reflects the spirit and emotions of Poland's Podhale region. Indeed, Szalas is like an ethnic museum showcasing excellent food with the artifacts and antiques used everyday in the homes of proud Highlanders. While enjoying a delectable treat, patrons can also feast their eyes on an originally designed, water-driven, rotating mill wheel, along with a large cozy romantic fireplace, winter sleighs and samples of the flora and fauna found in the beautiful Tatra Mountains. The menu is composed of delicacies and entrees based upon traditional Highlander recipes, but with a modern twist. This long-awaited dream took two years of renovations and hard work before it became a reality for owners Maria Lassak and Chris Zborowski. Recently celebrating its fourth anniversary, Szalas has been featured in numerous newspapers, magazines, and on television programs.

Head Chef,
Stanislaw Bobak

POTATO PANCAKES: Peel and wash the potatoes. Finely grate the potatoes and add all the ingredients to mixture. Heat oil in a large frying pan and spread mixture onto the pan. Flip pancake once edges start turning golden brown.

GOULASH: In a large oiled pan add the cubed pork and stir until it is lightly browned. Add 1 cup of water along with a quarter of a finely chopped red pepper, onion, and 2 chopped mushrooms. Add salt and pepper along with the Maggie seasoning, allspice and bay leaf. Allow the ingredients to simmer for about 20 minutes.

PRESENTATION: Place the potato pancake on a large plate, add goulash to the middle of the pancake, fold the pancake in half and pour out the remaining goulash on top of the folded pancake. If desired, sprinkle with mozzarella cheese and green onion.

SERVES 2

214

Szymanski's Deli ... Poppy Seed Rolls

INGREDIENTS

DOUGH

8 cups flour

1 pkg. dry yeast

1 stick of butter or margarine melted

5 eggs

3/4 cup sugar

1 tsp. salt

2 cups of warm milk

FILLING

1 lb. poppy seed

1 cup sugar

1 1/2 sticks margarine or butter

1 cup milk, hot

1 lemon rind

Combine all filling ingredients and beat well. Dissolve yeast in 1/2 cup of the warm milk. Combine the flour, sugar, salt, and eggs. Add remainder of the milk, butter, and yeast mixture. Beat until elastic. Sprinkle top with a little flour and cover with a cloth. Let stand in a warm place until double in size. Punch down. Divide the dough into two pieces to make two rolls. Put on floured board and roll out into a rectangle. Spread cool filling and sprinkle with raisins. Roll like a jelly roll. Place in greased pan and let stand to rise again. Brush tops with margarine or butter. Bake for 45-60 minutes in 350-degree oven.

SERVES 25

Born in Tarnow, Poland, Stanislaw Szymanski, at right, immigrated to the U.S. in 1984. In 1990, he established Szymanski's Deli and Liquors at 6014 West Irving Park Road. The first-time visitor senses the international flair: barrels brimming with sauerkraut, pickled soup, smoked fish, and Polish honey liquor. One finds long lines at the deli counter where customers pick up meats, cheeses, cheesecakes, and imported products from Central and Eastern Europe. "The Poles," says Szymanski, "have the best dried mushrooms. It's not surprising because they have so many unadulterated forests. The whole concept of organic is natural to the Poles." According to Stanislaw, his tripe soup and chalka *braided Jewish bread, along with his homemade sausage, are his bestsellers. Here at Szymanski's Deli, Polish Americans feel right at home."*

White Eagle Restaurant ... Veal Stew over Roasted Potatoes

White Eagle family owners and managers: Vicki Pindras, Ted Przybylo, Vivian Kolpak, and Alice Pawlicki.

The White Eagle is the largest and longest-running banquet facility in the Chicagoland area. The Przybylo family, in business since the 1940s, launched the White Eagle in 1966. The facility can accommodate from 50 to 1,500 people in its seven private banquet rooms. With classic elegance in a hotel-like setting, it specializes in weddings, anniversaries, family gatherings, fundraisers, trade shows, and memorial luncheons. The White Eagle Restaurant is open daily for both family style and individually plated dinners. It features old-world traditional entrees, freshly baked pastries, and a full-service bar. Both the banquet hall and the restaurant are managed and operated by the children of founders Ted and Alice Przybylo; namely, Vivian Przybylo Kolpak, Andrew Przybylo, Alice Przybylo Pawlicki, Ted Przybylo, Vicki Przybylo Pindras, and Althea Przybylo Kroger.

218

Ingredients

10 oz. onions, diced

8 oz. celery, sliced on bias

8 oz. carrots, sliced

1 clove of garlic, minced

3 1/2 oz. oil/butter

3 1/2 lbs. veal, cut into 2 oz. pieces

Salt to taste

Pepper to taste

1/2 tsp. caraway seed

1 1/2 tsp. paprika

1 tbsp. parsley, chopped

1 qt. veal stock (chicken stock/bouillon will substitute)

1 cup corn starch

1 cup sour cream

1 lb. cooked asparagus

. . . .

Sauté onions, carrots and celery in oil until translucent. Add the garlic and cook for 1-2 minutes over medium heat. Next, add the veal and the remaining ingredients except the corn starch and sour cream. Bring the mixture to a boil and then reduce the heat to a simmer for 2 hours. Bring back to a boil and add the corn starch slowly until you reach the consistency desired. Reduce heat and add sour cream (Do not overheat/boil). Serve over roasted potatoes, bow tie pasta or mashed potatoes, with cooked asparagus, and garnish with chopped parsley.

Serves 8

Swieconka (Easter meal)

Many of the rural customs and traditions of early Polish immigrants were impractical, if not impossible, to transfer to their newly adopted homeland. In Poland, living close to the soil, Poles grew their own food and raised their own animals. In Chicago, they purchased such commodities.

Nevertheless, Poles clung to many culinary traditions as is evident by the continued observance of *Swieconka* (the Easter meal). While in Poland, the *Wielki Post* (Great Fast) was an unwelcome reality with the main meal for the 40 days of Lent consisting of *zur*, made of fermented raw bread dough. As Lent drew to a close, Polish peasants took delight in burying the remnants of the *zur* and breaking the pot in which it was made.

Swieconka – everything and anything that could be prepared by the woman of the home was the joyous feast that awaited the family on Easter morning. Preparations began in earnest on Holy Thursday and Good Friday when women and girls began coloring eggs. This was to be done in secret with no men allowed. A cake in the shape of the Pascal Lamb (*baranek*) was baked and adorned with a red resurrection banner symbolizing Christ's victory over death. Butter, also, was molded in the shape of a lamb. Breads and other cakes were made from the better flour that was saved during the Lenten season. These included *babki* (in the shape of a hat) and *placki* (usually flat like a coffee cake). Today many of these items are store-bought with markings indicating an Easter theme. Ham, sausage, salt, vinegar, and *barszcz* (borsch soup) were included for many Easter meals.

After all items are ready for the *Swieconka*, they are placed in a basket, covered with a cloth and taken to church on Holy Saturday to be blessed by a priest. In Poland, the entire family would take the basket to church for the blessing. As immigrants settled in Polish American communities, women would take the basket with prepared foods and give younger children their own basket with a chocolate bunny or candy eggs. This practice of blessing food in Easter baskets for the family's *Swieconka* not only continues in Polish ethnic parishes but has spread to other churches throughout the Chicago area and with many who live in suburban areas.

Photo by Stanley Wlodkowski
Courtesy of White Eagle Restaurant

The Easter Basket

A young man takes his Easter basket to church for the Easter blessing with his great aunt. His mom, preparing her own basket, explains, "This custom was important to my busia *(grandmother).... It was imperative that each family have a representative take an Easter basket to the church for a blessing. At St. Stanislaus Bishop and Martyr, where our families attended, there was a series of continual blessings that lasted for several hours. I had the honor of taking our Easter basket for many years. It is a tradition I look back on with a smile. The baskets my mother and* busia *prepared had all the necessary elements and were works of art lovingly put together."*

An astute observer has commented, "In the old country, the size and contents of the basket were a matter of womanly pride; in America they were a tribute to tradition." Interestingly, that tradition seems to be gaining impetus and spreading to other nationalities with each generation.

The meal itself, the *Swieconka*, begins with an Easter prayer. Families will first taste the horseradish as a reminder of Christ's suffering on the Cross. Hard-boiled eggs are exchanged and greetings are extended. Generous portions of the contents of the basket are then made available.

Although *Swieconka* is usually celebrated with the immediate family in the home, it has also been observed in community settings bringing together families in a neighborhood or by members in a specific Polish American society.

For several years the PNA conducted an Easter Egg hunt on its spacious grounds at 6100 North Cicero Avenue.

The PMA's popular egg painting classes are an annual tradition. The 2006 class was taught by Mrs. Stanislaw Gasior, holding the platter in the center.

The blessing of the Easter baskets on Holy Saturday is a well-established tradition. On Friday evening, young girls were to prepare intricately colored eggs and other food to be blessed. Pisanki were made by placing a pattern in beeswax on the white egg shell and then dipped into onion skin water or other coloring. Kraszanki were colorful designs painted on the outside of the egg using one color made from roots or herbs. Malowanki were eggs made with a variety of colors and designs. Sometimes colored paper or straw was used to decorate an egg–these are called nalepianki. The above Easter basket blessing was at Holy Trinity Church.

Germany's invasion of Poland launched World War II. The United States entered the war after the Japanese attack at Pearl Harbor. As with World War I, Polish American young men enlisted in the Armed Services in proportionally larger numbers than enlistments in other areas in Chicago.

When they returned after the war, the neighborhoods they left behind were undergoing extensive change. This was especially true of the heart of old Polonia, Polish Downtown, which was still being referred to as the second largest concentration of Poles next to Warsaw. The geographic center of this area was the triangle formed by the intersecting of Milwaukee, Division, and Ashland streets.

Ed Marciniak, Loyola University professor, has closely studied this neighborhood. Largely untouched by the Chicago fire, this neighborhood was rapidly overbuilt. However, writes Marciniak: "Until World War II the [Polish Downtown] area continued to be a visitor's mecca, a charming old world neighborhood nestling in the shadow of modern skyscrapers, a port of entry for Polish immigrants, and a center of Polish culture, social life, and publishing…. With a population predominantly Catholic, churches were full. Parish schools overflowing…. Polish Downtown had survived the [Depression] as a solid working class neighborhood. There were few hints that trouble might be loitering around the corner."

That "trouble" would begin as returning veterans left their former homes and moved northwest along Milwaukee Avenue, some as far as Niles. In adjusting to a post-war economy that would result in 400,000 blue-collar jobs lost in Chicago by 1980, some Poles changed their names, others entered higher education, and sought positions in an economy starting to be determined by rapid technological changes.

With rents very inexpensive, other ethnic groups began moving near Polish Downtown. At St. Boniface Church, a German neighborhood

before the Poles arrived, there was a kindergarten teacher who taught the same class in Polish, Spanish, and English. Many signs at stores now informed customers, *Mowimy po Polsku*, *Se Habla Espanol*, and "We speak English."

However, the major "trouble"—the "snake in paradise" as some derisively called the plan—was the proposed 16-mile expressway from the loop to O'Hare Field. As word of the expressway spread in the early 1950s, it was learned that the "snake" would devour St. Stanislaus Kostka, possibly other churches, and the result, many feared, would be a decimated neighborhood.

Thousands of current and former parishioners protested. Expressway plans were revised. The city designated the area as "conservation" to prevent it from becoming a slum.

The Northwest Community Organization was launched in 1961 with the support of Polish American Catholic parishes and fraternals. Eventually 177 groups joined the cause to save the neighborhood and rally against city development projects—mostly high-rise buildings—designed to change the character of the area.

The city presented the Chicago 21 plan for the 21st century which said of, as it was now called, the East Humboldt Park area: "An older area which requires upgrading….population composition is changing and with it community needs." No specific recommendations were presented. The area continued to slip and, by 1970, was ranked in the lowest fifth of 75 Chicago neighborhoods with increasing low-income households, unskilled wage-earners, and more residents applying for welfare. Nevertheless, attendance at the area's seven Catholic elementary and secondary schools still outnumbered the four public schools.

In tribute to the ethnic history of the area, Chicago's City Council officially named Polish Downtown as "Polonia Triangle" in 1976 and set July 4th as the day of dedication. The event was cancelled.

Neither the remaining older Polish Americans in the area, nor the younger Polish American families seeking a better livelihood in other areas in and beyond the city, were enthusiastic about the proposal.

Indeed, the "Polish" flavor of the area was becoming diluted. Weber High School, the first school of higher education for Polish Americans within a block of the Polish Triangle, closed and moved to the northwest in 1950. Holy Family Academy, across the street, closed a few years later.

Major organizations would also leave the area. The PNA moved further north. Its Alliance Press set up offices several miles northwest on Milwaukee Av-

This Krawiec cartoon shows how the building of the Kennedy Expressway divided Polish American communities. Notice each church is identified with a Saint's name plus "owo," rather than just the name of the church. Polish Americans usually refer to an entire neighborhood inclusive to the parish boundaries, when "owo" is added to the Saint's name.

enue. The PWA moved to Park Ridge and the Polish Welfare Association relocated to the northwest.

However, the Polish Roman Catholic Union of America and Saint Mary of Nazareth Hospital did not leave. In fact, both made major commitments to expand their mission within the community.

Saint Mary of Nazareth Hospital built a larger hospital in the 1970s and, a few years ago, added a medical office building. "The Polish hospital" (as it was known) relished the publicity it received as "the hospital that wouldn't run away."

Other developments would affect Polish American communities in Chicago. Mrs. Matilda Jakubowski organized a campaign in 1974 to save St. Adalbert's on the south side, the third oldest church built for Polish Americans. She attracted considerable media attention for her effectiveness and was appointed an aide on ethnic affairs to Illinois Governor Jim Thompson. Two years earlier Congressman Roman C. Pucinski, representing Chicago's northwest side, sponsored legislation to enact an Ethnic Heritage Studies Center which passed with an appropriation of $15 million for the first year.

In the early 1980s, the Copernicus Foundation was opened in the former Gateway Theater near Milwaukee Avenue on Lawrence. The Illinois Division of the Polish American Congress also opened new headquarters on Milwaukee Avenue two miles north of the Copernicus Foundation.

In an effort to preserve the use of the Polish language, the Polish Teacher's Association of America was formed in Chicago in 1952. Its mission was to organize additional Polish Saturday schools. The first was probably the Casimir Pulaski school which celebrated its 50th anniversary in 2001. The

Lydia Pucinska, known as the Sunshine Lady, began a long and distinguished broadcasting career in 1936 with a daily program, Poranek Sloneczny *(Sunny Morning). She was a member of the Polish Radio Syndicate, organized in 1938, to structure the advertising market and improve the quality of broadcasts. In 1948, her program was re-titled* Godzina Sloneczna *(Sunshine Hour). Pucinska received many tributes in 1963, marking her 50th anniversary for work of social significance in the Polish American community. She is shown here with, left to right, Dr. Edward C. Rozanski, manager of Alliance Publishing and Printers, Chicago Mayor Michael J. Bilandic, and her son, Congressman Roman C. Pucinski.*

Benjamin A. Adamowski was elected to the Illinois General Assembly in 1930. He represented the largest senatorial district in the state, the 25th, and served five terms, becoming the Democratic Majority Floor Leader. In 1956, Adamowski was elected States Attorney as a Republican. He fought corruption on several levels, culminating in the Summerdale police scandal which exposed eight police officers burglarizing north side retail establishments. Adamowski unsuccessfully challenged Richard J. Daley in a close race for mayor in 1963. Eventually Daley ended his feud with Adamowski when he asked and Adamowski accepted an appointment to the Board of the Chicago Public Library.

number of schools rapidly increased after 1980 with the latest waves of Polish immigrants. By 1983, there were 18 schools with 300 students. By 2000, nine more schools were added with an enrollment of 14,000. The largest school in Chicago today is probably at St. Hyacinth's Parish, the Stefan Cardinal Wyszynski School, with 600 students. Other schools, reflecting the continued movement of the Polish Americans to the suburbs, are in Orland Park, Harwood Heights, Palatine, Elmwood Park, Summit, Addison, Arlington Heights, Park Ridge, Niles, Lemont, Schaumburg, Wheeling, Wauconda, Palos Hills, Bensenville, Bridgeview, Buffalo Grove, Burbank, Lombard, Romeoville, River Grove, Tinley Park, and DeKalb. There are 13 schools in Chicago proper.

Polish is also taught in Chicago's public high schools at Foreman, Steinmetz, Kelly, Schurz, Prosser Vocational, Sklodowska-Curie, Kennedy, and Taft.

There are also 35 Polish bilingual programs which teach in Polish and English for three years to prepare students for complete instruction in English.

Polish is also the language of liturgies in 36 Chicago churches and 24 churches in the suburbs. The largest attendance at a single church is probably St. Hyacinth's where some 7,000 to 8,000 attend Sunday Mass. Pope John Paul II issued a proclamation that was read by Francis Cardinal George on May 30, 2003 naming the church as a Basilica for its work on behalf of the Polish immigrants in Chicago. Reflecting that mission, visitors to St. Hyacinth's will see memorials to veterans of World War I and II. Other memorials include Pope John Paul II; Rev. Jerzy Popieluszko, a priest in Poland murdered by communists for his support of Solidarity; and Maximilian Kolbe, elevated to sainthood by John Paul II as a Polish missionary who died in a German prison during World War II when he took

the place of another prisoner slated for execution.

The Alliance of Polish Clubs (formerly the Alliance of Clubs of Little Poland) organized in 1928. Its clubs were named for the town or village in Southern Poland where the members lived before coming to Chicago. Club members prepared and sent packages of food, clothing, medicine, and other necessities to family and friends every month, if not more often. With the forced migrations of Poles during the war, the Alliance of Polish Clubs undertook massive aid programs. Between 1942 and 1945, 110,000 pounds of clothing were shipped to Poles in Iran, Iraq, Africa, and France at a cost of $220,000. In 1943, $500,000 of Polish war bonds were purchased. In 1945, 100 tons of clothing were shipped, followed by 500 tons of all new clothing in 1946-1947. Letters were received from over 1,000 areas in Poland confirming that all shipments were received and fairly distributed. The

What's on Polish radio in Chicago? Check page 104 of the 2007 edition of Informator Polonijny *which indexes some 200 Polish radio programs and personalities. This Polish version of the "yellow pages," with some 1,960 oversize pages, details a panorama of interests and needs of Chicago's Polish American community.*

Polish American Chicago Metro Population

The Polish American Association has published a comprehensive profile of the Polish American community in the Chicago area. This work, *The Polish Community in Metro Chicago: A Community Profile of Strengths and Needs*, details the locations and patterns of movement of Polish Americans up to and including the 2000 census. Useful charts, maps, and graphs are also presented.

There were 25,726 Polish immigrants in Chicago in 1890. By 1920, that population reached 151,200. Latest figures indicate 139,000 Polish immigrants in the Chicago area, a decline from the historic high of 165,000 reached in 1930. Nearly one-third of all Polish immigrants in the United States live in Chicago. Today, the Polish immigrant population in Chicago, at nearly 70,000, is the largest in the United States.

Many third- and fourth-generation Polish Americans may not be reflected in the 2000 census figures. Nevertheless, the number of Polish Americans in the metro Chicago area was recorded as 820,548. Chicago and suburban Cook County showed a decrease in the Polish American population since 1990, while Kane, Lake, McHenry, and Will Counties each had substantial increases.

Chicago areas that have Polish ancestry populations of more than 30 percent include: Archer Heights, Harwood Heights, Dunning, Garfield Ridge, Lemont, Portage Park, River Grove, Norridge, Hegewisch, and Burbank. In the suburbs, the largest Polish American population areas are: Naperville (13,936), Schaumburg (11,109), Arlington Heights (11,001). The top Chicago locations of foreign born Poles are Portage Park (12,894), Dunning (8,387), and Belmont-Cragin (7,878). During the 1990s, about 75 percent of new Polish immigrants coming to the area came directly to and settled in the City of Chicago.

Polish immigrants place a high value on acquiring citizenship. Currently about 40 percent of all Polish immigrants are citizens and nearly 90 percent of Poles who arrived before 1965 are citizens.

Of the 106,000 elderly Polish Americans in the metro area, one third live in the suburbs and two thirds live in Chicago, with 85 percent of those in Chicago owning their own homes.

chairman of this effort remarked, "we were able to clothe half of Poland."

Other major items sent to Poland include 500 horses at a cost of $100 per horse plus shipping costs. Eighty x-ray machines and other hospital equipment were also sent.

The Alliance of Polish Clubs, which had headquarters near Polish Downtown, moved to the northwest side in 1976. Its member clubs funded numerous construction projects in Poland resulting in many new churches, schools, community halls, fire stations, and other community facilities being built.

In 1992, the Alliance of Polish Clubs took charge of Polish Constitution Day (May 3) observances in the Chicago area. Previously, the PNA had organized the May 3 parade which originated at Holy Trinity Church in Polish Downtown when 10,000 marchers would pass PNA headquarters and march to the Kosciuszko statue in Humboldt Park. The parade drew crowds of 100,000 or more. The route was now in the Chicago loop and many marchers were not directly affiliated with Polish American groups.

The Alliance of Polish Clubs currently is focused on building a monument to Christ the King in Tarnow, Poland. It will also house a study center and provide meeting facilities for representatives of Polish communities who are visiting from anywhere in the world.

It is difficult to precisely state the Polish or Polish American population in Chicago since World War II concluded. Some 5,000 displaced persons were believed to have relocated in Chicago as a result of the Displaced Person Acts of 1948 and 1950. The quota set for immigrants in 1924 was modified in 1952 and 1965 allowing for more immigrants to enter the United States. Polish refugees and asylees were also granted permanent resident status between 1961 and 1992. If one accepts what an authority states, that is one-third of all newly arriving Polish immigrants went to Chicago, about 500,000 arrived between 1960 and 1996. Many were classified as visitors for pleasure or temporary workers and did not remain. In 1993, for example, it was estimated that 45 per cent of all who arrived from Poland returned to Poland within a year. Even official U.S. census figures can be misleading:

they do indicate "foreign stock" but do not record third, fourth, or fifth generation Polish Americans. Nevertheless, major media will probably continue to announce that Chicago has the second largest concentration of Poles in the world, even though many Polish Americans, especially the most recent arrivals, live and work many miles from the original Polish downtown.

After the failure of the Warsaw insurrection in 1944, many Polish Americans believed Poland would suffer further losses after the war, no matter how faithful an ally it was. A meeting of representatives of all Polish American organizations was established as the Polish American Congress. All officers and headquarters were in Chicago. With the U.S. national elections approaching in 1944, the Polish American Congress believed it could hold Franklin D. Roosevelt accountable for upholding the Atlantic Charter in regard to Poland so that the Soviet Union would return to Poland all Polish territory it had seized in 1939. Roosevelt met with a group of Polish American representatives in Washington sitting in front of a map showing Poland's prewar boundaries. The delegation left, encouraged

The Foreman Polish Club celebrated with Bishop Alfred Abramowicz when the Chicago City Council named a street in the bishop's honor. Dr. John Garvey, principal of Foreman High School, is shown with Bishop Abramowicz. At immediate right is Mrs. Czeslawa Kolak, club advisor and teacher.

The Chicago Intercollegiate Council dates its origin to 1927 when it affiliated with the Polish Student Association. On May 28, 1949 it adopted

its current name and continues to coordinate Polish American activities with Polish American students at Chicago area colleges and universities, support college scholarship assistance, and promote numerous educational programs such as its co-sponsorship of Elementary Knowledge Bowl in the Polish language. Officers and board members from 2001 include: (left to right) Camille Kopielski, Conrad Miczko, Peter Dykas, Ann Domogala, Lester Straga, Eve Penar, Agnes Penar, and Mark Dobrzycki.

Roosevelt's election, only to be shocked to learn Roosevelt had agreed with Stalin that this territory would be Soviet after the war. Polish Americans were enraged. They took a strong, anti-communist position as the Soviet Union continued to tighten its grip on Poland. Soviet-trained Polish communists took over the Polish government in 1947 following fraudulent elections.

The Polish émigrés–they did not want to be called immigrants–who arrived in Chicago after World War II insisted they represented the interests of subjugated Poland and would work for Poland's independence. As one historian has stated: "The needs of immigrants (especially immediately after their arrival) and the needs of the second, third, and later immigrant generations remained often at odds. While the former looked for housing, jobs, social services and strove to become familiar with the language and culture of the host society, the latter's primary goal was the maintenance of ethnic heritage and support for the established cultural in-stitutions.... As a result, in the late 1940s and early 1950s, both groups engaged in a heated debate about the nature of immigrant responsibilities, the essence of Polishness, assimilation, and loyalty."

Both sides were aggressively anti-communist. However, after the Hungarian Revolution was crushed by the Soviets in 1956, Poles in Poland, Polish Americans, and émigré Poles who were moving into control of Polish Affairs committees within the Polish American Congress, accepted the fact that an attempted insurrection in Poland would result in massive bloodshed.

Poland, however, was not forsaken by Polish Americans. In 1969, the Polish American Charitable Foundation arranged to have doctors from Loyola University teach new medical procedures in Poland. Although the communist regime would not allow foreigners to operate, accommodations were made to teach Polish doctors. Eventually more than $200 million in medical equipment and supplies were shipped to Polish hospitals. The Foundation then began working with Bishop Czeslaw Domin in Poland which resulted in the construction of three hospitals to care for children. For his efforts in these causes, Eugene Rosypal of Chicago was decorated by the Polish government with one of its highest honors, *Oskar Serca*, in Zabrze, Poland.

The 1980s proved to be a decade that changed the world. It began in Poland with the Solidarity movement and would end with Solidarity standing up to and causing the downfall of communism.

The passion that Solidarity evoked did dis-

Since 1999, seminarians from Poland have been preparing for leadership positions in Chicago's Polish American parishes. After one year of study at the Alfred Abramowicz Seminary in Chicago, the young men attend St. Mary of the Lake Seminary in Mundelein for three years. After ordination, they are assigned to a non-Polish-speaking parish to become more familiar with other parishes in the Archdiocese of Chicago, before appointment to a Polish American parish. From the left, Wojciech Oleksy, Karol Ksiazek, Tomasz Bochmak, Sebastian Kos, Rafal Ligenza, Francis Cardinal George (seated), Rev. Richard J. Klajbor, rector of the Alfred Abramowicz Seminary; Marcin Kania (behind Fr. Klajbor), and Pawel Zurawski.

"Adoramus," a singing group of Sisters of the Holy Family of Nazareth from Warsaw, Poland, came to Chicago in 1997 and entertained throughout the Chicago area including at St. Emily Church in Mt. Prospect, St Andrew Church in Calumet City, St. Camillus Church, Five Holy Martyrs Church, St. Hyacinth Church, PRCUA, and St. Mary of Nazareth Hospital Center.

sipate in many of its members who began arriving in Chicago during the 1970s and 1980s. As did the Polish émigrés following World War II, they believed their political agenda for the future of Poland was more timely and appropriate than established Polish American organizations in Chicago. Differences arose. Even language became an issue. Newcomers claimed that ethnic Polish Americans really did not speak "Polish." Many Polish Americans in turn looked suspiciously on this generation completely educated by a communist system.

In this context the Polish Welfare Association may be appropriate to mention. A PWA official explained, "There is an agency in Poland with the same name as Polish Welfare Association. This agency gives out money in Poland." Consequently, new arrivals came to the association with the same expectation.

Newcomers eventually organized their own groups: *Pomost*, Freedom for Poland, Brotherhood of Displaced Solidarity Members, and Polish-American Economic Forum. Although none of these organizations survived, they did influence more favorable U.S. policies toward Poland as both the newcomers and the established Polish American community cooperated in several efforts such as public demonstrations in support of striking workers in Poland.

The phrase, the "New Polonia," was being heard with increasing regularity as new arrivals became more involved in developing their own Polish imprint on a changing Polish American community.

Stopping Anti-Polish Bigotry

Polish Americans were the butt of many uncomplimentary and derogatory jokes during the 1960s and 1970s. U.S. media also began to blame Poles for the murder of Jews during World War II. Chicago's Polish American Guardian Society closely monitored negative portrayals of Polish Americans in television programming. NBC produced the TV series *Banacek* which was telecast for two years. Although the name suggested a Slovak and the Polish sayings were not really "Polish," Banacek was portrayed as a Polish American detective who solved cases others found impossible. The "Polish" sayings were clever and pithy. George Peppard received favorable comments and awards from the Polish American community.

In 1995, nationally syndicated columnist, Ann Landers, slurred Pope John Paul II and Polish people. PRCUA president Edward G. Dykla joined with many other Polish Americans who protested such defamation and was quoted in the national press demanding a public apology. Landers publicly apologized a few days later.

Jazz and other concerts in honor of Polish American Heritage Month (October) and other events have regularly taken place in the PMA since 1994.

Agnes Ptasznik, left, is the Polish Outreach Liaison on the staff of Illinois Attorney General, Lisa Madigan, right. A graduate of Loyola University where she was president of the Polish Club, Ptasznik was queen of the 2000 Polish Constitution Day Parade and active with the Polish Girl Scouts in her youth.

"Polish Political Posters, 1945 to 1989" from the collection of Piotr Dombrowski were featured in a PMA exhibit in 2000. The poster Zeby Polska była Polska (Let Poland be Poland) reflects a rallying cry during the Solidarity movement which was often heard in a popularized musical rendition which confounded the communist rulers in Poland.

There are several bookstores in the Polish American community which feature the latest books and other publications published in Poland. Among them are Polonia Bookstore, D & Z Dom Ksiazki (at left), Babilon Bookstore and Cafe, Eva Polish Bookstore, Exlibris, Odeon Bookstore, Golden Bookstore, Millennium, Quo Vadis, Zrodlo, Arkadia, Redyk Book and Card Shop, Nie-Bo, Polsoft, and Veritas.

Ewa Chrusciel reading her poetry at the D & Z Bookstore. Lectures, exhibits, and other cultural gatherings are common in many bookstores in the Polish American community.

While in Poland in 1987, a delegation representing the Polish American Congress placed a wreath at the Westerplatte monument commemorating the Polish soldiers who perished in the battle on September 1, 1939 where Germany attacked Poland to start World War II. In the Polish American delegation were Edward Moskal, PNA president, Helen Wojcik, PWA president, Edward G. Dykla, PRCUA president (center of photo), at the extreme right is Alderman Roman C. Pucinski.

Mike Royko wrote more than 7,500 columns over a four-decade career at the Daily News, Chicago Sun-Times, *and* Chicago Tribune. *He grew up in Chicago living in an apartment above a bar. His mother was of Polish descent and his father was of Ukrainian origin. In his columns, Royko created several fictitious mouthpieces with whom he could hold "conversations." The most famous of these was Slats Grobnik, the epitome of a working class Polish-Chicagoan. Royko's Grobnik columns generally took the form of the two men discussing a current issue in a neighborhood Polish bar. Royko died in 1997.*

Paczki Day

In Poland, the start of the pre-Lenten celebration is known as Tlusty Czwartek *(Fat Thursday).* Zapusty *(Carnival season) was ending. The well-to-do would no longer be holding elegant balls preceded by sumptuous meals featuring roast game and fine wines. Peasants would no longer be enjoying* zimne nogi *(pickled pig's feet)* kiszka *(blood sausage), and* kielbasa z kapusta *(sausage and cabbage) washed down with beer and* gozalka *(least expensive vodka available).*

On Tlusty Czwartek *both groups especially enjoyed* paczki *(plural of* paczek, *a doughnut). Since all the lard, sugar, and fruit had to be used up as it was forbidden during Lent, they made large amounts of* Paczki *to enjoy on Fat Thursday.*

Donated to Chicago by the artist, Agora *consists of 106 headless and armless cast iron figures, over nine feet tall, each weighing nearly 1,100 pounds. The figures are installed at the south end of Grant Park, near Roosevelt Road and Michigan Avenue, on land where the old Illinois Central Railroad Station once stood.*

At the dedication of Agora, *which means meeting place in Greek, officials noted that it "is a major sculpture by the renowned Polish artist Magdalena Abakanowicz (photo right).... Mayor Richard M. Daley enthusiastically supports the project and this invaluable gift is a gesture of friendship between the sister cities of Warsaw and Chicago."*

In America, this Polish custom was adapted to the Tuesday before Ash Wednesday. It is now commonly called Paczki Day as thousands of Polish Americans line up to buy millions of paczki throughout the United States. In the Chicago area Oak Mill Bakery quickly sells out the 15,000 paczki it prepares for the day. Other Polish bakeries are joined by many ethnic and commercial bakeries to produce all the paczki they can. Chrusciki *(angel wings), a very delicate, light pastry, are often prepared along with paczki.*

What was once commonly called Shrove Tuesday or Fat Tuesday is now known as Paczki Day in Chicago and other major cities throughout the United States.

COPERNICUS FOUNDATION

The Copernicus Foundation was established in July 1971 as a civic, educational, recreational, and entertainment resource. It helped raise $300,000 for the statue of Copernicus (at left) dedicated in 1973 in front of the Adler Planetarium near downtown Chicago.

Groundbreaking at the Gateway Theater (on West Lawrence Avenue near Milwaukee Avenue) was in 1979. The tall spire atop the theater has Poland's national symbol, a white eagle, (at right) which can be easily seen by thousands of motorists using the Kennedy Expressway just east of the theater.

The Gateway Theater (below) was dedicated as the Copernicus Foundation in 1981 after refurbishing and construction of three floors of office space, meeting rooms, and classrooms. Since 1988, the Lake Shore Symphony Orchestra uses the theater for its practice sessions and three annual concerts. Numerous other events are also staged here. A major attraction for 2007 is the 18th Annual Polish Film Festival scheduled to show 60 feature and documentary films at the Gateway Theater, Portage Theater, Gallery Theater at the Society for Arts, and Beverly Arts Center.

Many notables have attended events sponsored by the Copernicus Foundation. Chicago Mayor Harold Washington (photo above) was greeted at a concert at the Gateway Theater by Mitchell P. Kobylinski, the founder and president of the Copernicus Foundation for more than 25 years. President George H.W. Bush visited "Taste of Polonia" in 1992.

Since 1979, "Taste of Polonia," usually the first weekend in September, annually attracts about 30,000 guests. Non-stop Polish American musical entertainment and Polish culinary delights are provided. Many dancers attend in traditional regional Polish folk costumes.

Yachting

Chicago's Joseph Conrad Yacht Club began its sailing, educational, and social activities in 1969. Co-organized by Isidore P. Ryzak, Henry Luber, and Ireneusz Geblewicz, the club has grown to 150 members who sail 30 boats under the club's flag. Members and guests meet regularly at the group's clubhouse at 942 West Montrose.

Two sailboats which have brought attention to the club are *Lighting*, winner of the 2003 Mackinac Race in the open division and *Julianna* (shown below with the PNA sign). Known as the largest sailboat in Chicago, *Julianna* (at left) finished third in the "Turbo" category in the Mackinac Race in 2006.

Two annual regattas have become a tradition with the club: the Gold Button of the Commodore and the Cup of the Consul General of Poland. Other club sailing events include the NOOD Regatta, Verve Cup Regatta, the tri-state-race, and Venetian Night participation.

Isidore P. Ryzak, former commodore of the club for eight years, (photo below left, at the wheel of the 78-foot maxi-sloop, *Julianna*) has entertained Mayor Daley's camp kids on board and Casey Chlebek, current commodore, has been active in raising money for needy families in Chicago's Christmas Ship Program.

Basic coastal navigation classes are taught at the club headquarters and an active sea scouts program has been organized for young people who also are awarded scholarships for essays about Joseph Conrad. The namesake of the club was an avid Polish sailor who gained international fame as an acclaimed author writing in the English language. Other regular club events are participation in the Polish Constitution Day Parade, concerts, recitals with Polish themes, and an evening for sharing the wafer (*Oplatek*).

Chopin Theater

The Chopin Theatre, located in the heart of Old Polonia on Division Street between Milwaukee and Ashland avenues, is New Polonia's major contribution to both Chicago and Polish American theatrical and cultural aspirations.

First opened in 1918, the theatre served principally as a movie house showing films to capacity audiences. However, prominent Poles such as pianist Ignace Jan Paderewski appeared on the Chopin stage.

As many Polish American organizations began leaving the area in the 1950s, the theatre was almost abandoned until 1990 when Zygmunt Dyrkacz, photo left, came to Chicago, rebuilt the facility, and, as artistic director, launched a whirlwind of creative, challenging, and critically-acclaimed performances in the theatre's main stage seating 225 and in the 175-seat black box studio.

Averaging 500 presentations a year, Chopin is nearing 7,000 productions since its founding. Most are theatrical, but there are also film, poetry readings, music, and other events.

Many of Chopin's own productions have been from Poland. The Katowice-based Teatr Cogitatur was recognized as "a troupe that has done a superb job of passing on the techniques and traditions of the Polish avant-garde to a new generation of Polish theatre artists." They received high praise for their *La Luna* and *Aztec Hotel*, which, as one critic wrote, "despite more than two decades of international acclaim had never appeared in this country until Dyrkacz brought them here in 2003." More recently, Brandon Bruce was recognized with an award as director of *Tango* by Polish playwright, Slawomir Mrozek.

The Chopin Theatre actively promotes other artistic expression as cofounders and sponsors of art and music festivals such as Near Northwest Arts, Around the Coyote, and Paderewski in the Park Piano Festival.

On stage, Hamlet *presented by Signal Ensemble Theater, a resident company at Chopin Theatre.*

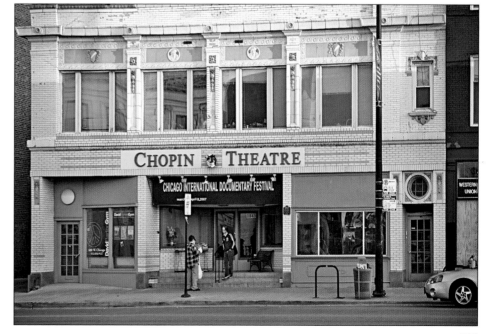

With Chicago's Buckingham Fountain and the Field Museum of Natural History in the background, Pope John Paul II concelebrates Mass with more than 350 North-American bishops in Grant Park before an estimated crowd of 1.2 million in October 1979.

St. Mary of Nazareth Hospital was the official City of Chicago welcoming site, August 20, 1976 for Karol Cardinal Wojtyla and a visiting delegation of bishops from Poland. Sister Stella Louise Slomka, CEO of the hospital, photo below, listens as Wojtyla addresses the gathered crowd. All photos above and below are from this event.

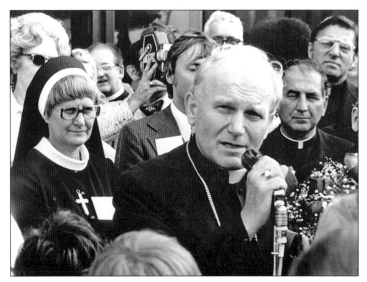

John Paul II celebrates Mass for the Polish American community in the parking lot at Five Holy Martyrs Church. A 40-foot mural to the right of the altar and the altar were both built for the Mass. Attendance was held to 17,000 fortunate ticket holders, leaving hundreds of thousands disappointed because of space limitations.

Pope John Paul II meets with Chicago's Polish American fraternal leaders in November 1987. From left, Edward G. Dykla, PRCUA president; Helen Zielinski, PWA president; and Aloysius A. Mazewski, PNA president.

Karol Cardinal Wojtyla meets with scouts at Five Holy Martyrs Church in 1976.

The connection between the Bobaks and Pope John Paul II began in 1979 when Frank Bobak had a personal audience with the Pope. When the Pope visited Chicago they were to meet again. Subsequently, the Bobak family has made several trips to Rome including this one in 2001.

Bibliographical Essay

An excellent introduction to Poland's history is Adam Zamoyski, *The Polish Way: A Thousand Year History of the Poles and their Culture* (New York: Hippocrene Books, 1995). British historian, Norman Davies' work, *God's Playground: A History of Poland* (2 vols., New York Columbia University Press, 1982) is also very popular and well written. Both are available in paperback. Another perspective is presented in *History of Poland* (Warsaw: PWN-Polish Scientific Publishers, 1968). Poland's most prominent historians led by Aleksander Gieysztor, Stefan Kieniewicz, Emanuel Rostkowski, Janusz Tazbir, and Henryk Wereszynoski contributed to this work. Sophie Hodorowicz Knab's, *Polish Customs, Traditions, and Folklore* (New York: Hippocrene Books, 1996) and Sula Benet's, *Dance and Customs of Peasant Poland*, (New York: Hippocrene Books, 1996) provide useful social and cultural information.

Rev. Waclaw Kruszka's 13 volumes of early Polish American history have been translated and are now available in four volumes: *A History of the Poles in America* (Washington, D.C.: The Catholic University Press, 1993). A highly regarded historian, who wrote principally in English, was Miecislaus Haiman. His *Polish Past in America, 1608-1865* (originally published in 1939; Chicago: Polish Museum of America, 1974) established the field of Polish American studies for future historians. Joseph A. Wytrwal, *America's Polish Heritage: A Social History of Poles in America* (Detroit: Endurance Press, 1961) and Theresita Polzin, *The Polish Americans: Whence and Whither* (Pulaski, Wisconsin: Franciscan Publishers, 1973) present a broader canvas and analyze the Poles assimilation into and influences on the American society in which they settled.

Although Chicago has been and remains the center of the Polish American community in the United States, there is no single volume which traces Chicago's Polish American community since 1837 when Poles began arriving and settling in Chicago. However, *Poles of Chicago, 1837-1937* (Chicago: Polish Pageant, 1937) documents Polish American activities in numerous fields of endeavor. Ed Marciniak provides insight into how and why settlement areas of Polish Americans dramatically and suddenly changed after World War II: *Reviving An Inner-city Community* (Chicago: Loyola University Press, 1977).

Specific topics related to Chicago's Polish American community have attracted the attention of many prominent historians. Victor Green, *For God and Country: The Rise of Polish and Lithuanian Ethnic Consciousness* (Madison: The State Historical Society of Wisconsin, 1975) explains how Poles developed their Polishness and why they remained so loyal to their Polish identity. Mary Patrice Erdmans, *Opposite Poles: Immigrants and Ethnics in Chicago, 1976-1990* (University Park, Pennsylvania: Pennsylvania State University Press, 1998) writes about the divisions and distinctions between the old Polonia—arrivals before World War II—and the new Polonia—arrivals after World War II—with specific reference to Poles who came to Chicago during the height of the Solidarity movement in Poland.

The overwhelming majority of Poles have identified with Catholicism for more than 1,000 years. Joseph John Parot presents extensive detail and insight of the meaning of religion in the lives of Polish Americans in *Polish Catholics in Chicago, 1850-1920: A Religious History* (DeKalb, Illinois: Northern Illinois University Press, 1981). Polish Americans as workers in industry and in the labor movement are the focus of Dominic Pacyga in *Polish Immigrants and Industrial Chicago: Workers on the South Side, 1880-1922* (Columbus: Ohio State University Press, 1991). Edward Kantowicz, *Polish American Politics in Chicago* (Chicago and London: University of Chicago Press, 1975) unravels the Polish American impact on Chicago politics. Joseph Migala devotes considerable attention to Chicago's Polish-language radio broadcasts in *Polish Radio Broadcasting in the United States* (Boulder: East European Monographs, distributed by Columbia University Press, New York, 1987).

A useful reference guide to some 1,700 items available in English is Joseph W. Zurawski's, *Polish American History and Culture: A Classified Bibliography* (Chicago: Polish Museum of America, 1975). *Polish America Studies*, published in English twice annually for more than 50 years, also has valuable bibliographies as well as numerous articles and book reviews, many of which pertain to Chicago's Polish American community.

Members of the Polish Genealogical Society of America, headquartered in Chicago at the Polish Museum of America, do extensive research at the museum as do many scholars, teachers, and other interested parties utilizing the extensive 60,000-volume collection in the museum's library which is open to the public.

Acknowledgements

Writing *Polish Chicago: Our History, Our Recipes* was a most challenging endeavor. It would not have been possible without the assistance and generosity of numerous organizations and individuals.

The PRCUA made its facilities available for numerous meetings and organizational work. Wallace Ozog, president, was a most gracious host. Anna Sokolowski, vice president provided much information on the fraternal's current activities. The rich collections of the Polish Museum of America, housed in the PRCUA building, were extensively and frequently utilized. The staff at the museum diligently and enthusiastically responded to numerous inquiries: Jan Lorys, director; Malgorzata Kot, head librarian; Richard Kujawa, operations manager; Halina Misterka, archivist; and assistants Krystyna Grell, Lisa A. Terlecki, Agnieszka Migiel-Lubiejewski, Leonard Kurdek, and Monica Nowak. Mrs. Joann Ozog, who conducts many of the museum's workshops, was also very helpful

PNA officials including Frank J. Spula, president, Paul C. Obrobina, vice president, Teresa N. Abick, secretary general, were most cooperative in directing us to important resources. Richard Piasecki and Wojciech Wierzewski tracked down and identified many photographs which helped tell the story of Polish Chicago.

PWA officials provided much useful information and shared items in their archives. Our thanks to Virginia Sikora, president; Sharon Zago, vice president; and Grazyna Migala, secretary general.

Many individuals shared personal memorabilia or provided insights which contributed valuable documentation to the range of topics *Polish Chicago: Our History, Our Recipes* attempts to present. These include: Susan Andrews, Stan Bobak, Joanna Borowiec, Paul Chabura, Chicago Public Library, Wieslaw Chodorowski, Rev. Fred Ciesla, CR; Maria Ciesla, Malgorzata Cieslak, Edward G. Dykla, Val Ensalaco, Sister Eulodia, CSSF; Alex Fiedotjew, Victoria Granacki, Romuald Hejna, Micheline Jaminski, Bill Jeske, Sister Katherine, CSSF; Rev. Richard J. Klajbor, Vivian Przybylo Kolpak, Camille Kopielski, Barbara Kozuchowska, Joe Krupa, Pola Kuczaba, Ed Madura, Wanda Majcher, Adrian Malec, Bruno Marczyk, Sister Mary Barbara, CR; Romuald Matuszczak, Robert Maycan, Dan McCarthy, Lycyna Migala, Adam Ocytko, John Ordon, Joseph Parot, Yolanta Pawlikowski, Mary Piergies, Agnes Ptasznik, Bogdan Pukszta, Isidore P. Ryzak, St. Mary of Nazareth Hospital Center Archives, Julie Satzik, Rod Sellers, Bill Skowron, Aleks Slota, Ted Swigon, Dr. Anna Szpindor, Tom Tarapacki, White Eagle Restaurant, Stanislaw Zagata, Marissa Zagone, and Helena Ziolkowska.

A special appreciation to the many professional and amateur photographers, both past and present, who have used their artistic talents to visually record the events and people that make up Polish Chicago. Most are unknown; those I am aware of and give credit to are as follows: Stanley Wlodkowski (p64-65, 220-221), Victor Jaremkiewicz (p189), Tina Leto (p25 from *The Archdiocese of Chicago* by Edward Kantowicz), Robert M. Jadach (dust jacket, etc.), Graig Stillwell/Adler Planetarium (p232), *Magazyn Plus* (p235), Julita Siegel (numerous), and Katherine Bish (numerous). My apologies to those names missed in the complications of production. A note of thanks also to Micheline "Misia" Jaminski for collecting the images used for the back end sheet.

Special thanks for their contributions are extended to Dominic Pacyga, a gifted historian who writes with insight about the "Polishness" of Chicago's early Polish American communities; Ed Gronkiewicz, keen observer of those elements which give Chicago so much of its Polish flavor; and Jan Lorys who, as director of PMA, brings attention to how Polish Americans have contributed to Chicago's and our nation's growth and development.

Thanks also to Julita Siegel, our recipe coordinator for this book, for her diligence and persistence in working with individuals and businesses contributing their delicious recipes. Also to Katherine Bish, our skilled photographer from St. Louis, Missouri, for her awesome images capturing the essence of Polish cuisine.

A very special word of appreciation to Brad Baraks of G. Bradley Publishing. His resolve to present this historical portrait of Chicago's Polish Americans twice necessitated expanding the scope and content of the work. The result is the most ambitious work ever attempted of our dynamic and active community.

My responsibility was to try to evaluate this overabundance of material and focus in on the values, goals, and deeds which have given meaning to the lives of Polish Americans in the Chicago area. I trust any shortcomings will not be directed at any of the organizations and individuals mentioned above as I bear final responsibility for this work.

To my wife, Marcia, my sincere thanks for her unending patience with my demanding schedule when writing and her always helpful assistance and understanding when most needed.

Epilogue

When Poles began arriving in Chicago in the mid-19th century, few would have predicted that in the early years of the third millennium, their number, and those who continued to identify with their Polish heritage, would now be recorded in the millions.

Indeed, the early Poles who settled in the historic neighborhood of the Polish Triangle (the intersection of Ashland, Milwaukee, and Division), who occupied the Pilsen area near 18th and Ashland, and who settled on the far South Side at 80th and Lake Michigan, were joined a century later by waves of immigration from Poland which continue to enrich the Chicago area. Today, however, the newer arrivals elect to settle beyond the city limits in Chicago's suburbs and neighboring counties which are experiencing dramatic growth in their Polish American populations.

Wherever the Poles moved, they retained their Polish heritage. As the Catholic faith was vitally important in the lives of most Poles, one of their first goals was to build Catholic churches. Major Polish American fraternals further unified Poles, not only in neighborhoods, but throughout the nation as Chicago was chosen as the national headquarters for all major fraternal organizations in the world.

The Polish language was and continues to be spoken in these former and newly established churches. Also, Polish Saturday schools teach the Polish language and help preserve Polish culture. Numerous social clubs embody and nourish the Polish spirit in their activities.

At its core, however, Polishness was best learned and preserved on a daily basis when sharing a meal. As successive generations gave way to future generations, preparation and presentation of food for a Polish table began to take on special significance. Holiday traditions were occasions eagerly awaited by everyone in the family. Often Polish dishes became favorites for all.

Polish food products, at one time not readily available, are now easy to locate in many new Polish neighborhoods. As the variety of Polish dishes continues to increase, it is important that older traditions be passed on to the next generation. I myself remember cutting the pierogi dough with a special glass, then helping my mother prepare the potato and onion filling, still my favorite. Although some consider Polish food to be heavy, there are many examples of numerous Polish dishes that require fresh ingredients prepared to be both tasty and healthful.

Our Polish American community continues to be dynamic and resourceful in many other ways. The more we look back with justifiable pride on our past, the greater our desire to assure a bright and rewarding future for our children, a future that will bring them success, a future that will bring contentment to their grandparents.

Polish Americans have so much to share and celebrate. Both Poland and the United States have always cherished the ideals of freedom and democracy. We continue to thrive in the opportunities our nation provides to express our love and devotion to these ideals. We are confident we will continue to grow in the awareness of our Polish heritage and we will expand not only our own horizons, but the horizons of all Americans.

Let us all step decisively into that inviting future.

Jan Lorys, Director
The Polish Museum of America

Polish Women Are Tough!

An elderly Polish man lay dying in his bed. While suffering the agonies of impending death, he suddenly smelled the aroma of his favorite pierogi with fried onions wafting up the stairs.

He gathered his remaining strength, and lifted himself from the bed. Gripping the railing with both hands, he crawled downstairs. He leaned against the kitchen door frame, where if not for death's agony, he would have thought himself already in heaven, for there, spread out upon waxed paper on the kitchen table were hundreds of his favorite pierogi.

Was it heaven? Or was it one final act of love from his wife of 60 years, seeing to it that he left this world a happy man?

He threw himself towards the table, landing on his knees in a crumpled posture. His parched lips parted, the wondrous taste of the pierogi was already in his mouth.

With a trembling hand he reached up to the edge of the table, when suddenly he was smacked with a wooden spoon by his wife.

"Back off!" she said. "Those are for the funeral."

Sieradz

Podhale

Rzeszow

Gorny Slask

Lubusk

Lowicz